CHAOTIC
NEUTRAL

CHAOTIC NEUTRAL

HOW THE DEMOCRATS LOST THEIR SOUL IN THE CENTER

ED BURMILA

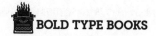

BOLD TYPE BOOKS

New York

Bold Type Books
30 Irving Place, 10th Floor, New York, NY 10003
www.boldtypebooks.org
@BoldTypeBooks

Printed in the United States of America

First Edition: September 2022

Published by Bold Type Books, an imprint of Perseus Books, LLC, a subsidiary of Hachette Book Group, Inc. Bold Type Books is a co-publishing venture of the Type Media Center and Perseus Books.

The Hachette Speakers Bureau provides a wide range of authors for speaking events. To find out more, go to www.hachettespeakersbureau.com or call (866) 376-6591.

The publisher is not responsible for websites (or their content) that are not owned by the publisher.

Print book interior design by Amy Quinn.

Library of Congress Cataloging-in-Publication Data

Names: Burmila, Ed, author.
Title: Chaotic neutral : how the Democrats lost their soul in the center / Ed Burmila.
Description: First edition. | New York : Bold Type Books, 2022. | Includes bibliographical references and index.
Identifiers: LCCN 2022003009 | ISBN 9781645030027 (hardcover) | ISBN 9781645030041 (ebook)
Subjects: LCSH: Democratic Party (U.S.)—History—20th century. | Democratic Party (U.S.)—History—21st century. | Democratic Party (U.S.)—Platforms. | United States—Politics and government—20th century. | United States—Politics and government—21st century.
Classification: LCC JK2316 .B79 2022 | DDC 324.2736/09—dc23/eng/20220611
LC record available at https://lccn.loc.gov/2022003009

ISBNs: 9781645030027 (hardcover), 9781645030041 (e-book)

LSC-C

Printing 1, 2022

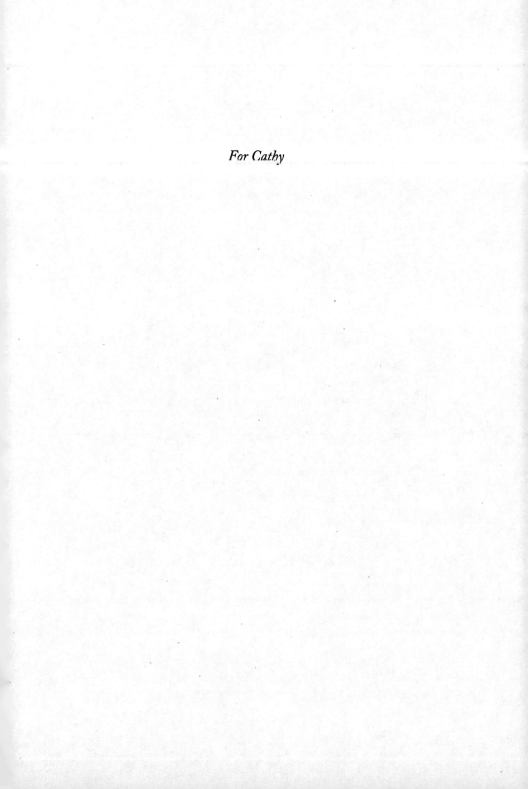

For Cathy

CONTENTS

INTRODUCTION

The Unshakeable if Vague Feeling That Something Is Wrong

I f you picked up this book, there's an excellent chance you feel like something about the Democratic Party is, well, off. Not quite right. Your relationship to the party is defined by either total exasperation or a veneer of enthusiasm covering a roiling cauldron of doubts you can't quite calm. You get your hopes up and are inevitably disappointed. You say things like "Well, it could have been worse" or "I guess that wasn't so bad"—a lot.

Democrats give up when they should fight. They say they know how to get things done and then spend their time in power explaining what they can't do. The victories they declare are strangely unsatisfying and require more asterisks, caveats, and qualifiers than a prescription drug ad. They use phrases like "better than nothing" and "half a loaf" like they have an endorsement deal with the concept of mediocrity. They seem to want the same things as the opposing party with disturbing frequency. They react to every failure—and these aren't rare—with "vote blue, harder!" and a barrage of fundraising emails so overwhelming that no filter yet devised is powerful enough to redirect them all to the spam folder. Sorry we massively blew that whole "protect abortion rights" thing; smash that donate button though! Even when Democrats are in power, the Republicans seem to be the ones in control.

You can't put your finger on it, but something is wrong.

Every voter who has been in the orbit of the Democratic Party experiences two important moments. The first is the moment of realization that what passes for liberal in the United States is closer to the political center by any meaningful definition of the term. For me, that moment was spread out across 2009 when Barack Obama—backed by a near supermajority in Congress—let Wall Street's masters of the universe off with a slap on the wrist as punishment for shit-canning the global economy, then insisted they get bonuses he previously described as "shameful,"[1] then concern-trolled about the deficit on a financial stimulus that was too small and far too weighted toward tax cuts,[2] *then* did worse than nothing to help the millions of Americans who were facing foreclosure.[3] When he walked out of his long-awaited sit-down with the CEOs of America's banking giants in March 2009 with assurances that everyone was on the same page and Wall Street was sincerely ready to help, I saw all too clearly that change was not going to be quite as radical as we were led (or had led ourselves) to believe. Even the greatest economic crisis in decades wasn't sufficient to obviate hand-wringing over the deficit, not only from Republicans, from whom it is expected, but from the Democrats, the party that is, in some abstract sense, the working-class party.

The second moment is the brutal one, and the one not everyone would-be Democratic voter is willing to face. It's the moment you realize that there is something deeply wrong with these people. They are not merely a little too eager to compromise, too moderate, or too trusting of Republicans who radiate maliciousness. Those things may be true, but the problems run far deeper. The way they see politics and the political world are, in a word, broken. For me, this moment can be dated precisely: February 28, 2017. Around 10:00 p.m.

President Trump had just delivered his first speech to a joint session of Congress, one of many occasions early in his presidency on which desperate pundits tried to convince themselves that Trump had "become president" and was about to start acting like an adult with object permanence (oops!). The Democratic response—always a thankless task for the minority party—was delivered by former Kentucky governor Steve Beshear.

Can you picture it, reader? Do you remember the visual that one commentator described as "Jimmy Dean [speaking] in a haunted diner"? Do you remember the darkened room, the white audience variously described as mannequins or hostages, as people instructed to "freeze all motor functions" for what looked like "a reverse mortgage commercial"?[4] It looked terrible. Somehow, the words were even worse:

> I'm here in Lexington, Kentucky, some 400 miles from Washington at a diner with some neighbors—Democrats and Republicans—where we just watched the president's address. I am a proud Democrat, but first and foremost, I am a proud Republican, and Democrat, and mostly, American.[5]

Let's think about this for a second.

Donald Trump has just been elected president over Hillary Clinton, whom Democrats broadly believed to be both a shoo-in and the most qualified candidate ever,[6] the obvious heir to the legacy of moderate liberalism embodied in Bill Clinton and Barack Obama. She lost to a sentient Twitter account, a complete imbecile, a shamelessly self-promoting C-list celebrity, the avatar of every American yearning for someone to tell them it's OK to be a narcissistic prick because there are no consequences (or shouldn't be), a man who quite possibly has never read a book to conclusion in his life. Trump's election was an existential threat to the country and to the Democratic Party. It wasn't a wake-up call; it was "WAKE UP!" engraved on a giant cartoon mallet that walloped Democrats in the face.

And this was what the Democratic powers that be (and still are) concocted. This was what they chose to do with their first big symbolic chance to show America that they weren't the sad-sack team in *Air Bud* that just lost a basketball game to a fucking dog. This was the way they thought they would inspire their emotionally shattered base and win over a country full of people grappling with the prospect of four years of President Father Coughlin.* "Hey, America," they could have said, "we got the message in November, and we are ready to fight!" Even if it was a lie, they

---

* Father Charles Coughlin, the "Radio Priest" of the Great Depression, was a direct forerunner of modern right-wing demagogues like Tucker Carlson and Donald Trump. Very popular for a time with working-class Catholics, his radio show was initially

didn't even try to sound a note of energy and enthusiasm. They went with *David Lynch Presents: Bipartisanship at the Cracker Barrel.*

Clearly, in the grand scheme of things, the response is epiphenomenal—it gets attention for the moment and then everybody forgets about it immediately. I wasn't troubled because Steve Beshear's response had meaningful consequences. I was troubled because everything about it was bad. Everything. It was bad in a surreal way, a DVD bonus material *Kids in the Hall* skit with no punchline. It was confrontationally bad, all but challenging the viewer to give up forever, to quietly walk into the ocean and be taken away by the waves. It was a cry for help, an old man blinking "please kill me" in Morse code while his captors, a pair of expensive Beltway consultants, exchange a high five off camera.

Any person chosen at random from a phone book could have come up with something better. Perhaps gather a handful of the Democrats' fresh new faces to imply some signs of life to disappointed or skeptical viewers. These younger, more energetic voices could come out swinging, maybe name some Democratic policy priorities and take appropriate potshots at the Republicans' pivot to pratfalling authoritarianism. They could have made a strong statement: Trump transcends mere partisan disagreement. He is dangerous. We will fight him without hesitation. America, we are up to the task. You can count on us. We understand what is at stake.

Instead, faced with the rise of a store-brand dictator, the perfect synthesis of Kim Jong-Il and Don Rickles, they decided on a message that vacillated between fear and appeasement. And to deliver it, they chose a septuagenarian retired governor from a state Trump won in a landslide, and they sat him in the dark, surrounded by a consultant's idea of what "regular folk" are like (gleaned from *Hillbilly Elegy* and four weeks campaigning in Iowa), saying "I'm a Republican" and describing his audience-hostages as Democrats "and Republicans" within the first five seconds, approximately the time it took the few viewers of the grotesque spectacle to ask, "Am I dead or do I simply wish I were?"

It was, in sum, a tableau of the ridiculous; a semester final project demonstrating that nothing was learned from losing to Trump, or

---

pro-Roosevelt and pro–New Deal, but by 1934 he had veered into anti-Semitism and open adulation of European fascists.

possibly ever. Given the opportunity to do whatever they wanted, this is what they did.

We are in trouble unless they learn to do better and fast. And I do not mean "do better" in a way that any simple, superficial changes can fix. I mean that there is something wrong with their worldview, with the way they think about politics, with what they think politics is. They are not showing up to a metaphorical gunfight against the GOP with a knife; they're showing up with a clarinet.

WHERE ARE WE AND HOW DID WE GET HERE?

This book has two goals.* One is to explain the evolution of the Democratic Party from the economic populism of the New Deal era to the nonideological lifestyle branding for better-off liberals it is today. This is the *how* and the *why* of the way the party is at present. The second goal is to identify and draw out the specific things Democrats get wrong, the mistakes they make over and over. Everyone can sense that *something* is wrong, and countless critics have already argued that the Democrats are too liberal, or not liberal enough, or whatever. I linger instead on the broader, more fundamental question: Why does watching Democrats govern always feel like watching a movie we've seen before? Why is it so predictable, not only that they'll underwhelm and disappoint but the specific ways in which they'll do it?

For decades there has been a thriving cottage industry of writing about "reinventing the Democratic Party."[7] If someone can sell a book every year or two about how to remake your party, often with cringey, trendy titles like *Democrats 2.0*, something is wrong. And that something goes beyond words, beyond messaging. Either the party lacks a coherent identity or, to the extent that it has an identity, voters do not like it. It is the kind of problem a party inevitably encounters when it defines itself by the opposition, as "not the Republicans."

And the wandering in the desert, which has been going on since at least 1972, continues to this day. Joe Biden's campaign theme in 2020 was unity. In 2016, Hillary Clinton used the slogan "Stronger Together."

---

* Three, if you count selling enough copies to circle the globe if laid end to end.

Barack Obama and Bill Clinton talked about bipartisanship and aisle reaching to the point of parody. But none answered the question: What are we supposed to do after we unify? Come together *to do what*? What do Democrats believe other than that they are very smart and should be in charge and that the GOP is bad? Does it make a difference whether we like each other if the core problems of our society only get worse? Wouldn't it be better if we hated each other but addressed some of those problems, like climate change, income inequality, and poverty, before they kill us? Perhaps most urgently, is there any value in "working together" when the other party's goal is to maintain power irrespective of election outcomes?

I have written about the Democratic Party because I can imagine nothing less challenging or interesting than writing about the Republican Party. It's a total write-off. The American right has categorically lost its mind, and everything to say about how terrible it is has already been said repeatedly. There are two points in this book—the 1994 Republican Revolution led by Newt Gingrich and the post-2008 Tea Party–era lurch to the right under Obama—that delve into the role of the GOP. But if you're looking for hundreds of pages of argument that Donald Trump and Mitch McConnell are bad, lie a lot, and embrace what a generation ago was the lunatic fringe of the right, wait for the next MSNBC personality to drop a book. That the GOP is vicious and amoral and broadly dedicated to malevolence is a given. You know it. I know it. I have nothing new to say about it, and you would learn nothing new from reading more about it. If you have yet to conclude that the Republican Party is a malignancy that needs to be destroyed rather than appeased or reasoned with, this is the wrong book for you.

Most democratic nations have a party rooted in economic populism; Americans have two warring factions of elites with meaningful differences but far too many important areas of overlap, particularly in terms of economic worldview. We have the high comedy of the Clinton or Obama years, bitter arguments over whether the top tax rate should be 36 percent or 39 percent in a system that lets the wealthy opt out of paying taxes anyway. I focus on the Democratic Party because it must, somehow, be turned into an effective counterweight to the Republican death cult.

Barring massive structural changes to our electoral system, most of which would require constitutional amendments that simply aren't going to happen, we are stuck with a two-party system—at the state and national levels, at least—for the foreseeable future. If all we have is one party representing the antidemocratic far right and one representing elite interests that find the GOP tacky and uncouth but don't mind "moderate" Republican policy or a little bit of fascism, as a treat, then this country has nothing to look forward to but brief periods of illusory normalcy leading toward eventual collapse.

It is not difficult to demonstrate that the Democrats threw in the towel on the working class and the poor a half century ago (and have been scratching their heads in wonder ever since about why those people won't vote for them anymore). Yet the "what's wrong with the Democrats" genre focuses, to the point of obsession, on the idea that *social* liberalism—positions on race, on women's rights, on LGBTQ+ equality, on abortion rights—is what has made the Democratic Party repellent to white working-class voters. What if that way of looking at the problem is completely backward? What if the real problem with winning over those recalcitrant white working-class stereotypes is that Democrats made a conscious choice that such voters no longer mattered and tethered themselves instead to a different kind of voter with very different economic interests? When the Democratic Party threw in its lot with successful, professional, often suburban, mostly white liberals, it created a trap in which everything it does to make itself more appealing to those voters *makes it less appealing to every other kind of voter it needs to assemble an election-winning coalition.* Unlike for the persistent belief that the problem lies with Democratic "wokeness," there is no easy fix here. It's no wonder so many people insist that Democrats aren't winning because they use the term *Latinx*. It's comforting to imagine that the problem is so simple and easily resolved.

My argument is not that Democrats have never done anything good or can never win elections. Recent decades have proven that once incumbent Republicans become so catastrophically unpopular that the opposition party could run cardboard cutouts and win, Democrats can win (see 2006, 2008, 2018). Since the great Clintonian reinvention of the

Democratic brand in 1992, however, they're incapable of staying in power for long. That is because they hold as articles of absolute faith ideas that produce failure over and over, and if this has not already created an untenable political reality, it will soon enough. An increasingly deranged, authoritarian-curious Republican Party is on the brink of fundamentally undermining the electoral process, and a host of social and economic problems—police violence, income inequality, the climate, a steeply rising cost of living, plummeting levels of trust and political efficacy—are getting worse instead of better. Rather than seeing the Biden presidency as a final chance to arrest looming disaster, Democrats continue to play by rules that exist only in their heads (the Republicans long since having discarded them) in the belief that what will boost their future electoral prospects is some good old-fashioned moderate compromises on spending bills.

The ultimate irony is that the political left—more on terminology momentarily—now finds itself in the position centrist liberals were in during the 1970s and 1980s before they took over the party. Back then, in the still-looming shadow of the New Deal, the Democratic Leadership Council (a group about which much more follows) lobbed criticisms at the Democratic Party that, word for word, mirror left critics of the Democratic Party today. Maybe critics of the party from the left can—this part will hurt—learn some things from the story of how the radical centrists remade the party in their own image. Or—and this may hurt too—maybe the party is beyond repair and there is no simple fix. Maybe primarying lousy corporate shill Democrats and replacing them with Democrats who will actually fight for something is a pipe dream given a party that, like any other institution, is controlled by powerful people with a strong incentive to maintain the status quo and resist change. Maybe the Democratic Party is, right now, exactly what the people leading it want it to be, and there's precious little you can do about that. If you have yet to consider that possibility, now is the time.

What follows is long on criticism and short on Panglossian solutions. I believe that books that promise you the answers, neatly summarized in a brief closing chapter, insult readers' intelligence. Those authors are deluding either themselves or their readers if they can lay out the path to solving such complex problems so breezily. Nonetheless, I will conclude with a frank look at what you can do as an individual and what the Democratic Party (which does not care what I think, so don't get your hopes up) could do to build a coalition designed for a future it long ago stopped planning for in favor of pining after a bygone era of political civility that—spoiler!—never was and never will be.

OUTLOOK NOT SO GOOD

Things have not gone especially well for the Democrats (or, not coincidentally, the nation) in recent years. The official party line would have you believe otherwise: that considering the dirty tricks played by the dastardly opposition, the Democrats have done well—or at least as well as anyone has a right to expect.

Whatever led us to this point cannot, by definition, have been a good strategy. A country does not simply wake up one moment and find itself in metaphorical or literal flames. That can only be the culmination of a long series of failures. Democrats were in power for some of those failures. Some they fought against. Others they abetted or outright championed. Too often they seemed content with losing, like they relish being in the political minority where nothing will be expected of them.

Voters certainly aren't convinced. Bill Clinton and Barack Obama, the only Democratic presidents elected in the forty years between the end of Jimmy Carter's lamentable presidency and Joe Biden's squeaking into office in 2020, each won two terms in the White House. Democrats have held House majorities for two four-year spans since 1994. After 2008, when Obama swept into the White House with large congressional majorities, the Democratic track record has been disastrous. At the state level the numbers have been ugly.

What's "ugly"? How about a loss of nearly one thousand state legislative seats between 2010 and 2018, a slight recovery in 2018, then losing even more in 2020. How about losing the House in 2010, regaining it in 2018, and losing seats again in 2020. Net losses of seven* and nine (!) Senate seats in 2010 and 2014, respectively, before clawing back to a bare

---

* Democrats lost one Senate seat in the January 19, 2010, special election to fill Ted Kennedy's seat, then six in the November election.

fifty-fifty split in 2020.* Holding twenty-eight governors' mansions in 2008 compared to just sixteen after the 2016 election (since recovered to a less embarrassing minority of twenty-two). Or losing the partisan fight over the Supreme Court to the tune of a 6–3 conservative bloc composed mostly of younger judges likely to serve for decades.

In the hope of painting a rosier picture, much has been made of Democrats regularly winning the popular vote in presidential elections—in fact, in every election since 1988, excepting 2004. Unfortunately, winning the popular vote and one bus ticket have the combined value of one ride on the bus. Even the enormous moral victory of vanquishing Donald Trump in 2020 was a closer shave than the popular vote implies. Biden's margins in three key states—Wisconsin, Arizona, and Pennsylvania—were vanishingly thin, as was the case when Trump won those states in 2016.

The failures and problems run much deeper than election results reflect. In power, Democrats have repeatedly failed to confront aggressively some of the most glaring problems in society, particularly if those issues disproportionately impact the working class, the poor, people of color, or anyone without a firm foothold in the "haves" category of a historically unequal economy. They have not merely missed some opportunities or made some mistakes; they've fundamentally failed to advance an agenda or stop their Republican opponents from executing their own. Everyone makes mistakes and misjudges politics, a nebulous arena of competition that is as much art as science. But the Democrats have failed in ways that are consequential well beyond a poor decision here and there.

I call the underlying flaws that have compounded the Democrats' problems *pathologies* because we need a term weightier than *bad habits* but less dire than *hesitation wounds*. A bad habit is something best avoided, like picking your nose; fundamentally misunderstanding the purpose of holding political power is a bigger issue. It's also important to avoid a term like *mistake* because that implies a lack of intention. Some of this stuff they do habitually and on purpose.

---

* All Senate counts throughout this book include independent senators who caucus with Democrats in Democratic totals.

These eight pathologies are the core of the problem, the "why" of why Democrats are their own worst enemy. Nearly any specific example from the past three decades of the Democrats underachieving, disappointing, failing, or backing down instead of fighting can be traced back to these flaws. Think of them as threads that connect disparate political moments over time, moments when something didn't happen that could have or did happen that shouldn't. They are woven throughout the five-decade-long story that follows.

In no meaningful order, they are as follows:

EXCESSIVE IDEOLOGICAL FLEXIBILITY

Throw out a couple of things the Democratic Party stands for—core ideas on which they will not compromise, period. Democrats have crafted an identity around competence (we are the adults in the room, the smart, high-achieving people you want in charge) and demeanor (look at how reasonable we are being). Neither of these is a replacement for ideology or a commitment to specific outcomes—to a coherent *agenda*. The closest the party comes to a hard line is on abortion, but even pro-choice views are optional (making it wholly unsurprising that by the time you read this, the long political battle over *Roe v. Wade* and abortion rights has been lost).[8] Democrats decry the left's purity tests, without understanding how much a purity test or two could help voters figure out what they stand for.

A key tenet of the centrist New Democrats who rose to prominence during the 1980s was that ideology is passé, a relic from a bygone political era. They argued that Democrats needed to focus on vaguely defined goals, often cribbed from the Republicans, while remaining agnostic about the means to achieve them, an important precursor to moving the party toward the center and away from its FDR-era roots in the social welfare state, government regulation, the empowerment of labor, and more. They convinced their fellow partisans that it made sense to embrace ideas outside traditional liberal ideology. There should be no Democrat ideas or Republican ideas, only *good* ideas.

The appeal of that approach is obvious, particularly when delivered by a good communicator like Bill Clinton or Barack Obama. We want the best ideas! The problem is that at some point openness to ideas—especially to the opposing party's ideas and extra-especially when the opposing party's worldview combines Gilded Age economic theories, social Darwinism, and thinly veiled white supremacist rhetoric—sounds less like taking a reasonable stance and more like suggesting that the party's position on any issue is infinitely malleable. If ideological inflexibility is off-putting, so too is ideological incoherence.

The result is that Democrats find it easy to appeal to successful liberals who have no pressing material needs and want to see a politics that conforms to their understanding of the world as a well-ordered, cooperative meritocracy. For these voters, most political arguments have an either-or quality: one outcome may be preferred, but life goes on either way. They're perfectly satisfied with access to health care, while other voters, namely the uninsured, *need health care*. They're impressed by smart housing policy as determined by the real estate industry, while others simply need housing.

Unavoidably, politics is about ideology and outcomes. It is the battle over resources and power. Arguing that you should be in control of those things without expressing clear intentions of what to do with them is, as you may imagine, unpersuasive.

REACTING TO PUBLIC OPINION (WHEN IT SUITS THEM) RATHER THAN TRYING TO SHAPE IT

The measurement of public opinion to inform policy—through polling, focus groups, and informal communication from constituents—became a Democratic obsession under Bill Clinton. Not only did the data speak to the technocratic affinities of the new generation of liberals, but in a democratic political system, public opinion *should* matter. Yet despite the central place public opinion occupies in their universe, Democrats constantly vacillate on whether and when it should be followed at all and apparently assume that, no matter what they choose, they themselves are powerless to shape it. Public opinion ends up being treated like the weather, an exogenous force that can't be controlled and provides a persuasive excuse for wriggling out of previous commitments and promises.

The first problem is more serious. When public opinion favors something Democratic leaders already want to do, they cite it to justify pursuing bad policy. During the George W. Bush presidency, Democrats had no interest in an antiwar agenda once they became convinced that a solid majority of Americans loved the troops, loved the idea of war, and demanded leaders who would project toughness on terrorism. In this case, public opinion was a blueprint, resulting in the absurdist theater of Democrats trying to out-Republican the Republicans on foreign policy.

But then consider the landmark 2009 debate in Congress over healthcare reform, during which Democratic leaders dropped the idea of a public option—a government-run alternative to private insurance—quickly and with little fight. The insurance industry obviously didn't like it, and while Obama claimed to support it, he did nothing to try to sell it to voters or Congress. So who did like it? According to surveys, nearly three-quarters of Americans.[9] Despite the clear signal, neither congressional Democrats nor the White House showed any interest in pushing for it, instead labeling it too controversial, a potential bill killer.

At other times Democrats have been willing to embrace extremely unpopular ideas with little regard for what the public wants. Cutting—er, "reforming"—Social Security is less popular than elevator farts, yet Bill Clinton, Obama, Biden, and other prominent Democrats have aggressively pursued it. In 1997, Clinton worked feverishly with Newt Gingrich to try to privatize Social Security, while in 2011 Obama was prepared to trade radical cuts to Medicare, Medicaid, and Social Security for—I'm serious—*a modest tax increase on the richest Americans.* Only the Monica Lewinsky scandal and Tea Party–era Republican intransigence, respectively, halted those deals. Overwhelmingly negative public opinion was irrelevant.

Democrats often argue that voters—or at least the all-important moderates—do not like liberal ideas, yet they do little or nothing to try to increase their appeal, ignoring their own role in that lack of popularity. Some of these ideas are unpopular precisely because it has been *decades* since voters saw or heard anyone making a strong case for why they are good.

BLAMING VOTERS

A core criticism New Democrats leveled at the liberal establishment during the 1980s was their tendency to carry themselves with a sense of moral superiority, suggesting—and explicitly saying, in some cases—that voters were just too stupid, too racist, too unenlightened to see that Democrats were right about everything. If an election was lost, it was not because the Democrats had failed to persuasively and adequately convey to voters why they were the better choice.

In the modern era, this tendency has returned with a vengeance. The lesson many liberals chose to learn from the 2016 presidential election was not that the Clinton campaign did anything wrong or that Democrats and their worldview are unpopular but that everything came down to the voters being defective. Yet the electorate in 2016 was composed mostly of the same people who had been eligible to vote in 2012, when Barack Obama won reelection. That didn't stop Obama himself from finding fault with the electorate, either, and in her popular memoir, Michelle Obama wrote of the disastrous midterms of 2010, "I'd been disappointed that millions of people had sat out during the 2010 midterm elections, effectively handing Barack a divided Congress that could barely manage to make a law." What an extraordinary statement! Instead of asking how Democrats might have failed voters, it focuses on how voters failed Democrats. Michelle Obama may not be an elected official, but she certainly moves within the highest circles of the Democratic Party. The assumption that voters owe Democrats their vote even when they refuse to deliver what those voters want is a fundamental misunderstanding of how electoral politics works.

There is no doubt that some voters, maybe even lots of them, hold objectionable beliefs. They are sexist and racist, believe things that aren't true, and/or have troglodytic views about the proper role of government. But this has always been true; if anything, the electorate today has fewer abysmal attitudes on these issues than in the past. Trump supporters were (and are) capable of expressing the most ridiculous and horrific beliefs, sometimes simultaneously. But racism, to take just one example, did not manifest recently. I've checked, and it turns out racism has been a problem in the United States for quite a while.

What the "broken voters" narrative omits is the crucial fact that as Democrats moved to the left on social issues, they *moved to the right* on economic ones, alienating their former blue-collar base. If elite liberals are right and working-class voters really are hopelessly backward knuckle draggers, then the GOP is offering them an economic kick in the teeth plus white nationalism. The Democrats, then, offer the same kick in the teeth—free trade, spiraling inequality, shrinking safety net, and trickle-down economics—without the nativist and racist appeals. Obviously, "get more racist" is not the way forward. What if, though, Democrats made a pitch like "the GOP offers you racism and an economy rigged against people like you, while we reject the racism and promise to improve your quality of life in clear, tangible, straightforward ways." White grievance and penury on one side, a dignified standard of living for every single American on the other. Many Democrats believe they already offer voters this choice, but they do so through complicated, partial, temporary, means-tested, and bureaucratically baffling policy that both confuses voters and, too often, doesn't work.

CONSTANTLY TRYING TO IMPRESS REPUBLICANS

In the 1990s Bill Clinton did lasting harm to the Democratic Party by introducing into its orbit two men, Dick Morris and Mark Penn, about whom more later. Penn's lamentable contribution, as a purported polling whiz, was to convince Democrats of something New Democrat moderates were already inclined to believe: getting nonvoters to vote is really hard. Most people who vote are partisans, and elections are a fight over a small number of persuadable voters on the fringes of the opposing party, along with a few true ideological moderates floating in the middle.

Thus began three decades of Democrats crafting their strategy to an embarrassing degree around appealing to moderate Republicans who might (really, we swear!) vote for a Democrat under the right circumstances. Joe Biden took this to its black-comedy extreme in 2020 by devoting an entire night of the Democratic convention to Bush-era Republicans. But that is only the most recent example. It is joked that Senate Minority/Majority Leader Chuck Schumer bases everything he does on how an imaginary middle-class family will react to it. Except this isn't a joke. It is an actual thing Schumer does. The made-up moderates even have names: Joe and Eileen Bailey (formerly O'Reilly, but I guess that was too ethnic). They live in Massapequa, New York.*

Oddly enough, what these imaginary better-off white moderates want is for the Democrats to admit that the Reagan-era GOP is right about most issues and do what Republicans want, only "better," "smarter," and without "going too far" as Republicans are wont. Despite having been committed to GOP Lite in many policy areas for decades, the electoral rewards for this strategy of moderation have been infrequent and insufficient. When they lose, the answer from Democratic sages is always to move further to the right. Despite being a not-especially-liberal party going on five decades, the problem can only be that Democrats are too liberal. When they win, the various moves to the center and the right are credited for the victory. When they lose, the moves to the right didn't go far enough.

In power, Democrats are convinced that Republicans will work with them "in good faith," a modern mantra that boils down to, look, they've lied to us about this a million times but this time they pinky-swear they won't. Charlie Brown, Lucy, football. Democratic presidents like Obama and Biden beam about appointing Republicans to their cabinet, a move that wins exactly zero concessions or votes from Republicans. On major legislation, Democrats make dozens of concessions—sometimes before even beginning negotiations with the GOP—for promised Republican support that almost never comes. On that note . . .

FAILURE (OR REFUSAL) TO LEARN FROM MISTAKES

I know it didn't work last time, but this time—trust me, it will.

Then it doesn't work.

How many iterations of this cycle have you lived through?

If the mainstream Democratic Party learned from its mistakes, you'd be reading a book called *Democrats: Not Bad, I Guess*. But in practice, the learning curve of the Democratic establishment is a flat line. Consider two examples.

---

* Goldberg, J., "Imaginary Friends," *New Yorker*, March 19, 2007. Please kill me.

In 1994, Bill Clinton bemoaned unpleasant budget cuts his administration endured in order to demonstrate fiscal responsibility by prioritizing deficit reduction. As a New Democrat he wanted to buck the "tax-and-spend liberal" reputation. Voters didn't seem to care about the cuts, which came as a shock. "Nobody knows we've got any spending cuts," Clinton moaned. "We've got the worst of all worlds. We've gotten all this deficit reduction. We've made all the hard, painful choices and nobody even noticed."[10] Doing Republican stuff didn't benefit Democrats, it turned out.

Fast-forward to 2014. Attempting to undercut criticism of Democrats' supposed leniency on immigration, Obama instituted harsh border policies, including the family separation policy that evolved into the infamous "kids in cages" under Trump. How many Republican votes were won over by this infliction of cruelty? Well, according to one veteran of the Obama White House: "There was a feeling that [Obama] needed to show the American public that you believed in enforcement, and [that we weren't pushing for] open borders. But in hindsight I was like, what did we get for that? We deported more people than ever before. All these families separated, and Republicans didn't give him one ounce of credit. There may as well have been open borders for five years."[11] OK, so zero. It won zero votes. Republicans accused Democrats of being open-border lovers anyway, and Democratic voters who cared about immigration felt betrayed, like they were sold out in an attempt to satisfy the right. Great.

The policy choices were bad here, but worse was the inability to learn that this kind of appeasement never works. Twenty years apart, two presidents who—especially in Obama's case given the ample time he had to learn that conservatives would never give him credit for anything, ever—should have known better walked into the same trap.

OVEREMPHASIZING NATIONAL POLITICS

Democrats have lost a spectacular amount of ground at the state and local levels since the Clinton presidency, a problem that is widely recognized by scholars but neglected at all levels in the Democratic Party. Elected officials, activists, and donors have repeatedly, consciously chosen to focus on national politics, while state organizations have been inefficient, ineffective, and poorly organized compared to their GOP opponents. The Democratic National Committee is a fundraising behemoth that can carpet-bomb supporters with solicitations for money but can't, for example, build upon the grassroots organizing and excitement drummed up during the 2008 Obama campaign.[12]

Republicans are a powerful presence in state capitols, where more legislation and policy that directly affects our lives is made than in Washington. A difference in culture among liberal and conservative activists is part of the problem; liberals see success as synonymous with a career in New York or DC, while Springfield, Illinois, and Jefferson City, Missouri, are considered backwaters without so much as a decent restaurant. A career in such places is indicative of personal failure. Worse, while plenty of money exists in the liberal universe, big donors see state-level policy work as unattractive.[13] It's a question of priorities, not resources, and Washington is where the action is, period.

The Democratic Party cannot exist as an entity that occupies the coasts plus Chicago and interacts with the rest of the country at two-year intervals. The effect during elections, as political scientist Theda Skocpol has noted, is of an organization that fans out from each coast to temporarily establish a presence in "flyover country" (a term that should be taken out behind the barn and shot). It rolls into town like the world's least entertaining circus and then disappears immediately after the election.[14] It feels thin and insincere on the ground because *it is*.

Republicans began their long march to power in the 1980s when activists targeted low-level local and state positions, as well as local GOP organizations, and built upon this to improve their national presence. Democrats continue to attempt the inverse and lose interest in anything down-ballot when they attain power in Washington. The result is that increasingly conservative policy—often unpopular or supported only by a plurality of voters—is normalized across the country, one state legislature at a time.

CONSTANTLY LOWERING AND MANAGING EXPECTATIONS

The nostrums of tech dudes rarely offer much enlightenment, but dammit if Steve Jobs didn't offer a very important observation after meeting

Barack Obama: "The president is very smart, but he kept explaining to us reasons why things can't get done. It infuriates me."[15]

Expectation management and post hoc excuse making are where this generation of elected Democrats really shines. Certainly, the Democratic Party does not hold a magic wand while in power. The problem is the Democrats don't even really try. They negotiate with themselves to water down their own proposals. They give up at the slightest pushback. They talk themselves out of trying to do something by explaining why it won't work. They go on endlessly about all the things they can't do and all the reasons you should accept that. There is *always* a reason. Whatever the size of the Senate Democratic caucus, the number of senators needed to achieve anything is and forever will be $n + 2$. They'd love to aim higher, but Ben Nelson. But Joe Lieberman. But Joe Manchin. But Kyrsten Sinema. What more can we do?

Under Bill Clinton the technocratic ideal of "getting something done" became the gold standard. We passed a crime bill, a welfare reform bill, a budget, a trade agreement. Whether those bills were any good was moot; in the face of Republican intransigence—just look at these guys, are they nuts or what!—Democrats demand to be rewarded for getting anything done at all. Curiously, the Clinton years are also when "bipartisan" replaced "good" as the preferred adjective to describe a bill or policy. Bipartisan meant that the Democrats, the grown-ups in the room, and some good Republicans put aside petty ideological differences and hammered something out. If it's bipartisan, it has to be good because everyone compromised, and compromise is good.

In reality, bipartisan became a way for Democrats to celebrate accomplishments that concede the ideological ground to conservatives. But a "bipartisan" bill sounds a lot better than "we gave them what they wanted, which I guess is also what we want now." The cumulative effect of this kind of leadership and the well-off professional class's lack of pressing material needs has been a constant lowering of expectations. Far from turning on their once-beloved elected officials as Republicans are quick to do, core Democratic voters are endlessly forgiving. The marginal or disillusioned voters Democrats want so badly to win over are not as lenient. After a while, they stop voting.

As a result, the Democratic establishment is accustomed to a base that demands nothing. They have preferences, of course, but not demands. The difference is crucial. A preference can be addressed with a shrug and any plausible excuse so long as the Republican alternative is worse. A demand often asks elected officials to do something hard and costs politicians their jobs if they don't deliver. Democratic leadership has a life tenure; leaders are never replaced no matter how poorly they perform or what happens during elections. There's no accountability because there are no real expectations.

Republicans, conversely, will ram their heads into a wall pointlessly and repeatedly, scheduling fifty Benghazi hearings or votes to repeal Obamacare because they fear what their core voters will do to them otherwise. They have end goals, like cutting taxes, deregulation, and stuffing the federal courts with conservatives, that are even more important than winning the next election. An excuse like "we can't do it, Chuck Schumer said no" would get a Republican Senate candidate tarred and feathered—once the audience finished laughing. Whether in the majority or the minority, congressional Republicans are always confident that they can deliver some of what their voters demand, or at least put up the appearance of a real effort. And *demand* is what GOP voters do.

STYLE OVER SUBSTANCE

Democratic voters may have next to no expectations policy-wise, but they absolutely demand their leaders function as a hybrid cool parent–best friend–favorite celeb. Look at this picture of the Obamas, are they beautiful or what? Kamala Harris wears such hip sneakers! Pete Buttigieg speaks eight languages, kinda!* Losing the federal courts for a generation is but a small price to pay for a stream of *epic clapbacks* to Republicans on Twitter.

---

* While campaigning in Iowa late in 2019, Buttigieg responded to an audience question about Gaza in Arabic, leading the *New York Times* to offer the best summary of elite liberalism ever written: "The overwhelmingly white audience, largely unaware of what he said, broke into raucous applause." Quoted in Herndon, A., "Pete Buttigieg Is an Iowa Front-Runner. Will That Help Him Anywhere Else?," *New York Times*, November 4, 2019.

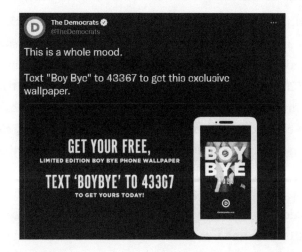

If you feel your chest tightening from cringe, seek immediate medical attention.

The Democrats' greatest national political success in the last few decades has come from the rise of charismatic individuals—Bill Clinton and Barack Obama—whose cool personalities were like the Swiss flag.* The power of coolness is sacrosanct now, with even not-particularly-cool figures like Joe Biden repackaged in the aesthetic. The Democrats' social media presence embraces online culture in that cringing way of adults using their kids' slang, possibly (hopefully) reaching a nadir in 2019 with the distribution of anti-Trump "Boy Bye" phone wallpapers. They even used of-the-moment phrases, such as "this is a whole mood," with the energy of a youth pastor trying to pepper his pitch on the overwhelming awesomeness of abstinence with relatable lingo.

This low-hanging fruit would be unworthy of comment except that it often replaces the substantive in Democratic politics. Sure, Nancy Pelosi inexplicably failed in 2020 and 2021 to insist on automatic renewal of pandemic-related stimulus if economic conditions didn't improve, something even the most moderate House Democrats begged for. But did you see her tear up Trump's speech? OMG!

The more the relationship changes from politician-constituent to celebrity-fan, the more forgiving voters become. Don't worry about what

---

* You know—a big plus. I regret nothing.

Obama did, just focus on how awesome Obama is. As with any celebrity, critics are simply haters who can be ignored out of hand. Instead of treating all political figures as fungible, there to do a job and readily replaceable if they fail to do it, this strategy succeeds in getting liberals personally invested in the success of specific characters in the drama. The personality cult around Ruth Bader Ginsburg, for example, elevated her sense of personal career fulfillment over the long-term partisan balance of the Supreme Court, which, by the time you read this, certainly seems a little more important. Joe Biden's appointment of Merrick Garland as attorney general in 2021 similarly gave the sordid story of Garland's obstructed 2016 Supreme Court nomination a pleasing conclusion. Yet it also saddled the country with a bad, timid attorney general whose lackluster performance stands out even to moderates as a glaring unforced error early in the Biden presidency.[16]

This stuff is simply not the point of politics. Politics is about attaining power and doing the absolute maximum you can do with it before, inevitably, you lose it again. Politics is, for millions of people, the difference between housing and being unhoused, between living crushed under a mountain of debt and having economic freedom, between cops shooting you in the back with impunity and living without fear of summary execution by the state because your taillight was broken. It's actually pretty important, big picture and small, short term and long.

That is, ahem, the whole mood. But the lack of focus and follow-through on these issues is made possible by Democrats' cultivating a base for whom politics plays the role of entertainment and signaling cultural values. The party functions quite well as a lifestyle brand for cool, urbane, successful, cosmopolitan liberals. It's a matter of having the right credentials (and lots of them!) and the right look and utterly rejecting—obliterating, even—any suggestion that one has anything in common with *those* people on the troglodytic right, even when you have the same policy preferences.* Liberals may be every bit as enthusiastic about showering police with money as any cop-worshipping conservative, but the

---

* The contradiction here with the liberal fetishization of Republican moderates or "good Republicans" is obvious. Republicans are disgusting people, except for the ones we have convinced ourselves might work with a centrist Democrat if sufficiently flattered.

"In This House We Believe" yard sign in front of a liberal's home lets you know who is the better person.

Can Democrats finally learn from their mistakes, or are they doomed to repeat them on a loop until Republicans and unchecked business interests wreck the country to the point that there's nothing left to fight over?

The clock is ticking. There won't be too many more chances to stop what began in the late 1960s, arrived with Ronald Reagan in 1980, blossomed in 1994 and 2010, metastasized in 2016, and took detailed notes on how to keep a stranglehold on power without winning elections in 2020.

On the plus side, you might be dead before some of the worst parts happen. See? There's always a positive.

A NOTE ON LANGUAGE

In his seminal *Why Parties?*, political scientist John Aldrich describes how the name of an American political party can refer to three different entities depending on context. First is the institutional party, the Democratic Party as an organization. The Democratic National Committee or the Corncob County Democrats are examples. Most people other than party activists who love attending meetings have minimal contact with this part of the party.

A second meaning is the Democratic Party in government, referring to the people elected or appointed to serve in some capacity under its label. A headline like "Democrats Criticize Trump's Proposal" refers specifically to the Democrats in Congress and context makes that clear.

Finally, the party in the electorate refers to everyone who identifies—formally or informally, strongly or loosely—with the party. "Poll: Majority of Democrats Want Trump Impeached" would refer to people in the general public who happened to be polled and identified themselves as Democrats.

In this book I will use the phrases "Democratic Party" or "Democrats" without always spelling out which usage is intended. Context will confirm to whom I am referring, I pray. However, when referring to a party organization I will always be explicit—for example, the Democratic National Committee.

When speaking about various ideological camps in the Democratic Party or in American politics, I try to avoid cycling through the confusing array of ill-defined terms used in our political discourse. Centrist and moderate are used somewhat interchangeably to refer to people who believe perceptions of the Democratic Party as too liberal are harmful and the party should seek to occupy the ideological middle. Liberal is the standard Democratic ideological position, as poorly defined as it is effective in practice. For liberal, read generic Democrat. Read Joe Biden, Nancy Pelosi, or Hillary Clinton. Read whatever basic issue positions come to mind when someone says "Democrats." (The troubled term *neoliberal* is addressed later.)

Progressive refers to people in the Democratic Party who believe that the party should pursue more liberal policies. Elizabeth Warren is an example; her criticisms of the Democratic Party are positioned from within it. The left, finally, refers to critics of the Democratic Party from the ideological left who no longer identify with (although often still vote for) the Democrats. On some issues, the left and progressives may hold similar positions, but the difference is in whether they believe change is best achieved working inside or outside the Democratic Party. A stronger left once existed within the party, but today much of the left is hostile toward or at least deeply cynical about it.

One final linguistic convenience is the acronym HEP—highly educated professional—which I will use to refer to the segment of the electorate on which the Democratic Party trained its focus in the 1970s and never looked back. Many terms, often derogatory, have been applied to this demographic: yuppie, suburbanite, PMC (professional-managerial class, by John and Barbara Ehrenreich), or the creative class (Richard Florida). The recent trend toward oblique references to "educational polarization"—that people with college degrees increasingly favor Democrats—gets at the same concept. HEP refers to a phenomenon that grew out of the transition to a postindustrial economy in the United States, in which less physical types of work required (or "required") credentials like a college degree. A new term was needed for this part of the labor force that wasn't proletarian or bourgeois but paycheck earners who nonetheless had clear economic and status advantages over many of their fellow paycheck earners. Future New Democrat stalwart Colorado representative Tim Wirth described it like this in 1981: "[Democratic] constituents are changing. They used to be labor, blue-collar, and minority-oriented. Now, as in my case, they are suburban, with two working parents—a college-educated, information-age constituency."[1] Despite his dated language, he hits several key HEP qualifiers: educated, savvy to the tech- and information-driven economy of the then future, and progressively oriented (a working married heterosexual woman was, in 1981, still a bit edgy).

With so much already said about this social-economic phenomenon, my goal with this acronym is simply descriptive. HEP is an attempt at a short, value-neutral descriptor for people who are successful (not necessarily wealthy but materially comfortable) and owe both their professional and social standing to knowledge and skills represented by educational credentials.

CHAPTER 1

DEPRESSION INTERCESSION

In 1934—the second year of Franklin D. Roosevelt's presidency—two employees of the Department of Agriculture invited struggling farmers in the Dust Bowl–ravaged town of Boise City, Oklahoma, to attend a meeting at the local movie theater to hear about a new government program aimed at helping people like them. Boise City, like most of the Great Plains, was suffering under a combined natural and man-made disaster* that buried crops under tons of dust brought across the prairies by biblical windstorms. This, of course, was in addition to the economic crisis that had already reduced many farmers to ruin even before the dust came.

The men from the government had an offer that was as bleak as the landscape and the shriveled crops: they were authorized to pay farmers one dollar per head to shoot and bury their skeletal, sick, dying cattle. If any of the wretched animals could still walk, the government would pay sixteen dollars to process them into food for distribution to the poor.[1] The plan was intended to put cash in farmers' pockets and reduce the supply of livestock in light of plummeting commodity prices.

---

* The Dust Bowl resulted from a combination of drought, federal land policy encouraging farming of marginal arid land, and unsustainable agricultural methods. See resources from the National Drought Mitigation Center at University of Nebraska–Lincoln.

Talk about grim. Farmers recoiled at the thought of simply shooting and burying their animals. But anyone could see that with no crops, no money, and no hope, the animals were dead already. And the federal government was offering cash in hand, plus temporary paid work disposing of the condemned animals. Slowly, farmers around the room assented. It was far from ideal, but the money was a godsend.

Try to imagine the impact this moment had on the lives of those farmers, few if any of whom were likely to have strong ideological beliefs about the proper role of government in the economy. Their only concern was that they had been ruined by circumstances, including some beyond their control, and now the traditionally distant and hands-off federal government was offering a lifeline. There was nothing abstract to understand, no "enhanced tax rebates for qualifying Zoroastrian households with no more than three dependents." And there were hundreds of towns like Boise City across the United States. Life had been reduced to the lower tiers of Maslow's hierarchy: food, shelter. Desperate times produced desperate people. They needed help, and here it was.

Upon election in 1932, FDR was already broadly supported by farmers and the poor; he promised help and followed through, aided by enormous Democratic congressional majorities that swept into office with him. Some previously politically indifferent Americans ended up not only supporting Roosevelt but adoring him. The New Deal solidified Democratic support among large segments of the electorate that would last for decades.* It did so by appealing directly to the economic interests of different classes—the poor, the middle class, and even some members of the plutocracy—and by investing in visible improvements in public goods to generate jobs in the short term and a better society in the long term.

The New Deal was not a social justice agenda; the harshest and most valid criticisms leveled at Roosevelt retrospectively involve his failure to address directly issues of racial inequality—a political calculation intended to placate prosegregation white southerners.[2] Yet FDR also broke

---

* From 1933 to 1995, Democrats had the House majority for all but two two-year periods (the 80th and 83rd Congresses).

the decades-long pattern of Black* voters as loyal Republicans. By offering help to the poor, a category in which Black Americans were disproportionately represented, Roosevelt inspired electoral loyalty even while
foot-dragging on issues like segregation.† As one Black interviewee explained to Studs Terkel in his seminal oral history of the Depression,
Hard Times:

> [FDR] broke the tradition. My father told me, "Republicans are the ship.
> All else is the sea." Frederick Douglass said that. [Black voters] didn't go
> for Roosevelt much in '32. But the WPA [Works Progress Administra-
> tion] came along and Roosevelt came to be a god. It was really great. You
> worked, you got a paycheck and you had some dignity.[3]

To understand how the Democratic Party has changed in the past half
century, it is necessary to look at where the journey began. Even though
nearly a century has elapsed since the New Deal arrived in Washington,
DC, American politics still takes place in its long shadow.‡

---

* Throughout this book I use the term *Black* for the stylistic improvement it offers over
writing "Black or African American" repeatedly or using the terms interchangeably and
inconsistently.

† Roosevelt also expressed racist attitudes in private, such as endorsing the then wide-
spread eugenic theories conflating race and intelligence. Critical discussion of FDR,
the New Deal, and race includes Sullivan, P., *Days of Hope: Race and Democracy in the
New Deal Era* (Chapel Hill: University of North Carolina Press, 2014); and Weiss, N.,
Farewell to the Party of Lincoln: Black Politics in the Age of FDR (Princeton, NJ: Princeton
University Press, 1983).

‡ Doing justice to the New Deal and FDR is obviously beyond the scope of a book chap-
ter. A partial list of thorough histories includes Cowie, J., *The Great Exception: The New
Deal and the Limits of American Politics* (Princeton, NJ: Princeton University Press, 2017);
Katznelson, I., *Fear Itself: The New Deal and the Origins of Our Time* (New York: Live-
right, 2013); and Phillips-Fein, K., *Invisible Hands: The Businessmen's Crusade Against the
New Deal* (New York: W. W. Norton, 2010).

THE DEMOCRATIC PARTY, PRE-1932

In the Beginning, there was FDR.
—Genesis 1:5*

The Democratic Party obviously did not begin with FDR, but an understanding of the *modern* Democratic Party has to start in 1932. The first century of history of the Democratic Party is of little relevance to events since 1970 and is largely omitted here.[4] A party called the Democratic Party existed by 1828 (and a Democratic-Republican Party dating to Thomas Jefferson before it) but bore little resemblance to its modern namesake.

Immediately preceding the New Deal was an era of Republican dominance from 1896 to 1932, which political scientists call the Fourth Party System. In that era the Democratic Party controlled the Senate for only six years and the House for only ten (in one case by a single seat). Only one Democratic president, Woodrow Wilson, was elected—with Theodore Roosevelt's third-party Bull Moose candidacy in 1912 splitting the Republican vote and assisting Wilson's win. The game of pretending, however, that Democratic and Republican mean today what they meant in, say, 1870 is best left to hack right-wing "historians." The concept of *realignment*—the process by which the parties and who supports them evolves and changes—makes the meaning of the party labels a moving target over time.

The coalition of reliable Democratic voters prior to 1932 was both geographically and ideologically scattershot. The power brokers in the party were the bosses of northern urban political machines and the ex-Confederate white southern landowner class. The former pulled white European immigrants into the Democratic fold, while the latter rallied rural whites and ensured that Black Americans had abrogated rights in many states. But this coalition was insufficiently large and too ideologically indistinct to seriously challenge the Republicans—the party of booming Gilded Age industrial capitalism and finance as well as some progressive social and political reformers—in the early twentieth century.

* Probably.

A Democratic Party rule mandating a two-thirds national convention vote to nominate a presidential ticket ensured that the former Confederacy—the Solid South—exercised a de facto veto over national Democratic politics for decades following the Civil War.

The United States had experienced economic collapses prior to the Great Depression; in fact, the phrase "Great Depression" was used prior to 1929 to refer to the economic downturn of 1837. What began in 1929, though, truly earned the adjective *great.** The depth and breadth of the collapse was without precedent, and it occurred in a United States that had grown considerably in population, economic power, and complexity since earlier economic crises.

FDR, who had adopted the party affiliation of his father James rather than his cousin Theodore, ended three-plus decades of Democratic futility by handily defeating Herbert Hoover in 1932. Democrats also took unprecedented majorities in Congress that year. Republicans lost a staggering 101 House seats—and then lost 29 more over the next two elections. In the Senate, the term *supermajority* understated Democratic dominance. By January of 1937, only 16 of 96 senators† were Republicans. Democrats may well have won in 1932 with a generic placeholder candidate simply by pointing at Hoover and saying, "Boo this man!" Roosevelt, however, seized the opportunity and built upon his success in New York state politics (where he had served in the state senate and as governor) by promising an activist role for government that, at the time, was a radical departure from traditional expectations of a president. The large, supportive Democratic congressional majorities gave him the freedom he needed to act aggressively.

HELP US, FDR; YOU'RE OUR ONLY HOPE

Numbers rarely tell a complete story in politics, but consider just a few New Deal statistics.[5] Its various programs directly built 212 dams and canals, 894 sewage treatment plants, 68,000 miles of firebreaks, 406 post

---

* The earlier crisis has been demoted linguistically to the Panic of 1837, which frankly sounds like it could be fun.

† Alaska and Hawaii did not attain statehood until 1959.

offices, 384 airports, 698 university buildings, 77,965 (!) new bridges, 325 fire stations, 407 public swimming pools, and 2,000 miles of levees.

It stocked lakes with over a billion fish, brought electricity to over a million rural households through 381,000 miles of power lines, commissioned almost 16,000 works of art for public spaces, made 1.4 million pieces of furniture for public schools, planted 2.3 billion trees, and built over 4,000 city parks. In its spare time it created Social Security to alleviate old-age poverty. Beyond the FDR years, the Democratic coalition assembled behind the New Deal went on to build the Interstate Highway System,* pass the Voting Rights Act, create Medicare and Medicaid, expand public higher education, and do other things that could feature prominently in a montage video called *America: We Used to Do Some Good Stuff.*

The statistics and alphabet soup of specific New Deal programs are less important here than its overarching purpose. Crucially, it was not an effort to impose socialism on the United States as its detractors claimed at the time and claim still. Contemporary and historical analyses have placed the New Deal firmly in the context of a larger, international shift toward state-managed economies that took place in 1933.[6] Yet unlike its European counterparts, the New Deal was explicitly an effort to *save* capitalism. It stopped short of creating a European-style social welfare state, let alone Soviet-style collectivism or fascist-style corporatism.[7] In a series of events that foreshadowed Barack Obama and the 2009 financial crisis, the Roosevelt administration faced the complete collapse of the economic status quo in 1932. Unlike Obama, FDR chose to (and was politically able to) make major reforms to that system. He made a clean break with the past in an era where it was clear to American business leaders and the voting public that reforms much more drastic than any proposed in the New Deal were a realistic possibility—Italy, Germany, the Soviet Union, and others stood as recent examples.

The core of the New Deal was a comprehensive set of ideologically liberal policy proposals aimed at ameliorating the worst effects of the Depression and preventing (or mitigating) future economic downturns.

---

* Signed by Eisenhower but passed by a Democratic House and, narrowly, through a divided Senate. Democratic Senate delegations in southern states provided the crucial margin for 41–39 passage of the House bill.

Importantly, Roosevelt's proposed means of bringing relief and managing the economy was to use federal power to intervene in the economy, create jobs, and reduce unemployment. Direct, long-term state takeover of industry was never seriously considered. Previously, American politics had featured a broad establishment consensus that the power, size, and role of the federal government should be limited. To Roosevelt, however, no other entity could handle a disaster of this magnitude.* A serious crisis required serious action, not incrementalism.

Understanding the New Deal as a crash program to save the free market makes it clear why some prominent capitalists supported Roosevelt: the powerful Du Pont family, much of the oil industry (to which New Deal price controls and cartelization under the National Industrial Recovery Act were especially appealing), and the banking industry outside of the J.P. Morgan empire, to name a few.[8] When executives from Standard Oil and General Electric helped FDR craft the Social Security Administration, for example, they weren't expressing the latent pinko sympathies of the ownership class. They believed that without significant reforms aimed at poverty and inequality, something akin to the Communists' rise to power in the Soviet Union could happen in the United States. This was not hyperbole. As the banking system teetered on total collapse, the prospect of radical social change was, if not exactly imminent, plausible to power brokers of the day, and the New Deal extended a lifeline that some corporate titans were in no position to reject on partisan or ideological grounds. A 1936 campaign speech Roosevelt gave in Chicago offers an example of his clear commitment to capitalism and liberal democracy:

> You have heard about how antagonistic to business this Administration is supposed to be. You have heard all about the dangers which the business of America is supposed to be facing if this Administration continues.
>
> The answer to that is the record of what we have done. It was this Administration *which saved the system of private profit and free enterprise* after it had been dragged to the brink of ruin by these same leaders who now

---

* Paraphrasing Admiral Ackbar, *Star Wars: Return of the Jedi*.

try to scare you. . . . Today for the first time in seven years the banker, the storekeeper, the small factory owner, the industrialist, can all sit back and enjoy the company of their own ledgers. They are in the black. That is where we want them to be; that is where our policies aim them to be.[9] (emphasis added)

So strike the idea that FDR and the New Deal were the American version of Lenin and the Five-Year Plans of the Supreme Soviet. The New Deal was an intervention in free-market capitalism that worked with, rather than existentially threatened, the titans of American commerce.

When the New Deal did veer toward more transformative change, it did so because of populist movements that forced the Democratic Party to the left. For example, radical leaders in organized labor altered the character of Roosevelt's National Labor Relations Act (NLRA). The administration had originally hoped to bring about orderly labor-management relations with a mild system of what effectively were company unions. Militant activism and waves of sit-down strikes initiated by the rank and file instead forced policy makers to recognize workers' right to bargain collectively through strong, independent unions.[10] The NLRA may not have been thrilling to bankers and industrialists, but the potential for something worse (from their perspective) was galvanizing.* Arguing in support of the NLRA, one congressman darkly warned that sit-down strikes and picket lines were small potatoes; without reform, the "gates of hell" would open and unleash labor radicalism across the country.[11] Way to threaten us with a good time.

THE GENIUS OF THE NEW DEAL

Presidents had entered the White House with grand ideas before. Notwithstanding the many achievements of the Progressive Era and earlier movements—1890s prairie populism, the brief World War I–era rise of the Socialist Party under Eugene V. Debs, militant labor activists, pioneering fighters for racial equality, suffragettes, and more—the New Deal promised the greatest expansion of the role of government in American

---

* The term *galvanizing* derives from eighteenth-century Italian physician Luigi Galvani, who discovered the concept of bioelectricity in animals.

history. It offered something tangible for almost everyone: north, south, east, and west, farmer or laborer, Black or white, rural or urban, rich or poor. Support for Roosevelt and the New Deal was never universal, obviously, but it achieved sufficiently broad popularity to give Democrats a winning electoral coalition for almost forty years.

The Gilded Age and the Roaring Twenties preceding the Depression proved that unregulated markets abused labor, produced corrosive levels of economic inequality, encouraged wild financial speculation, and pushed the externalities of economic activity (like pollution, corruption, and unsafe workplaces and products) onto the public and the state. The guiding economic dogma of the New Dealers was the then novel concept of Keynesianism, which argued that governments should respond to contractions of the economy by loosening rather than tightening the purse strings.[12] When the free market recedes, the government should fill the void. This would become politically controversial and, by 1980, discredited by many conservatives and neoliberals influenced by, among others, Milton Friedman and Friedrich von Hayek. For New Dealers, though, Keynes was the North Star.

Social welfare programs and direct assistance to people thrown into poverty and unemployment were largely unknown in the United States at the beginning of the Depression. The preferred solutions were charity, primarily administered by religious groups, and scolding the poor for their lack of character, as if real life were a Horatio Alger story where a rigged system could be beaten with luck, pluck, and diligence. FDR proposed an old-age pension plan based on lifetime contributions from workers and employers—Social Security—as the centerpiece of an economic safety net aimed at dulling the worst effects of poverty. Not all relief took the form of social welfare policies, though. Price supports for farm outputs, for example, greatly improved the economic lot of farmers while support for labor unions and workplace standards (maximum hours, overtime pay laws, minimum wages, health and safety minimums, etc.) increased the standard of living of millions of laborers. Direct aid to the poor was included, but economic policy oriented toward the goal of full employment favored the creation of federally funded jobs programs and other schemes to incentivize hiring. Accusations of socialism notwithstanding, the architects of the New Deal bent over backward to defer to the private sector.

Public works served two functions in the New Deal schema: creating jobs and improving infrastructure and the built environment for millions of Americans. The America of the time needed it badly; many areas of the country remained without basic services like electricity and plumbing. Public lands were underdeveloped. Outside major urban centers, the free market had done a poor job of bringing a higher quality of life to most Americans. The public goods and benefits the New Deal provided were rarely intangible—indeed, its biggest failures were in making progress on intangible problems like racial and gender inequality. It was brick-and-mortar politics, the politics of stringing up power lines, digging tunnels, laying bridges, building public services, and planting trees. Roosevelt aimed to do those things and bring paying jobs to otherwise idled workers in the bargain.

The New Deal sought to appeal broadly to politically marginalized groups like recent immigrants, women, and Blacks—but to make appeals that were economic, not rights based. Southern segregation, the lack of Black voting rights and equal rights for women, inequalities like residential and workplace segregation—none were problems Roosevelt wanted to tackle aggressively. Instead, the New Deal took the materialist view that if its relief programs and economic benefits were extended to marginalized groups, they would become members of the Democratic coalition even though other problems were ignored. It was a class-based and, frankly, cynical ploy to hold together a coalition that included immigrant and Black northern industrial laborers alongside conservative white southerners and farmers barely willing to admit that the Civil War had ended.* In the short term, this paid political dividends, as the Democratic coalition gathered under the New Deal was formidable. However, ignoring these obvious and important elephants in the room only increased the cost of confronting them later.

Historiographic accounts of the New Deal tend to depict it as a set of broadly popular and populist policy goals that brought a winning, majority

---

* It did. The Confederacy lost.

coalition of voters flocking toward Roosevelt. This is incomplete, if containing grains of truth. The coalition did not simply come together upon the shared realization that New Deal policies were good; Democratic Party organizations were instrumental in building and maintaining a loyal voter base.[13] Urban party machines, state Democratic parties, and the national Democratic Convention were all organized around maintaining cohesion, ensuring that all Democratic factions were satisfied, rewarded, or kept in line as needed.[14] Disputes among competing constituents were resolved in proverbial (and occasionally literal) smoke-filled rooms by party bigwigs, who exercised tight control over the range of acceptable issues and outcomes the coalition could unite around. Without the voting public directly involved in the nomination of candidates—a task reserved and jealously protected by the party itself—it was significantly easier for a handful of power players to cut deals and impose their will upon the rest of the party. The benefit of this brokered brand of politics was outward unity despite internal battles. The obvious downside was the homogeneity of the almost entirely white male party functionaries, elected officials, labor leaders, and business interests that dominated the closed system.

A final important ingredient in the New Deal liberal ideology came from the successors of the earlier Progressive movement. This was a crucial part of the Republican coalition at the turn of the century, led by figures like Theodore Roosevelt and "Fighting Bob" La Follette. The relationship between Progressives and Republicans was already disintegrating by 1932, with Teddy Roosevelt in 1912 and La Follette in 1924 running as presidential candidates of a separate Progressive Party against the GOP. With the promise of the New Deal attacking monopoly power (sometimes), minimizing patronage and corruption in politics, and adopting a good-government philosophy in the administration of its labyrinth of federal programs, many ex-Progressives became New Dealers.

With so many parts of the electorate attracted to the New Deal worldview, Republicans were left with a small base of support among white Protestants and certain segments of the business community that saw the pre-1932 economic order as natural and desirable. Regionally, only New England and a few urban centers with strong Republican political machines were reliable anti-Roosevelt bastions. During and immediately after World War II, Roosevelt and his successors hewed to popular, elite-consensus foreign policy that was initially isolationist, then aggressively interventionist, and always anticommunist. This ensured that the political focus remained on economic issues on which Democrats generally felt—with reason—they could not lose.

THE LONG NEW DEAL

At first, the Republican Party responded to the New Deal by fighting it tooth and nail.* Quickly, however, it conceded a need to make peace with some of the Roosevelt agenda's basic principles as a matter of survival. Social Security, farm and labor reforms, and structural economic reforms of banking and the money supply were too broadly popular to fight. Dwight Eisenhower, the only New Deal–era Republican president, enunciated the GOP policy of accommodation well: he identified as a Republican but was ideologically neutral and a realist regarding the most popular New Deal policies. He summed up his views: "Should any political party attempt to abolish social security, unemployment insurance, and eliminate labor laws and farm programs, you would not hear of that party again in our political history."[15]

He was wrong in the long run but correct in his moment. Eisenhower intuited that during the postwar economic boom, few Americans were eager to trim popular government programs on purely ideological grounds. Widely shared prosperity was a more effective argument than appeals to the abstract principle of small-government conservatism. Republicans learned with time how to score occasional victories within a framework of Democratic dominance, but they struggled until the 1970s to define a worldview that was both attractive to voters and sufficiently unique to overcome the structural disadvantages working against them. By accepting that Democrats had the upper hand, the GOP improved comity in Congress but effectively consigned itself to minority party status. Predictably, it could not achieve any kind of consistent success or develop

---

* "Tooth and nail" first appears in Thomas More's *A Dialogue of Comfort and Tribulation* (1534) to characterize Protestant-Catholic antagonism in Tudor England. When you must fight tooth and nail, imagine yourself dressed in Tudor fashions, and before long you'll forget what the fight was about.

a unique brand while admitting that the Democrats were correct about the economy and the role of government on a basic level. They let the Democrats define the premise, the terms of acceptable debate, and the range of achievable outcomes, all of which severely hampered Republicans' freedom to operate politically.

In Congress, they pursued a "go along to get along" strategy,[16] supporting the basics of Democratic economic policy in exchange for some concessions around the edges. Republican supporters would have to accept these negotiated concessions as the closest thing to victory they had any chance of achieving. If the New Deal could not be stopped or dismantled, Republicans hoped they could at least exert some influence over its implementation and perhaps limit its scope. It was a role that felt, and was, subsidiary. One analogy put electoral politics of the era in cosmic terms: Democrats were the sun and Republicans, the moon.[17]

The result of Republicans largely making peace with the New Deal was an era of unprecedented policy experimentation, investment in public works, and—eventually—social reform. Many historians and economists have pointed out that World War II, not solely the New Deal, pulled the United States out of the Great Depression for good. Still other critics from the left lambaste the New Deal as same-old exploitative capitalism in a shiny new package meant to bamboozle and pacify workers.* These critiques combine truth and oversimplifications. Some early reflections on the New Deal did treat it with something resembling prostrate awe, but modern scholarship both recognizes the antiradical foundations of Roosevelt's ideology and accepts the limits of New Deal accomplishments. It is clear, for example, that public works projects did not permanently reduce unemployment as policy makers intended. They did, however, function as a massive investment in infrastructure that made the economic boom that followed possible.[18] And crucially, the New Deal vision of government as a force for good persisted beyond FDR, enabling arguably the longest sustained period of increasing economic equality in American history. Without this core

---

* Prominent examples include but are not limited to Howard Zinn, Barton Bernstein, Ronald Radosh, and even the more critical consensus historians like Richard Hofstadter and William Leuchtenburg.

belief in government that was Roosevelt's political legacy, the push during the 1960s for antipoverty and equal rights legislation or the expansion of the social safety net would have been improbable.

TROUBLE BREWIN'

Like the Death Star, the New Deal Democrats were built with a fundamental weakness: by assembling a coalition around shared economic interests, other issues were pushed aside in the name of Democratic unity. Prominent Democrats throughout the era held and expressed racist attitudes and showed little enthusiasm for (or outright hostility to) addressing segregation, inequality, and other racial issues. It does not absolve those leaders to say their hands were tied by political pragmatism. The failure to address racial inequality was complete: political, moral, and ethical. The record is not entirely devoid of progress made on issues of inequality, but Roosevelt and his successors took a decidedly relaxed approach to America's glaring racial divisions. What desire for reform did exist among New Dealers broke against the rocks of a powerful and disciplined bloc of ultraconservative southern Democrats in Congress who held a practical veto over any civil rights legislation.

Outside either political party, though, a powerful movement for Black equality grew from the grassroots during the post–World War II era.[19] Support for Black civil rights was not neatly divided along party lines at first: northern Democrats and liberal Republicans tended to be supportive, while conservative Republicans and southern Democrats tended to be adamantly opposed. Whenever the Democratic Party made feints toward taking up the cause of the civil rights movement, southern Dixiecrats responded with outrage and threats to withdraw from the coalition.

No single date or event signifies the fracture in the Democratic coalition on issues of race; it played out over time. When Harry Truman desegregated the armed forces by executive order in 1948, for example, the short-lived States Rights Democratic Party formed to support the presidential candidacy of Strom Thurmond. While Truman was reelected, Thurmond received thirty-nine electoral votes from the former Confederacy, an early warning sign of political upheaval to come. The 1954 Supreme Court ruling in *Brown v. Board of Education* was met with vows of "massive resistance" from southern political power players, almost all Democrats. Strom Thurmond resurfaced to oppose the Civil Rights Act of 1957, to the point of staging a solo filibuster for twenty-four hours and eighteen minutes. It became law, with liberal northern Republicans overcoming conservative southern Democrats' opposition, but achieved little to advance Black voting rights, necessitating the subsequent civil rights acts.*

Prosegregation pressure groups and elected officials were not able to halt all progress, but they presented a serious threat to the otherwise dominant Democratic majority. Anti–civil rights figures both dabbled in third parties—Thurmond's Dixiecrat campaign of 1948 or the independent candidacy of George Wallace in 1968—and drifted toward the Republican Party. Much is made of the Republican Southern Strategy attributed to Richard Nixon, but the process of the Democrats becoming more liberal on race and equality while Republicans responded by becoming more conservative both predated Nixon and unfolded over the following decades.[20] The arch-Dixiecrat, Strom Thurmond himself, became a Republican in 1964—the same year Lyndon Johnson scored a landslide victory in the presidential election by winning every state *except* those of the Deep South.†

The New Deal era cannot be repeated, but more than fifty years later, it remains a holy grail for Democrats—if not in terms of policy, then for sheer electoral dominance. Even if divided on some issues, Democratic congressional majorities were for many years as much a fact of life as the seasons. But the New Deal era has been over for a long time, and Democrats now alternate between running away from that past and remembering it wistfully as an era in which they wielded great power. The story of how the Democratic Party became what it is today begins, then, where the New Deal ends.

---

* Follow-up legislation included the Civil Rights Acts of 1960, 1964, and 1968 and the Voting Rights Act of 1965.
† Barry Goldwater also won his native Arizona.

CHAPTER 2

THE TWIN TRAUMAS OF '68 AND '72

In 2013, then California attorney general Kamala Harris was a featured speaker at Chicago Ideas Week, where she gave a TED-style talk called—I hope you like buzzwords—"Innovation and Evolution in Our Criminal Justice System."* During the talk, well received by an audience of people who have unironically called themselves thought leaders at least once, she demonstrates a trait common to today's Democrats: emphasizing that she is not one of "those" Democrats. Not a *liberal*. You know, the starry-eyed, change-the-world, Kumbaya-singing variety, conjuring up stock caricatures of liberalism's past: the peacenik, the fist-clenched Black Panther, the bra-burning women's libber, the dope-addled hippie, and the spiritual successor of them all, today's delusional Bernie Bro. She defends her tough-on-crime record and mocks a favorite target of liberal bashing—Jesse Jackson—for suggesting the solution to crime is to build more schools rather than more prisons. *What a rube!*

---

* Full video available at Harris, K., "Innovation and Evolution in Our Criminal Justice System," Chicago Ideas, YouTube video, 18:57, www.youtube.com/watch?v=4bPRtLby CjY; thanks to Corey Robin for calling attention to it.

Not yet a household name in Democratic politics, it was essential for Harris to ensure nobody got the wrong idea about her. She understands the appeal of idealistic liberalism, of course: "We have these posters in our closet," she says of the protest slogans of younger days. But now it's time to grow up. Embrace the carceral state. Think about what really matters, like opportunities to increase shareholder value. That's the big reveal this rhetorical technique always builds to: I am a Democrat you can trust because I reject everything about liberalism that might threaten the status quo.

This defensive posturing has become a common palate cleanser for Democrats with ambition, a way of signaling to elites that they can be trusted not to upset any apple carts if elected to positions of power. Barack Obama similarly left the audience of a 2002 antiwar rally in Chicago in awkward silence by opening with:

> Let me begin by saying that although this has been billed as an anti-war rally, I stand before you as someone who is not opposed to war in all circumstances. . . . I don't oppose all wars.[1]

He repeated a version of the phrase "I don't oppose all wars" three more times in the short speech just to be safe. And if these examples were too subtle, Sen. Claire McCaskill (D-MO) closed her 2018 reelection campaign with radio ads telling voters she's "not one of those crazy Democrats." Somehow, she lost.

Some Democrats defend this kind of position taking as a smart way to appeal to an electorate they insist is unalterably conservative as being realistic, pragmatic, being an adult. In practice, they're conceding that the right is correct about a lot of things and agreeing that "liberal" is poisonous in theory and in practice.[2] They recoil at the idea of liberalism and then act surprised when voters fail to embrace any remotely liberal ideas.

Whether they realize it or not, generations of liberals-but-not-liberals are still reacting to the formative experience of Richard Nixon's 1972 drubbing of George McGovern, which followed the near disintegration of the Democratic Party live on television in 1968. These were deeply scarring experiences, particularly to baby boomers who reached voting age circa 1970.

How did liberal become a dirty word, and liberalism a taboo concept even within the nominally liberal party? What happened that so traumatized the Democratic establishment that it still trots out McGovern '72 as a warning about why it must keep moving to the right *fifty years* later? What sort of monster was this McGovern guy that Joe Biden's bland yet warm praise *in a eulogy at McGovern's funeral* was dug up and used to slam Biden in 2021?[3]

Moreover, why 1968 and 1972 instead of, say, the embarrassing Democratic defeats of 1984 and 1988? The short answer is that they were important mileposts on the journey toward the collapse of the New Deal coalition. Democratic politics have since moved in an entirely new direction that redefined liberalism, the ideology of the Democratic Party, and who makes up the Democratic coalition. The consequences of those changes are still playing out today.

1968: THE 2020 OF THE SIXTIES

Sure, 2020 was a bad year. Some new insanity seemed to happen every day. But in the tournament of terrible years, it faces stiff competition from 1968.

Two major national figures, Martin Luther King Jr. and Robert F. Kennedy, were assassinated in quick succession. Riots in the wake of King's death—rekindling racial tensions that had already exploded into serious urban rioting in 1965 and 1967—left at least thirty-nine people dead and several major cities on fire. American involvement in the Vietnam War escalated with events like the Tet Offensive, and such statements from military leaders as "it became necessary to destroy the town to save it" hinted that perhaps the war was not going quite as well as the Pentagon claimed. Police killed three antisegregation protesters at South Carolina State University and engaged in wild shoot-outs with Black activists in separate incidents in Oakland and Cleveland. The introduction of the National Guard into many American cities created an uncomfortable analogue to the Soviet invasion of Czechoslovakia taking place simultaneously. Other events too numerous to list here, from labor actions to campus protests, fed the atmosphere of tension.[4] The year, in short, deserves its reputation as a pivot point of recent history and, frankly, an overall bad time.

Events directly involved the Democratic Party at several points, from the assassination of one of its leading presidential candidates to the Johnson administration's increasingly unpopular involvement in Vietnam to the memorable chaos at the Democratic Convention in Chicago that August. The party that began 1968 in its fourth decade of national political dominance ended the year in disarray with an uncertain future. The key weakness of the New Deal coalition, recall, was the tenuous alliance among groups with shared economic interests but little else in common. By 1968, the movement for Black civil rights and desegregation, which gained momentum after World War II, had become an open battleground within the coalition, forcing Democrats to confront racial tensions within the party. Some southern Democrats who refused to accept advances in civil rights fueled the splinter campaign of segregationist and former Democratic governor George Wallace (of the infamous 1963 "stand in the schoolhouse door" to protest racial integration at the University of Alabama).

The Vietnam War became a major wedge issue that divided Democrats between younger, more liberal antiwar and older, establishment anticommunist factions. Those who could agree on civil rights suddenly found themselves divided on Vietnam, and vice versa. Even without the riots, violence, and assassinations, the 1968 election would likely have been chaotic for the national Democratic Party simply on the strength of its own internal tensions.

THE NOMINATION

The presidential nomination process worked much differently in 1968 than it does today. Some states held primary elections, but the results were not binding; they functioned as beauty pageants in which candidates tried to demonstrate that they were popular and thus the best choice to take on the Republican challenger. The convention delegates, selected by state parties and broadly the product of tight-knit local machine politics, chose the nominee irrespective of primary election results.

It was not immediately alarming, then, when a challenger emerged to run against the incumbent Lyndon Johnson in 1968. Sen. Eugene McCarthy of Minnesota, representing an antiwar peace platform, was hardly a figure on par with LBJ—master of the Senate, torchbearer of the legacy of FDR and JFK. While Johnson won the first-in-nation New Hampshire primary, McCarthy's strong second-place finish got all the attention. It was apparent that Johnson and the Democratic establishment had underestimated the strength of opposition to the Vietnam War among a significant minority of Democrats. That a middling senator—backed by an army of college kids who adopted the slogan "Get Clean for Gene"*— was a serious primary challenger to the incumbent president was interpreted, not unreasonably, as a sign of Johnson's waning popularity.

Seeing the writing on the wall,† Johnson announced in a dramatic television address on March 31, 1968, his refusal to seek a second full term (or to run if nominated). This created a political vacuum that Robert F. Kennedy hoped to fill, presenting himself as Johnson's logical successor. Unlike McCarthy, he had considerable standing among the party establishment as well as the afterglow of the still powerful aura around his martyred brother. Competing fiercely in the primaries, McCarthy and RFK traded punches until, finally, Kennedy appeared to strike a winning blow in California. Moments after delivering his victory speech at Los Angeles's Ambassador Hotel, he strode offstage and, surrounded by kitchen workers straining to shake his hand, met the same fate his brother had in Dallas in 1963. He died asking busboy Juan Romero, who pressed a rosary into Kennedy's palm, if everyone else was OK.

Some Democrats think more than a potential presidential candidate died that day. Kennedy positioned himself as the one candidate who could hold the New Deal coalition together. His idea of a Black-and-blue base composed of people of color and working-class white voters, united by working-class interests, is wistfully remembered by many

---

* To combat the hippie stereotype of young voters in that era, McCarthy's campaign volunteers tamed their wild 1960s locks, removed their beards, and dressed in business attire.

† This phrase derives from the Book of Daniel, wherein a disembodied, floating hand appears during a feast and writes the words "numbered, numbered, weighed, and they are divided" on a wall. Babylonian parties were *wild*.

progressive Democrats today as a missed opportunity. That Kennedy could have achieved that goal is not a given. He was not even assured the Democratic nomination let alone the presidency. And while his popularity among voters of color was very high,* like other Democrats of his era, he lagged among working-class and suburban white voters. Though as a Catholic and a Kennedy, he may well have kept more white conservative Democrats in the fold, RFK remains a compelling—but unknowable—what-if.

With political assassinations a distant memory for modern Americans, it takes effort to appreciate the impact this had on the election. Imagine how the murder of the leading candidate on June 6, mere weeks before the Democratic convention, would play out today. What happens next? Who gets nominated? What chance does that person have to win in November? With Eugene McCarthy something of a Bernie Sanders figure in 1968—polarizing among voters and an absolute nonstarter among the Democratic establishment—the nomination coalesced around a man who hadn't even run in any primaries.[†]

Convention delegates in Chicago settled, in every sense of the term, on incumbent vice president Hubert Humphrey as a safe, predictable, known quantity. Humphrey was a compromise that satisfied almost no one. Southern Dixiecrats considered him a racial liberal. Antiwar activists saw him as a warmongering extension of LBJ's Vietnam policy. RFK loyalists saw him as a bland, charisma-free placeholder unlikely to appeal to anyone except Democratic functionaries.

The infamously chaotic convention didn't become a fiasco when Humphrey secured the nomination; it was a fiasco from the outset. Televised scenes of police clubbing protesters in the streets outside the convention mirrored the chaos—with actual punches thrown[‡] and barroom

---

* This produced possibly the most cringe-inducing but largely forgotten moment in political history when, seeing the huge number of votes her husband received from Black voters, Ethel Kennedy exclaimed in front of reporters, "Don't you just wish that everyone was Black?"

† Humphrey received write-in votes but did not campaign or appear on the ballot in any state.

‡ Young CBS reporter Dan Rather was punched in the stomach and knocked to the ground on the convention floor.

challenges issued from the podium*—taking place inside. The convention delegates voted down a McCarthy-led antiwar platform, nominated the central-casting establishment Democrat, and fled under a cloud of tear gas. It was only mildly surprising, then, when Richard Nixon and his law-and-order-themed campaign (which focused on urban rioting with the attendant winking racial overtones) won over the divided and fractious Democrats.

That Humphrey made the election competitive at all was a credit to the mobilization efforts of his strongest supporters: labor unions. Though the union-party relationship was already fraying, 1968 showed that organized labor remained powerful electorally. Since most unions and their members were hostile to the "peacenik" and other activist factions that opposed Humphrey, they backed the vice president with zeal. It was a mini culture war, the beginning of a long struggle for control as the Democratic coalition fell apart. The stereotypical image of the era's conflict—youthful radicals clashing with the square-jawed establishment—played out both literally and figuratively. While Humphrey's victory represented a win for the establishment, in hindsight, he was the final Democrat propelled to the presidential nomination almost entirely by labor.

The Humphrey campaign was not merely supported by the unions; it *was* the unions.[5] Crucially, they blasted the abysmal labor records of Nixon and Wallace, both of whom made inroads among white union men with appeals to grievance politics but had explicitly antilabor views that threatened union livelihoods. This highlighted a battle for the white working-class voter that is still happening today, with Republicans offering reactionary culture war appeals and Democrats, in theory, countering with appeals to economic self-interest. What would the Democrats have left to offer if they lost their credibility and ability to appeal to working people's economic well-being? (That's called foreshadowing. All the best writers do it.)

The best efforts of organized labor were not enough to save Humphrey in 1968. Yet to demonstrate the depth and strength of the New Deal

---

* Chicago mayor Richard Daley can be seen shouting, "Fuck you, you Jew son of a bitch, you lousy motherfucker!" toward the podium as Connecticut senator Abraham Ribicoff accused the Chicago police of "gestapo tactics" with protesters. The national broadcast caught this moment clearly.

coalition, Democrats retained control of the Senate and the House. This underscores the difficulty in affixing a specific end date to the New Deal era. In presidential politics, 1968 clearly signaled a change in Democratic fortunes. But since incumbency is powerful and partisan loyalties tend to be stable, it would take decades before the consequences of the collapsing coalition filtered down ballot. Still, Nixon's victory amid the chaos made it clear that the Democratic Party had problems, and subsequent events would show that those problems, incredibly, were even worse than they seemed in 1968.

A NEW NOMINATION PROCESS

Seeking to avoid at all costs a repeat of the embarrassing display at the 1968 convention, the Democratic National Committee appointed a panel to study and recommend changes to the presidential nomination process and to internally reform the party. It was obvious that Democratic voters needed more say in the process—more than the "none" they had at the time—and that a nominee must be acceptable to different party factions. Officially called the Commission on Party Structure and Delegate Selection, history knows it by the names of the congressmembers who chaired it: the McGovern-Fraser Commission (MFC).* Party reform commissions are not, on the surface, riveting stuff. Take my word for it and never use them as a conversation starter on a date. Yet the MFC so profoundly changed the presidential election process that it deserves a closer look.†

The commission's major recommendation was to take the power to select delegates to the Democratic convention away from state parties and party bosses directly and give states the freedom to assign delegates in a more democratic process. Although it was not the intention of the commission to mandate primaries, states quickly found that a primary

---

* Sen. George McGovern and Rep. Donald Fraser headed the Senate and House delegations, respectively.

† The commission was an internal Democratic Party body, and Republicans were not bound by any of its findings. However, the GOP quickly *chose* to adopt many of the same reforms. That is why both parties have had similar nomination processes (but not identical) both before and since 1968.

election or caucus was an obvious alternative.* Not only did voters like the idea, but some states already held primaries; the changes initiated by the MFC meant that these were no longer just for giggles. The results would mean something, pledging to a candidate a given number of delegates. In broad strokes, this is the system that persists today: Democratic primaries use a proportional representation system that awards candidates a number of delegates roughly equal to their vote share in a given primary. Formally, nominations still happen at the convention, but the outcome is now predetermined by the primaries. Whereas in 1952 voters might hang on news of what was happening at the political conventions, in 2020 it was clear long in advance that Trump and Biden would be the nominees. Today's conventions are a hybrid pep rally–infomercial.

The Democrats also adopted rules to require diversity within state delegations (the Republicans merely "encouraged" it) and banned requirements like fees or literacy tests for any state-level Democratic nomination process. The unit rule was eliminated, meaning individual delegates could vote as they chose rather than how a party boss mandated—in theory. In practice and over time, the outcome of a primary (or caucus) in their state filled a similar role.

Because power flowed away from party bosses and toward voters thanks to its reforms, some interpretations of McGovern-Fraser characterize it as fundamentally weakening the Democratic Party as an institution. Indeed, many Democrats who were initially resistant to these changes feared that too much democracy would give voters the power to foist a truly horrendous nominee on the party. The 2016 Republican nomination exemplified this dynamic, with GOP insiders desperately trying to steer voters away from Donald Trump and toward a gallery of men with powerful Disney Channel stepdad auras.† Yet calling the reforms antiparty oversimplifies things. Especially for Democrats, party insiders retain an important role. There are, for example, the now-infamous

---

* Omitting a discussion of primaries versus caucuses—both remain in use today—is a gift to the reader. Masochists are encouraged to consult the *Routledge Handbook of Primary Elections*, edited by R. Boatwright (Oxfordshire, UK: Routledge, 2018), for an exhaustive discussion.

† Candidates included John Kasich, Ben Carson, Marco Rubio, Jeb Bush, and—do I need to keep going or is that enough?

superdelegates: about one-fifth of the total delegates at each Democratic convention are still chosen directly by the party organization because of rule changes adopted prior to the 1984 election—to retain a direct role for the party establishment in the nomination.[6]

POST-MCGOVERN YET PRE-MCGOVERN

The Democratic Party's post-1968 reforms are a case study in unintended consequences. To whatever extent the MFC reforms weakened party organizations, that was not the reformers' plan. Warring factions within the party after 1968 could not agree to link proposed party reforms to electoral (nomination) reforms. The result was that a raft of proposed reforms intended to strengthen national, state, and local Democratic organizations was rejected while reforms to the nomination process were accepted.[7]

The Democratic Party machinery and its close allies in organized labor had played an important role in resolving disputes among competing factions within the party. They kept the coalition hanging together, something that was considerably easier to do in an era in which elected officials, party bigwigs, and labor leaders were all but exclusively white men whose interests and rights were never seriously at risk.

Perhaps the biggest winners from the internal dissention and reform were interest groups. With the power of party organizations at all levels trimmed in the interests of increased democratic participation by voters, a void formed where the guiding hand of party power had been. Because the voters are not a well-organized group that can wield power coherently, these interest groups within the Democratic orbit were best positioned to fill some of the roles left vacant by party insiders. In that era, the best organized groups aside from labor unions were advocates of social reform from the world of issue activism: environmental activists, government reform advocates, antiwar activists, civil rights groups, groups focused on racial equality, the nascent gay rights movement, women's liberation organizations,* and so on. These groups had national and local chapters.

---

* Where appropriate, I use contemporary terminology to refer to these groups in historical context.

Members. Mailing lists. Meetings. Money. Media access. In short, they had many of the things required to organize collective action.

Before 1968, candidates hoping to please the Democratic establishment had a clear sense of how to seek electoral success by currying favor from party power brokers, largely behind closed doors. After McGovern-Fraser, however, Democratic hopefuls had to win the support of disparate activist groups with discrete and often quite different demands, in appeals that now took place openly for everyone to see. For a time, Democratic politics were reduced to an absurd degree to a process of serially obtaining the declared support of a collection of caucuses: the Black Caucus, the Gay Caucus, the Environmental Caucus, the Women's Caucus, and more. This implied, and often manifested as, a lack of unity or coherent party vision. Not surprisingly, the result could be a platform that felt like a collection of positions that didn't quite fit together. The transactional, box-checking nature of securing support from various groups struck some voters as unseemly or, in the case of groups they actively disliked, objectionable.

The Democratic machine built during the New Deal era was poorly suited for a transition away from materialist politics to intangible demands. Compared to promising constituents a new highway and making sure it got built, delivering on demands for women's rights or racial equality proved much more elusive and difficult.* Unions unavoidably saw their influence retreat—not only because of party reforms but also due to a breakdown of political consensus among rank-and-file union members and increasing downward pressure on labor costs in the manufacturing and extractive industries.[8] As union membership rates began a long decline, members became increasingly older, whiter, overwhelmingly male, and skeptical of liberal social attitudes—unrepresentative of the broader Democratic electorate.

A second major change unfolded over time: the growing need for individual elected officials and candidates to become adept at raising large amounts of money. Funding party activities had once been primarily a party function, and though Democratic Party organizations continued

---

* Specific policy promises such as the Fair Housing Act or the Equal Rights Amendment could clearly signal support, of course, but with complex social issues, even passing legislation rarely fixes the problem.

to have an important role in raising money, they would not fund the campaigns of everyone contending for nominations. But the expense of campaigning in primaries had to be met somehow, and the burden on individual candidates and their campaigns increased. As closely linked as politics and fundraising are for today's voters, in 1970 this represented a change from party-centered elections to a more candidate-centered process. Where parties once exercised powerful control over candidate selection and issue platforms, carefully balancing the various internal factions, candidates—their personalities, their goals, and their own beliefs rather than those of the official party platform—increasingly became the focal point of electoral politics.

Politics and America's moneyed interests did not meet one another for the first time after McGovern-Fraser, obviously. The two have a long and vulgar history. The introduction of federal regulations of campaign finances with the creation of the Federal Election Commission in 1974 temporarily held down the cost of campaigns, but time and the Supreme Court decision in *Citizens United v. FEC* (2010) have ensured that fundraising is subject to no limits beyond one's imagination and stable of tax attorneys. The importance of money has affected races at all levels. As a college undergraduate in 1998, I lived in the district that became America's first-ever million-dollar House race. This caused much wailing and rending of garments. Today a million-dollar race seems downright quaint, with spending across all House races totaling a hair under $9 billion in 2020.[9] Such numbers were not even conceivable in 1970.

After McGovern-Fraser, well-funded candidates with a strong showing in the first contests on the calendar would become instant frontrunners, gaining attention, headlines, money, momentum, and voters. National name recognition or popularity within the national Democratic Party would become less influential, and a lack of either could be overcome by campaigning hard and well in Iowa, New Hampshire, and the handful of other small early primary states.

The person who best understood the ways the Democratic Party, its politics, and its elections had changed was, unsurprisingly, George McGovern.[*]

---

[*] Fraser probably did too. Alas, his political ambition was to become the mayor of Minneapolis whereas McGovern eyed the White House.

While he wasn't brilliant and hadn't crafted these rules explicitly for his personal benefit, he did realize better than anyone else how the new process would likely work.

McGovern wasn't otherwise well positioned to run for the White House. He represented mighty South Dakota in the Senate and was not held in great esteem by national party figures. In 1968 he had offered himself up as a stand-in for the murdered Robert F. Kennedy but was pointedly rebuffed at the Chicago convention. McGovern, despite coming to politics in the New Deal era, was not a product of the Democratic political machine. Rather, he came from activist politics, notably the civil rights and antiwar movements of the 1960s and a stream of political thought that became known as the New Politics movement (and its cousin, the New Left). He was relentlessly (and easily) mocked by the party establishment as a caricature of activist politics, painted as the candidate of "acid, amnesty,* and abortion."

Whereas the New Deal coalition was held together with distributive, material politics—who gets what and how much—channeled through state and local parties,[10] abortion exemplified the New Politics shift toward higher-order goals aimed at creating a better world, what political scientist James Q. Wilson famously called purposive (ideological, intangible) goals.[11] McGovern's brief, dismal turn at the top was the Democratic Party's first experience with how difficult it could be to deliver rights and equality instead of farm subsidies and bridges. Gone were party bosses positioning themselves as simple distributors of patronage and pork; the new political environment required position taking on highly divisive issues.†

NEW POLITICS

New Politics was the label attached to a strain of American liberalism that grew out of activism, particularly the antiwar and civil rights movements of the 1950s and 1960s. It attracted younger, more liberal, more

---

* Amnesty referred to the debate over whether to punish Americans who evaded the draft during the Vietnam War. Jimmy Carter eventually declared an amnesty from criminal charges for violations of the Military Selective Service Act.

† This did not escape notice at the time; an example of contemporary and bitter criticism is Kemble, P., and J. Muravchik, "The New Politics and the Democrats," *Commentary* 54, no. 6 (1972).

issue-driven followers than the establishment Democratic Party. Fueled by an infusion of campus activists and other movement figures from the 1960s, New Politics Democrats explicitly sought to redirect the Democratic Party away from organized labor and the working class as its key constituency. They argued that social change was impossible so long as the Democrats were wedded to, bluntly, America's old racist uncles. New Politics activists repeatedly butted heads with the white working-class Democrats they considered holdovers from the New Deal era, finding them staunchly supportive of the military (and the war in Vietnam), lukewarm at best on equal rights, and hopelessly staid and hostile to enlightened thinking in general. Shake-up-the-system politics were the future, and the narrow economic focus of the New Deal was the past. Some contemporary commentators asked if New Politics was "a mood or a movement"; in other words, it prioritized one's state of mind and level of enlightenment over policy or practical politics.[12]

One anecdote sums up the diverging political worldviews of that era: philosopher James Miller was a key figure in the arch-1960s campus activist group Students for a Democratic Society (SDS). In his account of that era, *Democracy Is in the Streets*, he describes the difficulty SDS volunteers had in recruiting poor and working-class people to their new brand of enlightened liberalism. The young activists were stunned to discover that such people sometimes had positive feelings toward the military and the Vietnam War. Despite their low economic status and distrust for some institutions of government (particularly the police), they saw America as fundamentally good and committed to a noble mission on the global stage. Unable to square their own vision of liberalism with the reality of what some of the people they encountered believed, SDS volunteers quickly gave up on trying to reach "regular people" and instead focused their organizing efforts on college students.[13]

In place of the New Deal coalition, New Politics activists envisioned winning elections with "constituencies of conscience." Writing off the working class, the poor, and labor to reactionary racist and prowar politics, they would instead bring together enlightened people seeking institutional reforms: good-government activists, McGovern-Fraser party reformers, social justice seekers, civil rights activists, pacifists, and other groovy souls. Making the world a kinder place appealed particularly to younger activists (this is the generation, after all, that brought us the 1967 Summer of Love and founded a civic organization in 1968 called Up with People). While the New Politics movement ostensibly believed government should help the poor and the working class, in practice it had difficulty connecting with such voters because New Politics explicitly rejected the New Deal tenet that workers were a class with common interests.*

The New Politics movement envisioned a better world and aimed to fundamentally transform American politics to make that vision a reality. The intentions were good.† Ultimately, the Democratic Party's embrace of New Politics in 1972, as interpreted by and filtered through the McGovern campaign, did not merely fail. It failed in a way that left scars that have not healed a half century later. But first, a case study in the growing divide—ideological, cultural, and class based—within the Democratic Party of 1970.

HARD HAT RIOT

If you like your metaphors unambiguous and your symbolism right on the surface, the rupture of the New Deal coalition was exemplified by events in Lower Manhattan on May 8, 1970. Four days after the shooting of thirteen antiwar students at Kent State University, which killed four, a crowd of several hundred antiwar activists, mostly college students, protested outside the New York Stock Exchange.[14] The dead and injured Kent State students had been protesting the recent expansion of the Vietnam War into Cambodia, and the Manhattan protesters organized around the same issue.

Resentment between working-class and student-centered activist groups had been growing for years and was a contributing factor to violence at the 1968 Democratic Convention—the symbolism of blue-collar

---

* This point veers into the overlap between New Politics and the concurrent New Left movement. The two had commonalities, but the New Left viewed party organizations and leadership as inherently antidemocratic. Thus, the key difference—mercifully tangential here—is that New Politics led toward electoralism while the New Left described their end goal as revolution. For a thorough overview, see Coker, J., *Confronting American Labor: The New Left Dilemma* (Columbia: University of Missouri Press, 2002).
† Is there a more foreboding phrase?

Chicago cops lashing out at people they saw as privileged college brats trying to hijack *their* Democratic Party was not subtle. It is impossible to ascribe motives and feelings to every participant in an event that eventually involved around twenty thousand people, but the student-led protest in New York quickly attracted an improvised counterprotest disproportionately made up of tradesmen working on construction projects in Lower Manhattan. Like the reliably disheveled antiwar youths, these men appeared in perfect costume (white T-shirts, suspenders, hard hats) to create a visually compelling contrast for the cameras. Against the antiwar rhetoric, the counterprotesters shouted slogans like "USA all the way."

Fights broke out. Injuries piled up in the generalized mayhem. Luckily, nobody was killed. The event clarified what was happening in a way that even the Kent State shootings had not.* The scenes of stereotypical blue-collar workers—rough, white, defiant but patriotic—attacking young antiwar students (as disinterested police watched) captured the sense of being "fed up" that had manifested among some Democrats in 1968. A loud minority of working-class whites, many of whom were union members, complained of being beset on all sides. Then as now, the complaints and demands of this demographic were treated as tremendously important. Media coverage legitimized the grievances of the hard hats and depicted the students as deserving of a good ass beating. President Nixon expressed sympathy, telling the angry counterprotesters that he understood how they felt—that Nixon and, vicariously, much of America were eager to give those snotty kids a thorough pummeling too.

A recent book examining this event, though flawless on the facts, makes an unusual argument—not that the antiwar people deserved violence but that they were examples of how the left had gone too far and alienated the working class.[15] Liberalism and its adherents were the aggressor, conservative white voters their hapless victims. This is a curious interpretation given that the antiwar protesters were, in any view of their grievances, justified. The Kent State shootings *were* a grotesque overreaction to a student protest, and the American incursion into Cambodia and Laos did prove disastrous (and was very probably a war crime). Their

---

* In all areas including politics, things that happen in New York City are often given outsized significance and attention.

complaints were not only reasonable but certainly no less valid than the grievances of the hard hats. If the working men were fed up, certainly many other Americans with equally valid feelings also felt fed up with the war and other social injustices.

The event does not need to be relitigated, but it remains important as a manifestation of what was happening within the Democratic Party at the time. It also stands as a demonstration of common political and media biases that to this day exaggerate the importance and popularity of the views of angry white men. The narrative of left-wing hippies driving away the beleaguered white working class lives on, but intraparty tensions of 1970 were more complex than that. The New Politics movement had valid arguments: racism, environmental degradation, war, gender inequality, and other activist issues were indeed problems that needed to be addressed. The working class—white or otherwise—had equally valid grievances about its increasing economic precarity. Mediating the clash between these two groups of voters would dominate the next several decades of Democratic politics, complicated further by the party's goal to appeal to a new, different kind of voter with a worldview alien to New Deal Democrats.

NIXON 520, MCGOVERN 17

The most lopsided presidential election in recent memory was in 2008, when Barack Obama carried 365 electoral votes and 53 percent of the popular vote. In 1972, Richard Nixon—a venal, narcissistic, almost preternaturally dislikeable man with factors like Vietnam and a slowing economy working against him—won 520 electoral votes. Democratic challenger George McGovern? Seventeen. So, the first thing to understand about the lingering effects of 1972 on the Democratic psyche is that they got absolutely obliterated. Being on the receiving end of 520–17 leaves a mark.

Somehow 1972 was *worse* for Democrats than the Electoral College results suggest. For the first time in living memory, the AFL-CIO failed to endorse the Democratic nominee (although some more diverse unions like the United Auto Workers did). Powerful labor figures openly derided the new power wielded by liberal activists thanks to McGovern-Fraser. The Democratic convention, held in Miami, was as chaotic as Chicago had been in 1968, with procedural chaos among warring delegates pushing McGovern's acceptance speech to 2:48 a.m. on the night of what was supposed to be his big prime-time television appearance. Less than three weeks later, McGovern's chosen running mate was forced to withdraw upon revelations about his medical history.* The Illinois delegation led by Chicago's Mayor Daley, an avatar of the old, institutional Democratic Party, was barred from voting, and an alternate Illinois group coled by Jesse Jackson, which adhered to the new post-McGovern-Fraser rules, voted in its stead; the white-replaced-by-Black symbolism did not go unnoticed. In fact, it became a cause célèbre among opponents of the "new" Democratic politics. *Chicago Tribune* columnist Mike Royko, cataloging the racial, ethnic, and gender composition of the dueling delegations, declared that the "reforms have disenfranchised Chicago's white ethnic Democrats" before concluding that "anybody who would reform Chicago's Democratic Party by dropping the white ethnic would probably begin a diet by shooting himself in the stomach."[16]

The divide presaged the appeal of grievance politics that conservatives began to exploit. Disenfranchisement was a strange way to describe a group of people being told, for the first time in their political lives no doubt, that they were not the only people whose interests were important. Certainly, time has led to a better understanding that explicit quota systems like the McGovern-Fraser Commission initially recommended are not the optimal means of addressing a lack of diversity, and after 1972 the Democratic Party regularly updated and tried to improve its representation rules. If imperfect, though, the quota was an earnest attempt to remedy a situation in which the *entire structure* of a party was dominated by white men who actively excluded people whose loyal vote the party expected. That was untenable.

The Daley-Jackson drama was only one aspect of the messy convention.[17] High-profile activists like Chicago Seven figure Jerry Rubin staged

---

* Missouri senator Thomas Eagleton was revealed to have undergone electroshock therapy for depression. He was replaced by Peace Corps founder and Kennedy family member Sargent Shriver.

events around the convention center, adding to the surreal sense of multiple unrelated conventions being held simultaneously by people who detested one another. The discord was such that the establishment Democratic Party seriously considered *refusing to endorse its own candidate*, so desperate were some New Deal stalwarts to wrest control of the party away from New Politics activists.

The McGovern campaign emphasized an immediate end to the war in Vietnam as its top issue, discovering too late that antiwar sentiment was not enough to overcome voters' ambivalence toward McGovern on other issues, or his diffident, cold personality that even some allies found unappealing. Around one-third of Democrats would vote for Nixon in 1972, a staggering number of defections.* Winning only two-thirds of the vote from your own party is a bad sign, for the record. The lazy analysis was, and is, that the antiwar message combined with McGovern's methodically securing support from organized groups of liberal activists resulted in a metaphorical "Hard Hat Riot" at the ballot box.

In truth, the perception that McGovern represented radical liberalism that appealed only to far-out activists missed the point about how the Democratic Party coalition really *was* changing during that era. McGovern's most enthusiastic support (which, granted, isn't saying a lot) came from a growing cohort of young, educated, often suburban, free-market-oriented liberals who were openly skeptical of government and its ability to solve problems. Far from being acid-soaked rioters, they tended toward the fenced-lawn, 2.3-kids lifestyle synonymous with American middle-class normalcy. They represented the knowledge economy of the future, not the muscle economy of the past. It was these upwardly mobile office-worker types who gave some liberals hope for the future after a devastating loss. If the American economic base shifted away from manufacturing and toward knowledge-driven, education-intensive fields, then McGovern's supporters could be the building blocks of future success.[18] The difficulty would be finding a way to unite them in common cause with the other fragments of the Democratic electorate needed to piece

---

* For comparison, 7 percent of Democrats voted for Mitt Romney and 6 percent of Republicans voted for Barack Obama in 2012 per national exit polling compiled by the Roper Center.

together a winning coalition: the remnants of the working class, the poor, people of color, young people, issue-driven activist liberals, and the ideological left.

WHO NEEDS THE WORKING CLASS, ANYWAY?

Of the millions of words spilled in response to Nixon's victories and the meaning of the McGovern disaster, three books had an outsized influence on advancing the argument that the New Deal era was at an end and Democrats needed a radical reinvention.* *Changing Sources of Power* (1971) by academic and Democratic strategist Frederick Dutton was a widely read argument for the New Politics ethos, reimagining liberalism as politics of self-actualization instead of the crass distributive politicking of the New Deal. Second, sociologist Daniel Bell's *The Coming of Post-Industrial Society* (1974) is representative of the now-familiar narrative of postindustrialization and the inevitable economic future to which liberalism would need to adapt and in which the New Deal was unviable.[19] He offered an eerily accurate preview of the knowledge economy that became the national zeitgeist in the 1990s and was the foundation of the New Democrat ideology. Finally, strategist and future Clinton inner circle fixture Lanny Davis authored *The Emerging Democratic Majority: Lessons and Legacies from the New Politics* (1974), in which he makes explicit what is strongly implied by Dutton and Bell: that the political future would be determined by the growing demographic of highly educated, better-off, largely suburban professionals supplied by a bumper crop of children born between 1945 and 1960. Men in hard hats were the voter of the past, and managerial baby boomers—a group that included most New Democrats themselves, incidentally—were the future.

Changing Sources of Power is a remarkable document and not in a good way. It does not merely claim that the working class was becoming less

---

* Two other candidates for inclusion here—covering the same intellectual ground but with substantially worse predictions for the future—are the apocalyptically titled *One Last Chance: The Democratic Party, 1974–76* (Westport, CT: Praeger, 1974) by John G. Stewart, and *Transformations of the American Party System: Political Coalitions from the New Deal to the 1970s* (New York: W. W. Norton, 1975) by E. C. Ladd and C. D. Hadley.

important to the American economy. It actively asserts that the white*
working class is bad. Today, the struggle to win votes from this demographic is disproportionately central to partisan electoral politics; to understand how Democrats lost these voters in the first place, read Dutton.
He crystallizes the New Politics view of such voters as a burden that
must be shed so 1960s-awakened young liberals can achieve higher-order
goals. Only by rising above grubby working-class politics, with its obsti-
nate unions and selfish demands to get paid and treated decently, could
liberalism achieve its true purpose: helping middle-class white people attain self-actualization.

The reader is forgiven for wondering if I mischaracterize Dutton. This
demonization of hard-hatted America seems almost unbelievable. In his
own words and in context, he argued:

> The principal group arrayed against the forces of change is the huge
> lower-middle-income sector, "working America," made up of almost
> twenty-five million white families whose breadwinners are typically
> white-collar clerks and blue-collar workers. The left has long held as a
> testament of faith that "the workers" are the main historical agents of
> social progress, but an important portion of this group is now providing
> the most tenacious resistance to further broadening the country's so-
> cial, economic, and political base. Having gained a larger share of power
> institutionally during the last third of a century, this sector generally
> opposes—more accurately, is anxious about and therefore against—
> much additional change.

This characterization, right down to the term *anxiety*, is still a popular liberal frame for understanding white, working-class Trump supporters. Perhaps they have some legitimate gripes, but the root of the
problem is that they are *bad people*. Selfish. Materialistic. Stuck in the

---

* The antagonist to which Dutton addresses his argument is explicitly the "white ethnic Democrat," the stereotypical white, unionized tradesman in a hard hat. This was of
course not representative of the working class overall, and as the 1970s would prove,
the unwillingness of powerful unions to see common cause with labor they considered
unskilled and beneath them on the status ladder contributed to their waning influence.

past. Unwilling to change. Working-class America became something to be air quoted derisively and either lectured or pitied.

To be certain, prominent labor leaders—still a powerful political and economic force at the time—gave intellectuals like Dutton material to fuel this argument. The reaction of AFL-CIO chairman George Meany to the 1972 Democratic Convention is both brutal and revealing. Of the New York State delegation, he railed that "they've got six open fags and only three AFL-CIO representatives!"[20] He went on to regale a convention of union steelworkers with his perception* of the convention: "We listened to the gay lib people—you know, the people who want to legalize marriage between boys and boys and . . . girls and girls. We heard from the abortionists, and we heard from the people who look like Jacks, acted like Jills, and had the odor of johns about them."[21]

Meany epitomized the growing divide in the Democratic Party between its working-class New Deal traditions and its growing appeal among New Politics activists drawn largely from college graduates with liberal views on race, women's issues, gay rights, and other issues that qualified as novel inclusions in mainstream politics then.[22] With exceptions, such intangible goals as equality, peace, and environmental stewardship were not of compelling interest to organized labor or working-class whites.[23] Meany's speech also demonstrated the closing of ranks among unions to defend their ground during the economic upheaval then underway. As their role as a bastion of working-class power waned, unions began behaving like another entrenched, hostile establishment institution.[24]

Dutton said what many influential liberals felt: that the party could not move forward while tethered to old, boorish white men stuck in the 1950s. Despite the prevalence of less liberal, more Nixonian views among lower-income and blue-collar whites, their importance (along with white rural southerners, another group slowly trending Republican as the fight for civil rights escalated) to the Democratic winning coalition was underscored by the struggles of 1968 and 1972.† Dutton made

---

* Which was incorrect anyway; most Democratic delegates in 1972 were still from or closely allied with organized labor.

† The shift toward New Politics issues in 1972, along with other issues discussed earlier, opened the door wider for Republicans to appeal to disaffected working-class voters. The

an interesting—and, to liberal intellectuals, appealing—argument for a politics beyond material economic interest but did not explain how it would produce electoral success beyond assertions that constituencies of conscience would be brought together to deliver Democratic victories. If 1972 was any indication, that was far easier said than done.

Daniel Bell offered one part of the answer to this dilemma in *The Coming of Post-Industrial Society*. As if writing from the future, he offered a preview of the socioeconomic framework for twenty-first-century American life. He recognized that the unique advantages that enabled the post–World War II American economy to grow explosively—a strong dollar, the US-friendly Bretton Woods international monetary regime, cheap oil, exponential demand for manufacturing and raw materials the United States was uniquely positioned to provide—were ephemeral and had come to an end.

Among the developments Bell foresaw was the accelerating division of work between the educated, who would be successful and prosperous, and the "unskilled," who would be consigned to menial labor and low wages. Like Dutton, Bell envisioned a future in which blue-collar work would disappear. The children of New Dealers who worked on assembly lines for middle-class wages faced a choice: go to college and work behind a desk to achieve the same level of material prosperity as their parents or do unskilled service-industry work and wallow at the bottom of the economic ladder. Bell also predicted how transportation would be superseded by communication as the key infrastructure of the future. Technology would reign. His ideas presage what would become the elite consensus view of the American economy over the decades to follow.

It is worth lingering here a moment to note what a significant change in economic worldview this represented for Democrats and for American liberalism. Bell describes an economy that explicitly, pitilessly separates winners and losers. The guiding New Deal principle had been to raise the standard of living of all Americans and to pursue full employment,

---

AFL-CIO conducted an internal poll of union members in 1968, for example, and withheld the results after discovering that Wallace was supported by at least one in three union men. See Devinatz, V., "Donald Trump, George Wallace, and the White Working Class," *Labor Studies Journal* 42, no. 3 (2017): 233–238.

ensuring that every working person earned a dignified wage. In contrast, Bell warned that the lowest rungs of the economy were about to revert to conditions that had prevailed during the Gilded Age. The days when the "unskilled"—the taxi drivers, janitors, and assembly-line clock punchers—could live decently on their earnings was coming to an end. Only those motivated, smart, and deserving enough to provide more value to the economy would enjoy middle-class prosperity in the future. Sure, government would do a little here and there to help the poor, maybe. But falling in with the winners or the losers would be up to individuals. In one generation, liberalism was on the verge of a shift from Roosevelt's promise of freedom from want to "if you aren't successful, it's probably your own fault."

Lanny Davis, perhaps now best remembered as the most fanatically loyal dead-ender of the 2008 Hillary Clinton campaign, synthesized these ideas about liberalism and the economy while defining a winning electoral path for the future. In *The Emerging Democratic Majority*,[*] Davis argued a key growth area for Democrats was to begin appealing to the class of highly educated professionals set to flourish as baby boomers entered young adulthood and the workforce. He believed that while the egghead in the Adlai Stevenson mold had not been a winner for Democrats in the past, times were changing and this would be the template for the leader of the future. Knowledge, skills, education, and technology were the way forward. People who understood this would be not only the Democratic voters but also *candidates* of the future.

This idea had been working its way into the liberal worldview over time. Arthur Schlesinger Jr. aired similar thoughts in the *New York Times* on February 11, 1968. Although the headline "How McGovern Will Win" didn't age well, the novelty with which he announces that women and suburbanites will be a force in the future of politics says much about the era. Davis subjected Schlesinger's idea to some basic analysis of election results in 1972 and found that despite McGovern's

---

[*] Nothing better underscores the constant soul searching and rebooting of the Democratic Party since 1968 than the fact that a popular 2002 book by John B. Judis and Ruy Teixeira bore the same title as Davis's 1974 book. Almost three decades of "emerging"!

shellacking,* congressional and state-level elections, where the Democratic brand and its structural advantages from three decades in power remained strong, showed promise as a growth area for Democrats, for college-educated moderates and ex-Republicans fleeing that party's shift to the right.

The HEPs that so enchanted Davis, Schlesinger, and Dutton were at best a plurality of the electorate. To build an emerging majority requires, you know, a majority. Davis accomplishes this task with some hand waving about how growth among HEPs would combine with traditional Democratic base voters like workers, people of color, and New Politics activists (the communities of conscience). As we well know, this proved easier for Davis to write than to achieve in practice, as these groups often have different if not diametrically opposed interests. The cynical reality behind Davis's theory is the implication that people who had reliably voted Democratic would continue to do so with the right mix of promises and gestures even after the party ceased to advance their interests. That's one strategy, certainly.

Not every person who would wield influence in the Democratic Party between 1972 and 1992 read these three books. Nor did Democrats universally embrace these ideas. In fact, to modern audiences the ideological cast of Democratic Party characters in the 1970s looks bewildering. There was powerful Sen. Henry "Scoop" Jackson (D-WA), who combined passionate, uncompromising environmentalism with foreign policy views so hawkish and anticommunist that even Nixon-era Republicans thought him a bit too far to the right.† There was still a powerful southern coalition of Democratic conservatives who chose to evolve on civil rights rather than become Republicans as some Dixiecrats did, and who were nonetheless deeply leery of New Politics activism. The New Politics movement itself became a stratified, poorly coordinated universe of single-issue interest groups that all Democratic politicians wooed but

---

* Shellac, incidentally, is so named because it is made from crushed shells of the lac beetle.

† Jackson, whose environmentalism and belief in the welfare state were more strident than any current member of Congress, ended up embraced by the neoconservative movement due to his extreme hawkishness. So, Bush-era figures like Paul Wolfowitz remember him fondly while most Democrats ignore him. Politics is weird.

none convincingly united in a common cause. New Deal holdouts like Hubert Humphrey argued that the Democrats' past was the best blueprint for its future. But slowly a young generation of technocrats with impressive educational credentials, successful careers in hot professions like banking, and seemingly little love for traditional liberal views of the role of government accumulated in Congress.

CHAPTER 3

THE WILDERNESS YEARS

Watergate Babies, Malaise, and a New Liberalism

The changes in the Democratic Party over the past half century reflect a larger crisis in liberalism in the United States and around the
world. The pattern seen in recent American political history mirrors that
of other liberal democracies: 1960s upheaval, 1970s economic malaise,
the 1980s pivot to free-market orthodoxy, the reinvention of liberalism
as a commitment to free trade and markets in the 1990s, and the blind
stumble toward antidemocratic nationalism in the twenty-first century.

For the United States, the simplest version of "what happened?" credits
the end of the postwar economic hegemony Americans enjoyed. The rest
of the world caught up after rebuilding from the carnage of World War
II. Other economic blows, like the twin oil shocks of 1973 and 1979, are
important parts of the story too. To reach the heart of what happened to
the Democratic Party, though, we must do something unpleasant. Economic explanations are valid but insufficient. We must talk about—and I
am sorry about this—theory. About what "liberal" means.

The liberalism embraced by the Democratic Party during its high-
water years beginning in 1932 and lasting (roughly) until 1980 was

quintessentially American. It rejected the move toward central economic planning and nationalization of industry—toward "socialism," broadly— that most European nations experienced to varying degrees in the post– World War II period. The goal of the New Deal, remember, was to save capitalism. It was embraced by some of the business community because they feared that more radical changes to the economy might happen in the absence of some kind of reform.

Liberalism, in all its flavors, boils down to the belief that improving the human condition is possible with the application of rationality.* All traditions of liberalism emphasize individual freedom and private property, ensuring that collective efforts to solve problems do not evolve into totalitarianism. Liberalism broadly holds that given freedom and opportunity, humanity can get it right.[1] With the right international organizations promoting cooperation and the right combination of carrots and sticks, peace can be maintained. The right government initiatives can eliminate poverty. The right moral leadership and policy can ameliorate inequality. The right educational policies can turn out skilled workers and conscientious citizens. None of this is guaranteed, and different schools of liberalism propose different paths. But a better world is possible. We can do it, so to speak.

Modern liberalism is the closest tradition to what Americans today call liberalism without modifiers. It combines the liberal emphasis on civil liberty and private property with the belief in state intervention in pursuit of social justice, fairness, and equality of opportunity. It favors a more active role for government in the economy, within boundaries that respect private property and individual freedom. As FDR said in 1941, the liberal party

---

* Before you object, liberalism is famously difficult to define, hence Lionel Trilling's characterization (*The Liberal Imagination*, 1954) of liberalism as "a large tendency rather than a concise body of doctrine." Scholarly definitions similarly emphasize that liberalism "is not a clear-cut body" of doctrine (Laski, H., *The Rise of European Liberalism* [London: George Allen and Unwin, 1936], 14) or is "a complex of doctrines" (Geuss, R., *History and Illusion in Politics* [New York: Cambridge University Press, 2001]), combining, briefly, the elevation of freedom, reason, and tolerance with state intervention in the economic, political, social, and cultural well-being of the polity (Ryan, A., *Dewey and the High Tide of American Liberalism* [New York: W. W. Norton, 1995]).

believes that, as new conditions and problems arise beyond the power of men and women to meet as individuals, it becomes the duty of the Government itself to find new remedies with which to meet them. The liberal party insists that the Government has the definite duty to use all its power and resources to meet new social problems with new social controls—to insure to the average person the right to his own economic and political life, liberty, and pursuit of happiness.[2]

American conservatism has always emphasized the "his own economic and political life" part of that definition; the use of government as a remedy and a force for good without progressing toward socialism or the abolition of private property is American liberalism's counterargument.

During the Great Depression, American liberals experienced a surge in faith in the power of the state. The government needn't take over the economy, resorting to collectivization and central planning, but by harnessing the wisdom of experts and channeling ideas into collective action guided by the hand of government, social, economic, and political problems can be addressed effectively. Liberalism was, in its heyday, not "the left" but a path carved out between the left and right extremes of state socialism and Gilded Age–style laissez-faire.

This became untenable, the story goes, when the conscious decision to ignore issues of social inequality in the New Deal coalition exploded in the 1960s, just as the American economy faced its first serious threats since the Depression. That much is true. But importantly for this story, faith in government was already weakening within liberalism for reasons unrelated to economics. In the period leading to liberalism's 1970s emo phase, several antigovernment, promarket strains were already percolating in the Democratic ideological universe.[3] Eventually, this would evolve into the markets-not-government liberalism—neoliberalism, if you like—that is today's mainstream liberal worldview.

The probusiness, promarket views that eventually coalesced into the New Democrat movement were not new but a minority tradition with a long history in the New Deal coalition. But that was not liberalism's only government-skeptical faction. Black Democrats harbored mistrust of the state for reasons so obvious they needn't be drawn out here. The New

Politics movement, with its emphasis on peace, environmentalism, and social equality, was leery of the Democratic establishment and the institutions of the state that failed to address those problems. And another important movement of the era—the proconsumer, antibusiness crusade personified by Ralph Nader—was also inherently skeptical of politics and government.[4] Naderite consumer activism spoke to people angered by business's pursuit of private profit at the expense of the public interest and by a political process that indulged rather than tamed the excesses of capitalism.

So, activism-driven liberalism—the tradition that produced George McGovern and his disastrous 1972 presidential run—was not simply at odds with the Democratic establishment on the purpose and practice of electoral politics. It opened a growing rift over philosophical views of government, with a breakdown of consensus over what liberalism meant and to what extent it needed to be central to the worldview of the Democratic Party—just as the Republican Party was discovering new strength coalescing around a strong, shared vision of small-government conservatism.[*]

This created a clear cleavage in the (still-majority) Democratic Party that, by 1980, had brought the New Deal coalition to its knees, erupting in open warfare during the presidency of Jimmy Carter. Carter was in every meaningful sense a New Democrat before New Democrats had adopted the moniker, and his failure would be a key learning experience for the movement. But before we get to the internecine Democratic battles of the Carter years, a less famous figure's story illuminates the Democrats' battle for the soul of liberalism during the 1970s. His name was Wright Patman.

GROOVY PROFITS, MAN!

Not even the catastrophic McGovern campaign prevented Democrats from retaining control of Congress in 1972, and Nixon's subsequent self-destruction strengthened the Democratic position further. With skyrocketing levels of public dissatisfaction and mistrust in the wake of Watergate and the Vietnam War, the 1974 midterms saw a freshman

---

[*] In practice, of course, their commitment to small government is strictly rhetorical.

cohort—most of them Democrats—of unprecedented size, youth, and zeal for reform elected to the House.[5] Waggish journalists dubbed them Watergate Babies.

The Babies were cut from a much different cloth than congressional stalwarts of the New Deal era. Whereas the older generation remembered vividly the Great Depression and World War II, the Babies were born into postwar affluence. Many had graduated from elite colleges and were the proverbial corporate types, as natural in politics as in a boardroom. They detested the old ways of Washington—the backslapping, deal cutting, and three-martini lunches* integral to the politics of the old guard—and developed a political brand around openness, good governance, reform, respect for rules and procedure, and postpartisanship. Their loyalty to both the Democratic Party and the idea of government as a force for good was conditional and weak. Democrat meant very different things to New Dealers and Watergate Babies.

Two congressmen of the time exemplify the clashing generations. One was Watergate Baby Pete Stark, elected in 1972 but counted among the 1974 Babies cohort for his youth, promarket views, and enthusiasm for congressional reform. Stark was at once everything the Democratic Party was not and everything it would become. He held an MBA from the University of California, Berkeley. He was a former Republican who got rich founding Security National Bank and became a Democrat due to his opposition to the Vietnam War. He had the roof of his bank's headquarters (and its paper checks) emblazoned with large peace symbols. This kind of "cool capitalism" branding is ubiquitous now but qualified as transgressive in the stolid banking industry of the time.

---

* Fun fact: The congressional nuclear bunker built beneath The Greenbrier resort in West Virginia was, as of 1974, stocked not only with food, weapons, and medical supplies but with copious amounts of alcohol. So many members of Congress were known to be habitual heavy drinkers that emergency planners feared a wave of people simultaneously experiencing alcohol withdrawal while confined. For a fascinating history of federal efforts to curb the three-martini lunch with rules on reimbursement and tax treatment of food and beverage spending, see Thies, M. P., *The Rebirth of a Tax Deduction During a Global Crisis: Examining Three-Martini Lunch Tax Deduction*, Seton Hall Law, Seton Hall University, 2021.

Wright Patman was Stark's antipode. He had attended tiny Cumberland University, a private religious school whose greatest notoriety came from losing a college football game to Georgia Tech 222–0.* He entered Congress in 1928 and became an ardent New Dealer in 1932. He was a foreign policy hawk, including enthusiastic support for the Vietnam War, and had supported segregation early in his political career.† That career was defined by his relentless antagonism to concentrated wealth and power; this included big business broadly defined but focused most intensely on banks. Patman *really* didn't like big banks. Benefiting from rules that rewarded seniority, by 1974 Patman was part of an entrenched southern Democratic aristocracy that wielded great power as House committee chairs. His position atop the House Banking Committee was an ideal vantage point from which to conduct his crusade against the malign influence of big capital.

The contrast was almost too neat, the stuff of screenplays. Stark the peacenik, Patman the hawk. Stark the racial liberal, Patman the (former) segregationist. Patman considered bankers the natural enemy of the people; his crowning achievement in government was forcing the resignation of treasury secretary and legendary plutocrat Andrew Mellon in 1932. Stark's pride and joy was his small banking empire. Patman, the master of old-style informal deal making, Stark, the good-government reformer. When the two crossed paths in the House, Patman was aged but still a heavyweight; in 1975 he was fresh off a political triumph that initiated the congressional investigation of the Watergate burglary.‡

The Babies had big ideas about cleaning up the House, and that goal began with getting rid of the old tyrants who dominated committees and exercised effective veto power over the legislative process. Number one on their target list was Wright Patman. It was a clash of cultures, the old

---

* Unable to move the ball against their mighty opponent, Cumberland eventually resorted to letting Georgia Tech have the ball permanently, even after GT scored a touchdown. Pretty solid metaphor for modern Democratic strategy if you ask me.
† Following LBJ's lead, Patman eventually embraced civil rights and repudiated his earlier views, which included signing the segregationist Southern Manifesto of 1954.
‡ Using his investigative powers as committee chair, Patman tied several hundred dollar bills in the burglars' possession directly to the Nixon campaign, establishing unequivocally that the two were connected.

ways versus the new blood, reformers versus defenders of the status quo. To shorten a long story, the reformers largely won. Patman's politics—both his approach to Congress and his ideological underpinnings—were simply out of step with the era. He was an enemy of Wall Street, of banks, of big business, of monopoly power. He represented the Jeffersonian and Jacksonian strain of Democratic politics, the working-class and agrarian mistrust of urban capital. Farmers versus bankers, rural poor versus urban elites. It was as fundamental a conflict as exists in American politics.

The guard changing that took place during that era is little appreciated outside historians and political scientists who study Congress. For the Democratic Party, it was a crucial pivot between the future and the past. The idea of a party that defined itself as having populism at its core and being "for the little guy" ended during the tumultuous 1970s. Patman was not the only defender of the old tradition; he was one casualty of the changing winds as a new Democratic Party emerged from the New Deal's monumental shadow.

Having entered politics in an era when it was possible, thanks to New Deal regulations, to consider powerful economic interests well regulated, young boomers were not inherently suspicious of them. Big business or the banks or Wall Street did not seem obviously evil to members of Congress born in, say, 1946. This lack of skepticism would come to define the party under New Democrat control in the same way that crusading against monopoly power and villainous bankers had defined it under the New Dealers. As the Babies saw it, deregulation *was* populism. Airlines, banks, transportation, energy: they enthusiastically supported deregulating all of these on the grounds that it would mean, in theory, lower prices for consumers. With deregulated market competition begetting choice, being big wasn't necessarily bad. Big could be better. Bigger could mean cheaper.*

---

* This key philosophical divide can be seen in the story of Patman's bête noir, the once-dominant A&P grocery store chain. Patman crusaded against A&P for decades to protect small, independent grocers vulnerable to predatory pricing and distribution practices. Probusiness liberals, conversely, saw A&P as an example of big business helping the poor and working classes by offering them low-priced goods. See Levinson, M., *The Great A&P and the Struggle for Small Business in America* (New York: Hill and Wang, 2011).

Watergate Babies did not dream of creating the largest concentration of elite economic power since the Gilded Age, but thanks to their credulity toward the biggest economic actors, that's what happened. At the time, many younger Democrats were unconvinced that concentrated wealth was a problem. Big business seemed entirely compatible with a healthy democracy and good government. Populist nostrums sounded to them as relevant as the Third Amendment.* It would take time to find a leader who could sell voters on a radically reoriented kind of liberalism that accommodated these changing views. The first person to try—Jimmy Carter—failed spectacularly. Like McGovern, Carter's failure would be formative to his New Democrat successors. He showed them what to do—and the wrong way to do it.

PEANUTS

Thanks to his skillful understanding of the primary-focused nomination process that emerged from the McGovern-Fraser reforms, Jimmy Carter won the nomination in 1976 and bested Gerald Ford for the privilege of governing a nation with clinical depression and a teetering economy. Adroitly sidestepping the growing Democratic disharmony by running a post-Watergate campaign emphasizing "moral clarity" and administrative competence (a quality that columnist David Broder called "managerial moralism," and that would become increasingly central to the Democratic brand with time[6]) the peanut farmer (and nuclear engineer!) entered the White House with a rare two-thirds House majority and a filibuster-crushing sixty-two senators.† But while that looked great on paper, in practice the Congress was ideologically fractious and decidedly undeferential to the White House.[7] It was increasingly divided among New Deal holdouts who wanted Carter's economic policy to focus on full employment, Watergate Babies who championed government reform and free markets, and a conservative faction from the South and West demanding fiscal austerity and deregulation.

---

* It protects you from being forced to quarter King George III's soldiers in your home in peacetime.
† Sixty-one plus one Democratic-caucusing Independent.

Carter meanwhile staked out a third way position with no natural constituency. A southern Democrat rooted in his faith, he embraced balanced budgets, deregulation, increased defense spending, hawkish anticommunism, and free-market economic solutions. He alienated Democrats without winning over Republicans or building a new base of support that cut across existing ideological boundaries. He epitomized the risks of occupying the middle. By refusing to see Congress as a pair of opposing parties but instead as an endless buffet of possibilities for assembling alliances, Carter was left with "merely transient coalitions and friendships" rather than a solid base of consistent support.[8]

While Republicans painted (and still paint) him as a wild-eyed liberal, policy during his presidency shifted sharply to the right. Economist Thomas Palley has argued that the neoliberal economics of Reaganism became the official Washington Consensus not under Reagan but under Carter. He passed a tax plan that slashed capital gains and increased Social Security taxes on workers. He also signed the Hyde Amendment, which banned federal funding for abortion and handed the nascent anti-abortion movement its first major victory in Washington.

His politics were unusual enough that some of his contemporaries had a hard time understanding; Christopher Lydon in the *Atlantic* summarized Carter in 1977 as a Rockefeller Republican (meaning GOP Lite).[9] Carter's close confidante Hamilton Jordan characterized him as nonideological.[10] Arthur Schlesinger Jr. was less charitable, lambasting Carter as nothing less than a total break with the Democratic Party's conception of liberalism. Noting that the problems of the Carter era were not "amenable to these everyone-for-himself, devil-take-the-hindmost, private-market solutions favored by the Carter administration," he concluded that "what pretends to be a Democratic administration has deliberately and methodically chosen Republican policies." Then, the dagger:

The Democratic party will never succeed as a timorous, respectable, standpat, conservative, pro-oil company, anti-government party, luxuriating in the alibis of public impotence. It will succeed only as it reclaims its heritage of concern and reform, of innovation and experiment, of commitment to the poor and the powerless.[11]

Sound familiar? Forty years on, this debate remains unresolved.

Carter also exemplified a shift away from the New Deal ethos of a just society and toward the southern Democratic preference for rhetoric of responsibility and belief that unequal outcomes were the natural order of things. He rejected the populist approach implicit in Martin Luther King Jr.'s Poor People's Campaign or Robert F. Kennedy's similar call for a "black-blue" coalition of Black have-nots and working-class whites, instead showing the distinctly conservative tone of post–civil rights southern liberalism. Upon signing the Hyde Amendment, Carter helpfully noted that "there are many things in life that are not fair, that wealthy people can afford and poor people can't. But I don't believe that the Federal Government should take action to try to make these opportunities exactly equal." In 1973 he chaired the probusiness Southern Growth Policies Board, a regional Democratic effort to reshape economic policy away from organized labor and redistribution to benefit extractive and labor-intensive industries that dominated the southern economy. All that stuff your dad told you about Carter as a bleeding-heart liberal was wrong.

The Carter presidency took place in the context of an energy crisis best remembered for long lines at gas stations after the OPEC-led oil embargo of 1973 and the price volatility following the 1979 Iranian Revolution.[12] With inflation and unemployment both reaching shocking levels by today's standards, the decade was an emphatic end to the postwar economic boom. After years of increasing wages, productivity, and profits, all underpinned by a seemingly endless supply of cheap energy, Americans were ill prepared for the changes.

Carter's approach to energy policy managed to alienate nearly everyone. Unlike antimonopoly New Dealers or environmentally minded New Politics liberals, Carter was sympathetic to the (largely southern) oil industry. He favored deregulation over the existing policies, which included government-administered allocations (a complex technocratic plan intended to distribute oil to each state proportionally based on its share of American oil use in 1972) and various price controls to protect consumers from rising heating oil and gasoline costs.* Carter asserted that the free

---

* In a stunning display of ideological flexibility, Nixon assented to congressional Democrats' preference for government intervention to stabilize prices but stopped short of

market would raise prices with the twin effects of forcing consumers to use less and incentivizing the oil industry to produce more. With this odd approach for the time, Carter found some supporters among congressional moderates, in the Beltway media, and among academic deregulation enthusiasts. He found little, though, among rank-and-file Democrats angered by higher prices and deeply cynical about the oil industry.*

Even the apparent elite consensus was tenuous under Carter. Energy Secretary James Schlesinger noted, "The basic problem is that there is no constituency for an energy program. There are many constituencies opposed."[13] The poor, organized labor, many environmentalists, consumers, and New Dealers hated it. Carter learned that a Democrat pitching a Republican policy solution lives on an island. Failing to please everyone (or satisfy them completely) is one thing; actively displeasing everyone is another. Carter did the latter.

Carter compounded his problems by trying to build public support in the worst conceivable way. Instead of the optimism that FDR, Reagan, Clinton, or Obama would bring to the public-facing presidency during a crisis, Carter went to voters with what looks to modern sensibilities like an unfathomably bleak message of hard times delivered in tones of a stern Sunday school lecture. He moralized and scolded, treating working people as spoiled children ruined by affluence. He spoke of "malaise," of a "crisis of confidence," of grim warnings that everyone must get used to using less and having less. He promised sacrifice, austerity, and "difficult and unpleasant" choices. All of that sounded like, and in fact was, a warning that the weight of the economic and energy crises would fall on working people.

The dreary messaging had two goals. One was to portray Carter as a leader willing to talk straight, to speak of hard times when hard times were at hand. The second was to cement his appeal to the emergent suburban middle class—to HEPs—a "rapidly expanding segment of the

---

instituting gasoline rationing preferred by more liberal Democrats. Dabbling in energy populism contributed to Nixon's decisive 1972 victory.

* A popular conspiracy theory at the time held that oil companies left tankers full of oil waiting offshore until prices rose; in other words, the industry itself created the energy crisis.

electorate that is tired of being taxed, is frightened by inflation, and is wary of the Federal government's ability to solve the nation's problems."[14] Results were . . . mixed. Carter did appeal to the growing professional middle class that was coming to dominate Democrats' long-term thinking, but there were too few of them to form an electoral majority. As for leadership, Carter came off at best as a cold technocrat and at worst as a hectoring scold. More alarmingly for a technocratic problem-solver, Carter's "solutions" didn't work. Deregulation punished consumers, did little to boost the economy, and promised benefits (increased oil production, innovation) that would not materialize for years. Nobody was happy except, for a while, the oil industry, which was now free to charge what it pleased. Carter even rejected a golden opportunity to go all-in on renewable energy on the grounds that it would require an unwelcome expansion of government to manage it; to New Deal liberals that was precisely the point—industry would not invest in renewable energy of its own volition, but government could.*

The 1978 midterms gave Democrats a chilling preview of the Reagan years. The center position Carter had staked out offered the worst of all worlds: New Deal liberals were alienated, the poor and working class were punished, and conservatives bashed Carter simply for being a Democrat even as he embraced parts of their approach. Historian Meg Jacobs noted that Carter too often "sounded like a Republican, without that party's confidence and gusto and without the massive tax cuts it was offering" as a panacea.[15] Most bafflingly, Carter simply resigned himself to the belief that "we cannot satisfy the normal desires of important elements of the Democratic Party: blacks, mayors and governors, and labor."[16] How Democrats could win elections without keeping core constituents satisfied was not explained.

Democratic leaders who cut political teeth in the New Deal era were appalled. Tip O'Neill—"almost a caricature of a New Deal liberal" with whom Carter had an awkward relationship[17]—flatly rejected Carter's initiatives, inveighing that he "did not become Speaker of the House to dismantle the programs that I've worked all my life for."[18] Veteran

---

* They were right. When oil prices cratered starting in 1981, private sector interest in renewable energy vanished.

congressional Democrats could be read in newspapers saying things about their own party's president like "all consumers heard from the president was talk of Sacrifice and higher prices, and neither seemed necessary or helpful to them."[19] Members representing both rural and urban House districts complained to the *New York Times* that "their constituents seemed to bear the brunt of [Carter's] budget cuts."[20] Talk of a primary challenge to Carter, which culminated in the 1980 Ted Kennedy campaign, was open and enthusiastic among liberals.*

The most consequential departure from traditional Democratic orthodoxy for Carter was his selection of Paul Volcker as chair of the Federal Reserve in 1979. Volcker's economic prescription was to wage all-out war against inflation, which in 1979 and 1980 reached record levels: 11.3 percent for 1979 and over 14 percent for the first half of 1980. Inflation, interest rates, and unemployment are interrelated; reducing one often results in increases in the others.† Carter shared Volcker's belief that inflation must be reduced at any cost; the cost turned out to be an increase in already high unemployment and interest rates. Volcker's recipe for reducing inflation by forcing a sharp recession—"The sooner the better, as far as I'm concerned" as he put it in 1979[21]—fit the tone of Carter's televised addresses preaching austerity and telling the nation, in essence, to shut up and take its medicine.

The late-Carter and early-Reagan recession was enormously consequential to today's political landscape. Carter and the Democrats were saddled with a reputation for economic blundering even though Carter's economic policy drew heavily from the conservative playbook, while Ronald Reagan would later reap the benefits of the "Great Moderation"—a period of highly unequal economic growth that followed the Volcker recession far too late to help Carter.‡ Given the leading position of the US economy and the dollar, it also initiated a global realignment toward neoliberalism. As Gérard Duménil and Dominique Lévy argued in *Capital*

---

* Kennedy's candidacy collapsed partly due to his unresolved 1969 scandal involving the death of Mary Jo Kopechne, a passenger in his car during an accident caused by Kennedy's negligent and probably impaired driving.

† This is complicated in reality, of course, but this is the Econ 101 version.

‡ Crucially, a glut on the global oil market plunged gasoline and heating fuel prices throughout Reagan's first term.

Resurgent (2004), the 1970s presented a crisis of governance for liberal democratic states around the world as deteriorating economic conditions resulted in rising unrest and working-class militancy that would either break governments or be broken by them. Volcker's shock treatment of sky-high interest rates triggered a recession and higher unemployment, giving eager conservative movements and the ownership class an opportunity to reorient the economic landscape in their favor.

Domestically, employers used the crisis to break organized labor and usher in a new era of deregulation, while internationally the spiraling interest rates created debt crises throughout the global South that allowed neoliberal international institutions like the International Monetary Fund to impose capital-friendly policy changes through "structural adjustment programs" combining loans and smaller-government policy mandates.[22] In short, Volcker was appointed by Carter to create the economic world we live in today, dominated by free trade, stable prices, powerless labor, unequal prosperity, and concentrated economic power. Carter did not merely oversee the collapse of the postwar political and economic order; he actively advanced it.

Some New Deal–era holdouts raised alarms over Carter's inflation obsession. Senate majority leader Robert Byrd warned in 1979 that soaring interest rates and tight monetary policy were the same tools Republicans used unsuccessfully in 1974 to combat inflation. Moreover, Byrd warned that "attempting to control inflation or protect the dollar by throwing legions of people out of work and shutting down shifts in our factories and mines is a hopeless policy."[23] He grasped that no amount of good economic data would satisfy voters thrust into unemployment, poverty, or precarity. The working-class voters on whom Democrats had always relied knew nothing about Milton Friedman but knew what stable employment and decent wages meant to their lives. Inside the White House, liberal holdouts like Vice President Mondale explicitly warned Carter that apparent indifference to unemployment and the suffering of ordinary people would cost him the presidency in 1980.[24] He was right.

Carter's reputation, which bottomed out with his 1980 trouncing at the hands of Ronald Reagan, has risen in his postpresidency, and presidency scholars have argued that the political context of 1976 was such that no Democrat of any ideology could have succeeded.[25] Yet what happened in 1978 and 1980 was a worst-worlds scenario for Democrats. They increased their appeal to middle-class professionals with technocratic, smaller-government sympathies that stopped short of Republicans' anti-government zeal—and lost badly in the process. Too many voters Democrats relied on justifiably felt betrayed or ignored.

The question was and remains: What kind of liberalism did Carter's formula leave? Is it, to circle back to the rudimentary definition of liberalism that began this chapter, an ideology that truly believes that a better world is possible? Or is it a liberalism that implicitly accepts that some will experience great prosperity while others grind away in precariousness or poverty? A liberalism that accepts the inevitability of a winners-and-losers economy may not be *identical* to American conservatism, but it's certainly within hailing distance. It can be true simultaneously that Republicans and Democrats are different in important ways and that the differences in economic worldview are insufficiently important to people in the lower strata of the economy. One party promises the whip, the other promises the whip with some sympathetic words and advice on how to increase one's odds that the whip falls on someone else next time.

For the Democratic Party, an even more important practical question arose: How can a party work against, slow walk, or disregard the interests of its former working-class base to curry favor with a different, better-off part of the electorate without losing votes? Disappointing Peter to impress Paul only works as a political strategy if you don't need Peter to vote for your party every two years. A group of ambitious younger Democrats from the South and West, including a governor from Arkansas, thought they knew how to do it.

THE NEW DEMOCRAT WAY

American parties are good at some things but defining their issue positions is not one of them. That is largely left up to candidates, changes over time, and is subject to fierce fighting among activists, interest groups, and ideological factions within the party. Party organizations like the Democratic National Committee are neither expected nor eager to be policy workshops; their purpose is organizational and as support structures for candidates.[26] So this is the story of the group of activists—the Democratic Leadership Council (DLC)—that won the battle against the New Dealers and New Politickers to chart the new course. They molded the party in their image by being better organized, better funded, more persistent, and more persuasive at the elite level than competing factions.

The New Democrat movement brought together two different factions searching for answers after the electoral disasters of 1968 and 1972. One was a group of New Englanders with affinities for the fast-growing tech industry in places like Massachusetts's Route 128 corridor as well as for the growing Boston-to-Washington corridor financial industry. These men—and as we will see, white men led the New Democrat movement to a degree that would eventually embarrass it—included young, affluent moderates like Bill Bradley (NJ) and Michael Dukakis (MA). Their enthusiasm for then novel developments in computers, robotics, high-tech manufacturing, and telecommunications was such that one infamous wag[*] labeled the group Atari Democrats—Atari being the embodiment of high technology in that simpler time.

A second group hailed from the Sun Belt: the rapidly growing South and Southwest, as well as their border regions like Tennessee and Colorado (which produced New Democrat stalwarts Gary Hart and Tim Wirth). Southern Democrats had always hewed closer to the moderate or conservative Democratic tradition, but the generation that would become the New Democrats was unique. Their résumés often showed elite educational backgrounds, and their political personas exuded youthful energy and charm, pointedly rejecting the growling racism stereotypical of earlier southern Democrats. Bill Clinton (AR), Albert Gore Jr. (TN), Bruce Babbitt (AZ), and Dick Gephardt (MO) were all examples of the cohort of younger southern and western moderates who entered politics during or shortly after the era of McGovern and Watergate.

While they didn't engage in the vicious antigovernment rhetoric that would come to define Republican politics under Reagan, these younger Democrats grew up seeing both the successes and failures of liberal social policies. As they saw it, the primary enemy of growth and

---

[*] It was Chris Matthews. This, in 1982, was the last interesting thing he said.

problem-solving was bureaucracy, which created rules that begat rules, stifled innovation, propped up failures, and reduced opportunity.* Only with innovation could entrepreneurs create the high-tech economy of the future described by Daniel Bell. Innovation would produce growth; continuing to invest in the failed industries of the old economy would not.

Economic growth was something of an obsession for the New Democrats. They were deeply influenced by *The Zero-Sum Society* (1980) by Lester Thurow, an economic theory depicting old Democratic politics focused on distribution as a dead end. It was misguided, Thurow argued, to view politics as a matter of deciding how much of the metaphorical pie would go to various constituents. Meaningful solutions could only arise from making the pie bigger. In the economic malaise of the 1970s, a growing number of Democrats with no allegiance to transactional Democratic politics of the New Deal era became convinced that the government was limiting growth by focusing on fights over distribution. These Democrats believed that a better role for government would be providing direction and encouragement to the private sector to generate growth. If FDR believed in the power of the bureaucrat and the federal program to direct economic activity, New Democrats believed in the entrepreneur and unobtrusive government support for promising industries.

The key to making their worldview work was an almost fanatical faith in the power of education to make workers smarter, more creative, more skilled, and more productive. As the implied meritocracy of education— where the smartest succeed based on their abilities—had been key to the personal career success of people like them, New Democrats believed that it could unlock a promising and more rewarding future for everyone.† Unskilled labor, as they saw it, would inevitably be replaced by automation or

---

* The economic malaise of the 1970s was global, with the oil crisis of 1973 and the end of what the French called Les Trente Glorieuses—the thirty glorious years from the end of World War II—exposing every industrial economy to similar stresses. The formation of a "new" liberalism based on core tenets of neoliberalism took place in many countries, for example, Tony Blair's New Labour. See Mudge, S., *Leftism Reinvented: Western Parties from Socialism to Neoliberalism* (Cambridge, MA: Harvard University Press, 2018).

† Cue the famous speech from Aaron Sorkin's postideological corn syrup bong *The West Wing*: "Education is the silver bullet. Education is everything. We don't need little changes. We need gigantic revolutionary changes. Competition for the best teachers should be fierce. They should be getting six-figure salaries. Schools should be incredibly

by ever-cheaper unskilled labor. Workers of the future needed to obtain, if not higher education, then skills and training that were appropriate to high-value, high-tech work. The government could help workers in this regard (or at least lecture them sanctimoniously), but ultimately it was the responsibility of each individual to make themselves economically attractive. The alternative was to get left behind.

The basics of this economic worldview align with that troubled term *neoliberal.* But politically, the neoliberal worldview extended beyond economic theory. This generation believed that free-market capitalism was the solution not only to macroeconomic problems but to a range of thorny social and political problems: the environment, poverty, inequality, discrimination, inefficient bureaucracy, crime, underperforming schools, a lack of affordable housing. Market-based approaches were the answer in every case. Competition, profit motives for individuals and businesses, and the pure creative energy of America's innovators would do what government could not do by fiat and bureaucracy. Neoliberal politicians came to see free-market capitalism not only as an enlightened economic system but as the ideal organizing principle for society. Capitalism would fix what government had (or could) not.

Conservatives obviously endorsed neoliberal ideas as well, as promarket thinking was already in line with the preferences of the American right. The Republican Party used the 1960s and 1970s to rebrand based on a style of hawkish, antigovernment, revanchist conservatism that first flowered in California—and then the national stage—under Ronald Reagan.[27] No doubt New Democrats saw the political benefits Republicans extracted from "running against Washington" and anti-tax zealotry. It is oversimplified, however, to paint the New Democrat movement as merely the adaptation of a successful GOP gimmick. New Democrats and Watergate Babies reached their belief in this worldview on their own. They may have disliked bureaucracy and excessive regulation, but unlike Republican neoliberals who were hysterically antigovernment and treated the very idea of government as an evil, insidious force undermining the American way of life, New Democrats simply had greater faith

expensive for government and absolutely free of charge for its citizens, just like national defense."

in markets to resolve problems. They envisioned a better, more efficient, more effective government playing a key role in supporting growth and innovation. That was the idealized outcome, anyway.

On cultural and social issues, New Democrats were less coherent. The Atari Democrats from New England tended to have very liberal views on abortion, women's rights, gay rights, race, and other hot-button issues of that era (and ours). Sun Belt New Democrats gravitated toward moderate views on these same issues in the belief that cultural-social liberalism was what was driving away working-class whites (recall George Meany's caustic complaints in 1972). Throughout the 1970s and 1980s, speeches, media accounts, and books by and about the New Democrats were redolent with euphemisms for white voters who did not warm up to McGovern-era New Politics issues (or, more darkly, advances in civil rights), the kind of voters who defected to Nixon and later became Reagan Democrats. When in 1985 DLC mainstay Lawton Chiles (D-FL) criticized the Democrats for having "a caucus for every group but Middle America," it wasn't hard to figure out who he was referring to.[28] Main Street, average Americans, ordinary folks, the mainstream, the middle class, hardworking Americans: the context surrounding these terms made it clear that New Democrats, particularly those from the South, were concerned about the party's waning appeal to white, non-college-educated voters.

It may already be apparent that a contradiction lay at the core of what New Democrats believed. They argued simultaneously that

1. Liberalism needed to reject New Deal economic populism aimed at full employment and a decent working-class standard of living in order to free the forces of innovation and the market, leading to economic growth.
2. Working-class people abandoned the Democratic Party because of its liberal positions on noneconomic issues like civil rights.

If you're wondering why Democrats have settled on the second point *but not the first* as the reason it lost the white working class, you're in good company. Some mental gymnastics are required. But even during the heyday of the New Deal, there was a probusiness Democratic faction that believed in the kind of supply-side economic solutions that eventually became synonymous with American conservatism.[29] At the core of the New Democrats' embrace of this approach is a narrative of inevitability about the changing economy, an assumption that would be brought into high relief by Bill Clinton. Globalization, economic change, the death of old industries and the birth of new ones—all were inevitable. They could be resisted, as liberal governments in Western Europe were trying to do, but not successfully or for long. Thus, New Democrats did not think of themselves as "abandoning" the working class. As they saw it, they wanted to use government to assist workers in weathering economic changes that could not be stopped. They were the pragmatists who saw, and were brave enough to say, that the working class was doomed.

LET'S BE FRANK

That is a description of New Democrat ideology as they saw themselves. But a more cynical view, both contemporary and historical, saw them as soulless yuppies, relentless climbers who were willing to throw the poor and working class under the bus to secure the socioeconomic equivalent of a gated subdivision for college-educated, high-earning, mostly white baby boomers.[30] Contemporary observers labeled them "self-serving cognoscenti," "vacuous" and "blow-dried," and donor-appeasing "PAC-men." In 1986, Arthur Schlesinger Jr. declared in the *New York Times* that the "quasi-Reaganite" DLC were dooming the party to failure with economic "me-too* Reaganism."[31]

A glaring problem was the repackaging of personal responsibility rhetoric, appealing to white voters (and higher-income voters in general) by crapping on the poor, especially the Black poor, and attacking racialized issues, especially welfare and crime. In 1986, DLC chair Chuck Robb of Virginia said Democrats needed to face "uncomfortable truths" about Black poverty and shift the narrative from "racism—the traditional enemy within—to self-defeating patterns of behavior—the new enemy within."[32] In 1984, Mondale's loss was met with waves of complaints that special interests dominated the party, with pointed mentions of Jesse Jackson to

---

* This phrase obviously did not have the connotations then that it does today.

clarify exactly who the special interests were. No wonder Jackson referred to the DLC as Democrats for the Leisure Class.

New Democrat appeals on welfare reform bordered on race-baiting. And the border was frequently crossed. In 1988 then senator Joe Biden penned an editorial that explained how welfare "relieved recipients of the incentive to take control of their future" after opening with a reference to a welfare queen in a luxury car—a stereotype he categorized as potentially harmful and false but definitely a real thing Democrats needed to attack anyway. In a truly remarkable article for *New York Magazine* in 1991, Joe Klein—Bill Clinton's personal chronicler, later the author of *Primary Colors*—argues in "Deconstructing Duke" that failed 1991 Louisiana Republican gubernatorial candidate and former KKK grand wizard David Duke is right about welfare, and only Arkansas governor Bill Clinton, among leading Democrats, is brave enough to see it. Americans, Klein explains, are right to be resentful of having their money taken to pay people who don't work, and by the way, urban crime (*wink!*) is skyrocketing. Then he offers a list of typical white stepdad grievances about Black culture glorifying violence.

Democrats, who "fear alienating the black leadership," ignore this and support "racial-preference programs" that nobody likes. Democrats have been "far too timid, though, in condemning the irresponsible behavior of the poor." Finally, in declaring that no issue is more important in 1992 than "anarchy in the slums," Klein concludes that "selfishness, greed, and desperation" dominate among the poor. For some odd reason this article is not available online from *New York Magazine*, nor does Klein list it among his works.

Joe Klein may be "only" a journalist, but he was unquestionably a journalist close to Bill Clinton and the New Democrat circle when that was written. Bashing welfare was certainly a part of the late 1980s, early 1990s New Democrat (and Reagan Republican, obviously) playbook. To be clear, poverty, crime, and the social safety net are important issues that belong in the discourse. But the New Democrats used them too often in a way meant to let well-off white liberals feel liberal (they're supporting *Democrats*, the liberal party, after all) while venting hostility at the mooching, undeserving, ungrateful poor—especially the "urban" or "inner-city" poor. It is hard to view their rhetoric as anything other than an attempt to capitalize on resentment toward the poor among the better-off and toward Blacks among white voters of any economic stratum.[33]

The New Democrats' neoliberal economic ideas had a similarly self-congratulatory appeal to a professional class that viewed its successes as the well-deserved product of their exceptional credentials and skills.[34] Not unlike Reagan's trickle-down economics, New Democratic proposals to address poverty involved a convoluted theory about how giving more money and opportunity to the most successful members of society would eventually help the poor. What if economic growth— making the pie bigger—simply resulted in the rich helping themselves to more? Even a glowing contemporary take on the emergent New Democrats concedes that "if one thing rings false in all the rhetoric of neoliberalism, it is that the 'national interest' may be nothing more than the special interests of the upper middle class."[35] It did not require excessive cynicism to conclude that New Democrats aimed to flatter a new constituency at the expense of one deemed superfluous.

Above all, New Democrats liked to depict themselves as nonideological or postideological; if it worked, they wanted to do it, regardless of where the idea originated. This was intended to dissociate them from the Democrats' unpopular tax-and-spend reputation, as well as from the antiwar, women's rights, civil rights, and environmental movements that were by that time perceived as powerful special interests out of step with mainstream (*wink!*) America. Economic growth was positioned within New Democrat circles as the ideal nonideological issue—who opposes economic growth? That sounds nice, and it appealed to an electorate in which the political parties were not held in high regard. But their ideas were as intensely ideological as those of any other political faction. There is nothing nonideological about focusing on economic growth while excluding distributional questions, which over time has aided the staggering increase in income inequality. Turning the middle class against the poor and working class—and doing so with framing that included obvious racial overtones—is ideological. The belief that seismic changes to the economy could be addressed with government programs to train and educate workers for different careers is ideological. That worldview may be right or wrong,* but calling it nonideological is bunk.

NO ALTERNATIVE?†

A key component of the centrist narrative is the assumption of inevitability. The way things happened beginning in the late 1960s is the only way they could have happened. Democrats (and their counterparts internationally) moved to the center because they had to.

History is written by the victors. In this case, the victors want to disavow responsibility for choices that had devastating consequences or are a bad look for modern liberal sensibilities. No Democrat, still holding out hope of wooing working-class votes, wants to brag that they gave up on an entire class of loyal voters because they found a better, more affluent demographic to target. So presenting the changes as a pragmatic response to external circumstances is good cover.

The relationship between labor and the Democratic Party that unraveled in the McGovern era involved a third, omitted group: the working class. Organized labor or unions and the working class, often treated as interchangeable terms, are not the same. Unions won much for their members and sought, logically, to protect what they won. Their political focus shifted from the Depression-era emphasis on legislating better conditions for the working class to what labor historians call private-sector welfare: benefits packages won through collective bargaining.[36] For example, rather than fighting for Congress to provide health care for all, unions used collective bargaining to win generous health benefits for their members, within a given industry or from a specific employer. For the unionized workers who benefited, that was great, but it also served to undermine a broader movement toward universal solutions benefiting all workers. By the 1970s the most powerful unions were not interested in a mission of building broad-based working-class solidarity. They confronted growing economic uncertainty by closing ranks and defending what they had won for themselves. Crucially, the cultural "Archie Bunker" aspect of union members' openness to reactionary

---

* It's wrong.

† Great album, incidentally. Holds up.

politics in 1968 and 1972 is oversimplified as a function of racism and hostility to feminism and other New Politics movements. This sidesteps the important fact that predominantly white union members *considered themselves middle class*, not working class, and as the working class grew increasingly diverse, unions, as the institutions they had become, saw no common cause. The union steelworker saw himself as a skilled professional, socially and economically above unskilled—and increasingly female, Black, and Hispanic—workers in fields like retail, agriculture, or light manufacturing, all of which happened to be growth areas in the American economy during the unions' decline.

Both the Democratic Party and establishment labor unions turned their focus away from the working class as it was evolving away from traditional manufacturing and extractive industries. Some unions like the Teamsters grew reactionary. Among the lowest points in US labor history is the Teamsters standing beside law enforcement to help suppress farm workers' organizing efforts in California. The Teamsters saw enemies—unskilled and identifiably foreign—not fellow workers with common interests.

The early 1970s were, make no mistake, a period of working-class and labor activism without precedent since the Great Depression. Independent truckers hurt by the oil crisis of 1973 engaged in nationwide wildcat strikes; auto workers bucked the UAW leadership and pushed a new generation of activist leaders; and Cesar Chavez organized some of the most powerless, disenfranchised working people in the country. But local bursts of activism and organization like the 1972 Farah, Texas, garment workers' strike withered rather than expanded as the institutional labor movement failed to support them, and rank-and-file activists in the United Mine Workers union saw their chosen leader Joseph "Jock" Yablonski denied leadership in a rigged election and, when that failed to stop him, murdered in his home by corrupt president Tony Boyle. Meanwhile, working people everywhere bristled against dull, unfulfilling, dangerous work for wages that didn't go far in the face of inflation and other macroeconomic changes.

We cannot say definitively that something like a Poor People's Campaign of working-class solidarity—political and economic—would have worked. What is certain is that the establishment Democratic Party and organized labor chose not to try. They pursued a different strategy. Democrats saw a future in which the working class was not central to winning elections and unions traded solidarity and militant activism for protecting their hard-won status quo. Rather than a concerted effort to replace each Archie Bunker who recoiled at Democrats' liberalism on issues of equality with a member of the young, diverse, struggling working class of the future, political actors embraced the neoliberal worldview that organized labor and empowered working people were simply obsolete.

CHAPTER 4

INSURGENT MODERATES

The Rise of the New Democrats

The Democratic Leadership Council occupies an odd position in the long story of American politics. It never had many members. It was satisfied to remain anonymous outside the Beltway and the purview of political junkies. Its heyday was brief. Yet its timing was impeccable. When the Democratic Party was at a low ebb, it thrust one of its own into the 1992 presidential election, and he proceeded to rebrand the party in his ideological image. How did a small group of moderates from the political hinterlands succeed in remaking a major political party to its liking, with ripple effects still felt decades later?

THE OBLIGATORY ORIGIN STORY

If two people less well known than Gillis Long and Alvin "Al" From had a greater impact on modern American politics, their names have been lost to history.[1]

In 1980, the Republicans took the Senate while Reagan swept Carter out of the White House. With the House the last bastion of Democratic power at the national level, in 1981 Rep. Gillis Long (D-LA) became the chair of the House Democratic Caucus. Its executive director was Al From, a former adviser to Jimmy Carter and staffer to Sen. Edmund Muskie (D-ME). A cautious, moderate New Deal liberal, Muskie had been Hubert Humphrey's running mate in 1968 and saw his own campaign for president in 1972 derailed, likely for the only time in US political history, by his alleged use of "Canuck" as a slur against Americans of French Canadian heritage.[2] From was known in Democratic circles as a reliable policy guy but hardly a revolutionary. He listed as one of his proudest professional accomplishments the ushering of the fiscally conservative Congressional Budget and Impoundment Control Act of 1974 into law—not the kind of achievement that would thrill many liberals. To From, that was the point.

From believed that the Democrats no longer presented a coherent, big-picture worldview to voters. He mistrusted the New Politics movement, which he believed alienated conservative voters with its liberal social views. He was also critical of mainstream Democrats' refusal to break with the New Deal, continuing to cater to unions representing declining industries and failing to address what he considered the hyperbolic growth of government.[3] In this sense, From's critique of what ailed the Democrats was far more sophisticated than those who boiled the party's problems down to white backlash against civil rights. Certainly, the politics of race were a factor. Yet From watched the ascendancy of Ronald Reagan's brand of conservatism and concluded that voters disliked two pillars of what Democrats had long believed: that government is a force for good as a regulator of social and economic issues and that organized labor (and prolabor federal policy) is a net positive. It's difficult at this remove to grasp how alarming it must have seemed at the time to suggest Democrats had to jettison perhaps the two most crucial parts of their political cosmology. It was like telling Julia Child that she needed to tweak her show by cutting out all the cooking. What's left?

Gillis Long shared From's vision of what was wrong with the party. In 1981, he established the Committee on Party Effectiveness (CPE) to serve as a forum for policy ideas and to reinsert members of Congress into the process of defining the direction of the party.[4] Long and From felt that since the McGovern-Fraser reforms, the party had ceded control of its ideology to interest groups and activists while sidelining elected officials and candidates. The CPE drew from Democrats of all factions, so it was only a spiritual, not direct, predecessor to the New Democrats and Democratic Leadership Council; though not all CPE participants became New Democrats, most of the important early New Democrat figures were involved. Among the names that would eventually become prominent were Al Gore (D-TN) and Dick Gephardt (D-MO).

One belief CPE participants shared was that the election of 1980 was not a fluke, nor were 1968 and 1972. The Democratic Party was in trouble and retreating into delusions that it could make tired New Deal politics popular again. Long and From believed strongly that the answer was for the Democrats to win back some of the voters they had lost by focusing on free-market solutions rather than old economy institutions like unions and bureaucracy.[5] This contrasted with the view of activist groups who saw nonvoting as a matter of lack of resources and of alienation from the political process and social institutions; they believed they could appeal to nonvoters and turn them into (or back into) Democratic loyalists.

The CPE could not be accused of slacking. For nearly two years leading up to the 1982 midterm elections, they met at least weekly to produce a loosely connected set of policy recommendations. The resulting document, *Rebuilding the Road to Opportunity: A Democratic Direction for the 1980s*, didn't exactly light up the bestseller list, but it was noticed by Democratic politicos who saw the party as unavoidably in transition. The report offered an informal platform intended to suggest new directions for the future—and the title kind of gave away what the authors saw as the answer.[6] To counteract the dreaded perception of tax-and-spend liberals advocating handouts and welfare, the CPE centered opportunity. The most widely noticed paper from the project—by Gillis Long and House colleagues Tim Wirth and Dick Gephardt—argued for a philosophical shift away from redistribution and toward growth and opportunity.[7] Some in the labor movement were concerned enough with the neoliberal economic tone of these proposals to pen a response accusing the CPE of patching potholes rather than building a road.[8] The unions were not wrong to interpret the CPE's nascent manifesto as a red flag. "Opportunity" and "growth" sounded like Chamber of Commerce slogans, not the reassuring commitment to the welfare state and blue-collar work that labor was accustomed to hearing from Democrats.

There was no real coherence to the proposals in *Rebuilding the Road to Opportunity*, and its impact outside the narrow universe of Democratic political operatives was nil; it played no role in the Democrats' good showing in the 1982 midterms.* As a product of the House, the CPE had to appease too many different ideological preferences to articulate a single worldview. So From and Long formed a new group, the National House Democratic Caucus (NHDC), in 1983. It included many House members but also Democratic figures outside Congress and from the business world, think tanks and academia, and the ranks of former elected officials whose reputations Long hoped would bolster the group's standing. Unlike a caucus of sitting members of Congress, an outside group like the NHDC could more clearly articulate preferences and advocate for specific policies. In 1984, the group released an updated version of *Rebuilding* called *Renewing America's Promise.*† Again, it received some light applause and marked From as an important policy guy without really affecting politics more broadly, elevating his profile in what was a rarefied but not terribly large Democratic inner circle.

THE FINAL STRAW

Al From and other like-minded Democrats felt unable to influence the direction of the party in 1984, an election they considered Exhibit A of everything Democrats did wrong. Walter Mondale, a New Deal liberal and prototypical establishment figure, secured the nomination by methodically horse trading for the support of what the DNC had declared in 1982 its seven official caucuses: women, Blacks, Hispanics, gays, Asians, liberals, and business professionals.[9] What he lacked was any kind of

---

* With the lionization of Ronald Reagan, rarely is it remembered that 1982 and 1986 were disasters for the GOP. Democrats picked up a net seven governorships in 1982, as well as Senate and House seats, while in 1986 they added eight Senate seats to retake the chamber. Reagan was not magic, and the Reagan-era GOP was far from a political juggernaut.

† See National House Democratic Caucus, *Renewing America's Promise: A Democratic Blueprint for Our Nation's Future* (Washington, DC: NHDC, 1984). Barack Obama would crib the title of this NHDC document for a position paper at the beginning of his presidency in 2009. Foreshadowing!

unifying ideology or larger vision for the country, a significant handicap in a race against Reagan, who exceled at grand, soaring rhetoric. To emphasize how completely the Democratic Party had lost its New Deal roots in the working class and organized labor, Mondale's campaign put forth no jobs creation plan. Not a bad or an insufficient plan—no plan at all. He went down to a defeat nearly as lopsided as McGovern's in 1972.

It is unlikely that any Democratic nominee could have defeated Reagan in 1984, and there is no practical difference between losing by one electoral vote or four hundred. But Mondale represented a final straw among the activists who felt that a new Democratic Party was needed. Rather than rebounding from the low points of 1968 and 1972, efforts to revive the party seemed like they were making things worse. The sense of drift and disunity was increasing. After the 1984 Democratic Convention in San Francisco, Long and From decided that they would not be able to effect change from the inside; moderates like them held too little power. Instead, they felt that an organization not formally affiliated with the Democratic Party would give them time and freedom to build strength. That is the short version of how and why, in 1985, Al From founded the Democratic Leadership Council.

Originally, the group was open only to sitting members of Congress and consisted primarily of southern and western Democratic moderates seeking to bring the party back into what they saw as the mainstream of American politics.[10] Moderates in these regions were especially concerned that the negative perception of the national party was hurting them. Eventually, DLC membership would expand to include governors, lower-level elected officials, and political professionals, like consultants and pollsters, who shared these concerns. But it was never a mass-membership group that counted thousands of supporters. It was more like a very well-organized and exclusive club for Washington insiders.

The group emphasized that Democratic candidates were doing relatively well at every level of politics except the White House. For governorships, state legislatures, and Congress, Democrats remained competitive if no longer dominant. The reason, the DLC felt, was that the national Democratic Party lacked a coherent and appealing vision and was stereotyped as a bunch of elite liberal single-issue activists and special interests like unions and Black voters. Candidates were therefore forced to appeal to voters by repudiating the Democratic Party's national image. The media sensation of Reagan Democrats (yet another euphemism for white, conservative-leaning, working- and middle-class voters) emphasized that voters who had long worn the Democratic label were unhappy with the party even while continuing to vote for incumbent Democrats down ballot.[11]

In hindsight, From described the first four years of his organization as accomplishing little.* Convening policy forums showed that the DLC was a serious group of serious people, not the usual loose coalition of Capitol Hill creatures who occasionally met for cocktails and network-ing. While the policy discussions had substance, they were not specific enough to draw sharp contrasts with the rest of the Democratic Party because "by not being overly specific about its aims, the DLC maximized membership."[12]

The first modest goal of the DLC had been to put forth a centrist candidate for the vacant DNC chair position in 1985. To underscore the powerlessness of the new group, the DLC both failed to come up with its own candidate (all promising contenders declined to run for the position) and exerted no influence on the outcome of the race. Worse, the spiritual godfather of the New Democrat movement, Gillis Long, died of cancer in 1985.† But From did have an eye for political talent; he used the DLC relentlessly to promote young prospects like Bill Clinton, who seemed like he had been built in a lab to be the perfect glad-hander, and Al Gore, a walking binder of white papers and unrestrained gush about the prom-ise of technology to transform the future.

It was clear that the beliefs of active DLC members were neither purely liberal nor conservative, but a new kind of radical center, with the rheto-ric and youth of activists and idealists but with distinctly un–Democratic Party views on government (too big) and free markets (always good). But, too weak and too new to take on the Democratic establishment, the

---

* From a revealingly titled chapter of his own retelling, "The Illusion of Power," in *The New Democrats and the Return to Power* (New York: Macmillan, 2013).

† Long was preceded in his House seat by Speedy (his actual name) Long, his cousin, and followed by his wife Catherine Small Long. Cousin Speedy defeated Gillis in 1964 after the latter was accused of casting a procedural House vote to facilitate the Civil Rights Act. This is the Louisiana version of King Lear.

group calculated that playing to party unity and staying friendly with the DNC was important for its survival. So when the new DNC chair, Paul Kirk, prevailed upon From to align the goals of the DLC with the broader Democratic Party, the DLC complied as part of a strategy to play nice, bide time, and make allies. At the same time, it sounded a drumbeat of criticism against one of the dominant players in Democratic politics.

In the DLC's view, unions were the problem. A big problem. They were, from the New Democrat perspective, powerful and corrupt organizations that protected jobs that no longer made sense to the American economy. Appeasing unions meant keeping the Democratic Party shackled to the past. Implementing reforms aimed at breaking the stranglehold of the old Democrats on the party was an early priority for the DLC. It sought to change DNC rules on the presidential nomination to elevate the importance of Super Tuesday in the primaries. The idea was to boost the profile of southern and western states (where union influence lagged) by grouping them into one megaprimary early in the process. This would not only reduce the influence of Iowa and New Hampshire, which they considered unrepresentative (and, in the latter case, too liberal), but also, due to the less strident liberalism of southern and western Democrats, increase the odds that a moderate in the mold of Jimmy Carter could become the frontrunner for the nomination. (Why they felt that Carter's presidency was something to be replicated is unclear.) The DNC took these changes to heart, ostensibly agreeing with the DLC about the need for a less ideologically liberal presidential candidate. They also agreed to shorten the 1988 platform to reduce the apparent influence of special interests, another point where DLC goals aligned with the establishment party.

With the new Super Tuesday rules and the platform changes in place, the DNC was gambling that it could undermine the DLC, which it saw as a threat to its authority. If the Democrats won the White House in 1988, the DNC could politely thank the DLC for its helpful advice and move on, leaving the DLC to disappear in the absence of any obvious reason to exist. But if the Democrats lost, then the panic and rage among centrists and moderates would only increase. So the DNC rolled the dice: 1988 would either break the DLC's momentum or multiply it.

It didn't break it.

THE LAST FINAL STRAW

Super Tuesday didn't elevate a moderate southerner to the nomination in 1988 like the DLC had hoped. In fact, the nominee was the Republicans' caricature of a Democrat: soft-spoken, elfin Massachusetts liberal technocrat Michael Dukakis. His lack of charisma negated the lack of charisma of the Republicans' chosen successor to St. Ronnie, George H. W. Bush. Dukakis's laconic personality made him vulnerable to attacks to which he did not respond vigorously, effectively, or at all. But Democrats' low opinion of Bush and their success in retaking the Senate in 1986 had convinced them that Reagan's hold on the electorate's imagination was weakening. This election, they felt, was winnable.

Dukakis did not win it, though. The best that could be said is that he did better than Mondale. In the end, Dukakis's beliefs, ideology, and record were less important than the perception that he was a meek nonentity Republicans could paint as yet another big-government liberal from "Taxachusetts." The GOP, sensing the changing political landscape, saw the benefit in campaigning against every Democrat as if he were half Lenin, half Jane Fonda. The GOP both fed and played to the stereotype, not necessarily the reality, of post–New Deal Democrats as criminal-coddling, big-spending, commie-appeasing, enviro-feminist dweebs. Every joke in existence about liberal activists of the New Politics type was hung around Dukakis's neck. That he was essentially moderate, bordering on dull, did not matter. Dukakis also hurt himself repeatedly, as with the legendarily ludicrous "Dukakis in a tank" stunt and, fatally, his insistence that the election was about competence not ideology.

But as prominent New Democrat (and ex–Carter White House) strategist Pat Caddell pointed out in no less an outlet than *The Mainstream Democrat*, the official magazine of the DLC, politics without ideology made no sense:

> The reason Dukakis lost was because he had no message. Good jobs at good wages is not a message. Saying that the election is not about ideology but about competence is a joke. Elections are about ideology. They're about values and what you stand for. We didn't offer any vision for the

future, any argument for change. The kind of change we were offering said, "We'll get rid of their hacks and put our hacks in."[13]

Caddell had a point. Competence is only a meaningful attribute in politics if voters have a good sense of what exactly the government intends to do competently. It was like telling passengers to board a plane without knowing the intended destination because the pilot was very nice and good at flying.

If the insurgent moderates of the DLC were angry after 1984, after 1988 they were incandescent. Working inside the big tent of the Democratic Party, withholding criticism against other party factions, and accepting small concessions like rule changes and tweaks to the language in the platform had failed—and From knew it. Like modern Democratic progressives or the left, the DLC moderates found trying to change the party from within a fool's errand. The Democratic establishment would patronize them but would never give them power. Most vexing was the realization that the DLC's biggest mistake in 1988 was not to have its own top-tier candidate in the presidential fight. Gore and Gephardt ran in that year's primaries, as did DLC-curious Sen. Joe Biden (D-DE), but all flopped. The DLC now made the decision to challenge the establishment Democrats head-on for control of the party. By being well organized and dogged about raising its own visibility, the DLC confidently positioned itself as a young, energetic, intellectually vibrant alternative to the creaking, unpopular, bickering party machinery. This meant offering a distinct policy platform to contrast with the party's garbled attempts to enunciate a post–New Deal ideology. That the DLC had connections to powerful people who could raise money and were taken seriously within Democratic circles made this parallel party strategy viable.

Early in 1989, the DLC established the Progressive Policy Institute (PPI), an affiliated think tank for scholars and researchers to work full-time fleshing out policy ideas that could serve as platform alternatives. The PPI was intended to turn ideas into detailed, specific plans. Think tanks, particularly when they are well funded and considered serious (that is, within the ideological range acceptable to Washington Consensus views), can be very effective at legitimizing ideas. They provide academic and intellectual heft, the kind of depth that garners invitations to prominent conferences, appearances on Sunday panel shows, and contact with elected officials.

It takes some effort today to recognize what a departure from the Democratic normal the DLC's distinctive ideological brand represented. The centrist worldview is familiar now because it became deeply rooted in the Democratic mainstream, but at the time not everyone knew what to make of it. As they sought to hold on to an existing base of support without driving away voters who liked the idea of free markets and less government, a big component of their strategy was to take existing Democratic commitments to issue activists and propose new, more broadly appealing ways of achieving the same goals. For example, the DLC did not repudiate environmentalism; instead, it argued that environmental stewardship was compatible with economic growth, and in fact economic prosperity was a necessary precursor to protecting the environment. Entrepreneurs, not EPA bureaucrats, would lead the way to a better environmental future. This too would become ingrained in the Democratic DNA—the ability to weave activist issues like criminal justice reform, environmentalism, equality, and more into the market-centered economic worldview that insisted capitalism, not government, would produce solutions. In their growing insistence that no matter the problem, the answers would come from the private sector, the DLC sounded, in fact, suspiciously like Republicans.

The New Democrat worldview was most fully spelled out in a 1989 PPI paper by William Galston, an academic, and Elaine Ciulla Kamarck, a PPI fellow, called *The Politics of Evasion*.[14] The title alluded to establishment Democrats' resistance to confronting the obvious problems facing the party as long as plausible excuses were available. It is the closest thing the New Democrats had to a manifesto and remains important more than thirty years later, though in reality its framing of prevailing Democratic views was already dated by 1989. The paper focused on three myths. First was the myth of liberal fundamentalism—that the path to success lies in moving left, returning to the proverbial faith of their New Deal ancestors. Second, the myth of mobilization holds that nonvoters can be turned into voters if correctly targeted. Third and final is the myth of the congressional bastion, that nothing can be seriously wrong with the party while it continues to do well in congressional, state, and local races.

All three arguments pointed to similar conclusions: the Democratic Party cannot solve its problems by resorting to liberalism because liberalism is unpopular. It cannot appeal to nonvoters because nonvoters will not become voters. And if something doesn't change soon, the collapse could become more general. The third point certainly played out: Democratic success down ballot did collapse shortly after this article was published. The first two points, though, would deeply influence Democratic thinking moving forward. If nonvoters can't be turned into voters and liberalism makes things worse, little insight is necessary to see where these criticisms lead: moving to the right is both the best and the only way Democrats can do better.

A particularly difficult issue for the New Democrats was how to keep people of color—whom Democrats were more electorally reliant on than ever—in the Democratic base while also winning back white, blue-collar types, who Democrats believed had been driven away by liberal positions on racial equality. Americans, especially white Americans, had subsumed racial issues of the civil rights era—notably segregation and Black voting rights—into other issues like crime, poverty, and welfare. As political scientists Edward Carmines and James Stimson explain in their classic *Issue Evolution*, by the 1980s it was no longer politically viable to campaign with flagrant bigotry like George Wallace did, advocating Jim Crow and using racial slurs the way most people use prepositions. That doesn't mean that racist politicking ended; it just got incrementally more subtle, cloaked in a layer of plausible deniability. Words like *urban* and *inner city* became proxies, and socially undesirable labels like *unwed mothers* and *welfare recipients* took on racial connotations.[15] And some issues that were explicitly racial, like school busing and affirmative action, remained obvious ways for politicians to play on racial resentment. Racial politicking evolved. In the infamous description of Republican strategist Lee Atwater,

You start out in 1954 by saying, "[redacted racial slur]." By 1968 you can't say "[redacted racial slur]"—that hurts you. Backfires. So you say stuff like, uh, forced busing, states' rights, and all that stuff, and you're getting so abstract. Now, you're talking about cutting taxes, and all these things you're talking about are totally economic things and a byproduct of them is, blacks get hurt worse than whites. . . . "We want to cut this," is much more abstract than even the busing thing, uh, and a hell of a lot more abstract than "[redacted racial slur]."*

Thus, when New Democrats talked about being tough on crime and favoring welfare reform, they were delivering twin messages. One was that, as Democrats, they were willing to reject liberal ideas like emphasizing rehabilitation over punishment in the justice system. The other was the unspoken message to voters who had deserted the party in 1968 and 1972: *You think Democrats are too racially liberal and we hear you.* Saying *urban poor* with some implied winking was clear enough and gave politicians, especially Democrats, cover against accusations of racism.

Reagan and the Republicans had a track record of getting political mileage out of welfare, in particular, because it was easily, if disingenuously, characterized as the government taking money from white people who worked and giving it to people of color who didn't work.[16] Conservatives encouraged and popularized this idea, playing it up for maximum political advantage. New Democrats took note and positioned themselves as advocates of reform on topics like welfare and crime, hoping to sound more palatable to Democratic voters who had been wooed by Reaganism, but in many cases advocating the same kinds of harsher policies preferred by Republicans.

In essence, the New Democrats thought that ideological moderation could blunt or eliminate the most common negative stereotypes about Democrats. Their economic worldview, they hoped, would overcome tax-and-spend charges. By proposing a less conciliatory, more interventionist foreign policy, they would no longer be weak on defense. And most of all, by proposing tougher criminal penalties and more policing, combined with welfare reform, they could never again be labeled soft on crime or

---

* Yes, the redacted word is what you think it is. For discussion and transcription of Atwater's remarks, see Perlstein, R., "Exclusive: Lee Atwater's Infamous 1981 Interview on the Southern Strategy," *Nation*, November 13, 2012.

the party of handouts (*wink*). After all, if Democrats stopped acting like Republicans accused them of acting, then Republicans would no longer be able to attack them. Truly an airtight plan.

The establishment Democratic Party's response to the surge in DLC activity after 1988 was to do nothing. The DLC had a hard time picking fights with the DNC or with the more liberal wing of the party because no one would respond to defend the status quo. Only Jesse Jackson, with his independent Rainbow Coalition organization, pushed back with his own competing vision of a Democratic future that did not involve moving to the right.[17] Like something out of Monty Python, the Democratic Party refused to stick up for the Democratic Party. And by the time the institutional Democratic Party realized the DLC had become a major threat—for example, scheduling its own competing convention in 1991— it was too late to stop it.

But what the DLC really needed was its own candidate running on its own ideas. They needed someone to take the New Democrat ideology to the big stage and win over voters, not only with ideas but with those magical qualities recent Democratic candidates had so singularly lacked: charisma, personality, charm, call it what you will.

Al From was pretty sure that he knew a guy.

CHAPTER 5

IT'S BILL CLINTON'S DEMOCRATIC PARTY NOW

Just seventy-eight days into Bill Clinton's presidency, before the 1994 Republican Revolution upended the partisan political landscape, Bob Woodward recounted the following outburst in the Oval Office when penny-pinching won out over Clinton's campaign promises for investment in education, clean energy, and a middle-class tax cut:

"Where are all the Democrats?" Clinton bellowed. "I hope you're all aware we're all Eisenhower Republicans," he said, his voice dripping with sarcasm.

"We're all Eisenhower Republicans here, and we are fighting the Reagan Republicans. We stand for lower deficits and free trade and the bond market. Isn't that great?"

In context, this is an odd moment. No individual is more responsible than Bill Clinton for pushing the Democratic Party toward Eisenhower Republicanism. He was shouting at himself.

Clinton did not invent the idea of moving the Democrats toward the center and even the right, but he presided over the official death of the

New Deal and radically changed the way his party understood politics, elections, and governing. It is not always clear whether Clinton himself led these changes or was merely representative of them—the man at the helm when American liberalism finally settled on a post–New Deal rebranding that seemed like a winner. Bill Clinton won—twice. To Democrats who had struggled to win the White House for two decades, that counted for a lot.

All presidents leave an imprint on their parties, but Clinton was uniquely situated to have an outsized influence on a party in flux. He won the White House at a time when the Democratic Party was at a low ebb, at the tail end of twenty-five years of futility in presidential elections and increasingly losing its grip on Congress. He delivered what had started to seem impossible. Accordingly, his influence on Democrats was greater than any single actor in the party since LBJ. In 1992, reporters often called him a "kid,"[*] but for Democrats—and particularly for the centrist DLC of which he was a member in good standing—"golden child" is more like it. The Democratic Party that existed when Clinton[†] left the White House in 2001 would have been unrecognizable to Democrats of 1968.

Democrats remain aggressively fond of Bill Clinton, but depicting him as a success story conveniently omits what the party conceded on his watch. That Clinton accomplished more of Reagan's agenda than Reagan did, that he governed as a moderate Republican, that his answer to the ongoing Democratic identity crisis was to pursue conservative priorities but "better" and "smarter," that his solution for combatting conservative anti-government rhetoric was to endorse and embrace it—all of this has been argued and documented elsewhere. What is overlooked are the many ways in which Clinton's methods—his electoral strategy, his way of thinking, his way of governing—became the default, the baseline, of the modern Democratic Party. The conventional wisdom we hear today from Democratic sages is not drawn from FDR or Grover Cleveland but overwhelmingly

---

[*] In a speech in Manchester, New Hampshire, after winning the state's primary in 1992, Clinton thanked voters for making him "the comeback kid," and reporters covering the otherwise dull nomination contest ran with it.

[†] Throughout this chapter, I hope that context will make clear that "Clinton" is Bill Clinton, whereas when Hillary Clinton is the subject, I use her full name. In later sections when Hillary is clearly the subject, I reverse this.

from Clinton and other Democrats who rose to positions of influence in the 1990s.* Bill Clinton's influence on the party is more than the sum of his issue positions and presidential actions; he did nothing less than redefine what Democrats believe they need to do to win and—this is crucial enough to merit a font change—even *what winning means.*

THE CONFUSED KID

It took Bill Clinton a long time to figure out who and what he was politically. But the characteristics that would come to define him to a public that either loved or loathed him were apparent from the moment he entered politics in 1972 with an unsuccessful bid for Congress. He was charming (critics said "smarmy") and eloquent, and well, there was just something about him. Charisma. He could give a speech and leave people who were variously for or against a topic believing he agreed with them (a rhetorical talent contemporaries also attributed to FDR). He wiggled his way out of difficulties with a combination of southern boy aw-shucks and Ivy League gentleman manners. He was, at the core, slick. The traumas of 1968 and 1972 were part of his politically formative years; he was twenty-six when he and Hillary (twenty-five) worked together on the McGovern campaign. Both came to Democratic politics as an old party was collapsing and uncertainty reigned about what the new one would look like. Like many in the baby boom generation they represented, they lacked attachment to New Dealism and had their faith in New Politics liberalism shattered in 1972.

Clinton came to the attention of Al From and what would become the DLC early in his political career for several reasons. He preferred moderate politics and internalized the intellectual revolution of his young adulthood: the neoliberalism of Hayek and Friedman that promoted free markets and denigrated big government. He reflected the latent southern probusiness strain of the Democratic Party that also produced Jimmy Carter. He was highly educated and believed education was the key to the economic future. He was electable in a southern state. He liked big ideas, white papers, and the idea that technocracy (distinct from bureaucracy)

---

* In Cleveland's case, wisdom was imparted on two occasions, nonconsecutively.

could craft policy solutions—put the smart people in charge, give them freedom to innovate, and they'll sort the mess out. But perhaps most importantly, Clinton stood out because he had the innate political talent other future DLC figures lacked. The DLC had plenty of ideas people, including From himself, but they could charitably be described as a bit dull, with political ceilings well below the White House. Clinton, though flawed and of limited experience, was the closest thing the DLC had in its circles to someone with the elusive "it" factor that makes a strong presidential candidate.

The DLC rarely passed on an opportunity to get Clinton exposure: at conferences he was often featured as a speaker, and hardly an issue of *The Mainstream Democrat* passed without a story about or penned by Bill Clinton. No doubt some in that circle considered the boyish Clinton a potential candidate of the future, but From and the DLC leadership had the political instincts to recognize their opportunity in 1992. After Joe Biden, Al Gore, and Dick Gephardt ran in 1988 and received a combined total of about ten votes,* primary voters were hardly clamoring for more of that trio. Progressive bigwig Jesse Jackson declined to run in 1992. Contenders from other Democratic camps were beyond uninspiring: California governor Jerry Brown, parodied as "Governor Moonbeam" and slapped with the fatal special interests label,[1] represented the New Politics tradition, while tepid Massachusetts senator Paul Tsongas and Iowa senator Tom Harkin ran as bland fiscal conservatives, the kind of candidate you forget before he finishes speaking.

Brown's candidacy was easily dismissed as McGovern redux. Tsongas and Harkin could best be characterized as inoffensive holes in the atmosphere.† Given the uninspiring alternatives, a little-known baby-faced Arkansas governor could have a chance. Sure, Clinton's first moment on the national stage was a 1988 Democratic Convention speech so bad that the audience literally erupted in cheers when he said "in conclusion,"‡ but other than insiders and politics junkies, who would remember that?

---

* An exaggeration, but only slightly.

† For Bill Bryson and Mr. E. T. Stotesbury.

‡ Boos can be heard throughout the rambling thirty-three-minute address; see Clinton, B., "The 1988 Democratic National Convention Speech by Gov. Clinton,"

Clinton, enthusiastically backed by the DLC, dove headlong into the weak field. His 1992 campaign messaging veered from traditional Democratic ground (labor, government programs, the welfare state) and aimed at the successful middle- and professional-class knowledge economy demographic, the very people Lanny Davis and Frederick Dutton were writing about in between the Humphrey and McGovern presidential campaigns. He talked a lot about opportunity, about being "a different kind of Democrat."[2] The New Democrat label he introduced to the public was novel enough to require explanation both on the campaign trail and in the media,[3] yet it was always clearer what he wasn't (a liberal, a New Dealer, a union guy) than what he was: "a middle-class moderate offering radical change" while reaching out "for new voters in the suburbs, among Reagan Democrats, and among Independents."[4]

Against the patrician, promise-breaking, recession-overseeing plutocrat caricature that was George Bush, Clinton came off as authentic, empathetic, and almost human. He repeated the phrase "middle class" like a magical incantation, speaking to the politics of "forgotten" white middle America while carefully sidestepping George Wallace– or Nixon-style reactionary appeals. He explored every aspect of the art of saying white voters without saying "white voters." But the campaign also veered into more explicit, if still coded, appeals. It took a conspicuously strong and un-Democratic position on welfare, with an expensive (at the time) ad campaign in key states famously vowing to "end welfare as we know it."[5] Anti-welfare sentiment was less about a specific government program than a sweeping gesture of animosity toward the poor, especially the urban Black poor.[6] Crime, another issue on which Clinton was vocal in bucking Democratic orthodoxy, functioned as a similar dog whistle.[7]

Despite the strong support he received from the DLC, Clinton's campaign and early presidency were much more about tone and feeling* than about detailed policy prescriptions.† On the trail he told voters he felt

---

C-SPAN, July 20, 1988, clintonlibrary42, YouTube video, 36:12, www.youtube.com /watch?v=g0TdQwyd08A.

* I believe the kids these days call this "vibes." Bill Clinton was all vibes.

† At one point in 1993, the DLC grew so frustrated with Clinton's unwillingness to advance their specific agenda that he was briefly considered an apostate (though quickly absolved).

their pain and sounded like he meant it.* His campaign pitched populist tones but emphasized moderation, offering empathy without specifics, hope with minimal substance. It famously focused on "the economy, stupid" without doing a ton to clarify how the economy could be fixed beyond the comprehensive promise that growth would create jobs, opportunity, and middle-class prosperity.

Somehow, it all worked in 1992. Despite Clinton's hesitancy about fully embracing its ideological agenda, the DLC was crucial to his ascension in several ways.[8] First, as a well-organized (if top-heavy) organization, it opened doors in DC otherwise closed to a minor-state governor. The DLC didn't get millions of people to support Clinton, but it was crucial in getting some of the *right* people to support him. Second, the DLC created a policy playbook Clinton readily drew from. Presidential candidates have to act like they have an answer for everything. Clinton was intent on making his answers different from what voters associated with Democrats. And whenever his personal stash came up dry, he had a bag of white papers and wonkery he could reach into. Finally, the DLC outorganized, outfundraised, and generally outhustled the other factions of a moribund Democratic Party and took action when it saw an opportunity. They didn't talk themselves out of pushing Clinton when it became apparent that the field of Democratic contenders in 1992 was historically weak.

A myth worth dispelling about 1992 is that any Democrat could have won due to the poor economy and Ross Perot's cannibalizing of Republican votes. There was a pronounced recession throughout 1990 and 1991, but economic growth was trending up throughout 1992. If anything, these economic improvements pointed toward a win for the incumbent Bush.[9] Perot's actual role was to drive an increase in turnout among voters who would not otherwise have bothered voting and to *reduce* Clinton's margin of victory.[10] Clinton won with a meager 43 percent of the popular vote, but it was neither a total fluke nor a victory handed to him on a platter. True, Clinton's newfangled ideas did little to tip the scales for the

---

* Clinton's original "I feel your pain" moment came during a tense exchange with an AIDS activist heckling him during a March 28, 1992, speech. He noted how well the crowd reacted to the line and reused it on the topic of economic pain during a presidential debate on October 15, 1992.

Democrats; voters didn't even digest the then novel idea of a New Democrat until much later. In 1992, they simply liked Clinton and trusted him on economic issues.[11] That was enough.

CLINTON THE NEW OLD DEMOCRAT, SORT OF

Clinton's quest to find his ideological level was apparent during the early months of his presidency, where he was torn between traditional liberal ideas and the New Democrat ideology he loved. In an infamous example, he kicked off his presidency with the disastrous "Don't Ask, Don't Tell" policy to address gay and lesbian military service—a classic New Politics play directed at an activist constituency with ideological goals, but with the New Democrat twist of being tailored to avoid (in theory) upsetting traditional values enthusiasts.* Ultimately, the compromise disappointed everyone: opponents considered it a libertine policy presaging the downfall of Western civilization, while LGBTQ+ advocates largely resented the implication that staying in the closet was the solution.[12]

More surprisingly, Clinton spent considerable early political capital on the North American Free Trade Agreement. NAFTA upended domestic American politics perhaps more than any single economic issue since Andrew Jackson battled Congress over the National Bank in 1833. That a Democrat supported a policy that opened trade borders so American businesses could access cheap foreign labor was truly jarring. George H. W. Bush, a big NAFTA fan, could not get it passed through a Democratic Congress.† But, with a coalition of neoliberal or conservative Democrats and customarily probusiness Republicans, a Democratic president could. For this faction, which had embraced the winners-and-losers economy and rejected the New Deal ideas of full employment with a decent standard of living for every working person, NAFTA was an expression of the New Democrats' core economic beliefs.

In hindsight, it is easy to see NAFTA as a betrayal of the working class and the end of blue-collar America's hope for a middle-class lifestyle.

---

* Homophobes.

† After signing NAFTA, Bush asked Congress for fast-track authority to ratify the agreement but was rebuffed. His presidency ended before further action was taken in Congress.

And that narrative is compelling. Yet at the time, Clinton and the New Democrats argued—and perhaps even believed—that it would improve the lot of American workers. Neoliberals framed NAFTA as the best response to *inevitable* change. Globalization was coming, period. It was the future. Nothing and nobody could stop it. All America could do was get with the program. While the villainous GOP couldn't care less what happened to workers whose jobs migrated to low-wage countries, New Democrats wanted to help workers by promising them that through education and retraining they would acquire new skills and better-paid jobs. Yes, the factory job would disappear—but it would be replaced by a far better job! Something high-tech, or whatever.

In the book-film *Primary Colors*—Joe Klein's (remember him?) lazily fictionalized retelling of Bill Clinton's rise—a key scene shows Clinton (ahem, "Stanton") speaking inside central casting's rusting, dilapidated idea of a factory. He faces the grim-looking workers and explains the story of globalization, the new economic reality that simply is and will be. He intones empathetically: "Muscle jobs are gonna go where muscle labor is cheap—and that's not here. So if you want to compete and do better, you're gonna have to exercise a different set of muscles, the ones between your ears." A woman mutters, "Uh-oh." The governor shoots back: "Uh-oh is right."

In the film version, two aides watch impassively. "He's lost them," one whispers. The other responds, "Fuck them. *He's got me!*"*

The melodrama perfectly encapsulates the pitfalls of the new path the Democratic Party was taking. Regular working-class Americans might hate the new economy, but fuck 'em; look how much the right people—educated, with-it people like political consultants!—love it. The role of the working class is to realize that its days of high living are over. Adapt or die.

You'll recognize the rhetoric around jobs, NAFTA, and globalization because so much of it remains unchanged today. In practice, of course, what happened is that the factories closed, jobs disappeared, and "retraining" in some vague, unspecified way remains the answer. Learn to code, I guess! Wages spiral downward as workers are diverted into impermanent,

---

* Please kill me.

low-paying service industry work and, more recently, the gig economy. Democrats present themselves as the saviors—or at least the only thing standing between economic precarity and a Republican abyss—in a crisis they played a decisive role in precipitating. Some voters, believe it or not, remain peeved at the way globalization sounded the death knell for vast regions of the country.

Whether Bill Clinton anticipated what NAFTA would do, secretly hoped for it, or sincerely believed it would improve workers' lives is unknowable and, for our purposes, unimportant. NAFTA was pitched by a faction of moderate Democrats who were growing in influence as a new idea for a new economy—for the future, not the past. And in their words, it promised benefits, not pain, for the working class. The novelty, the downright weirdness of a Democratic president embracing a business-friendly reform that even some Republicans questioned can easily be missed today.* Now endorsements of the key tenets of neoliberalism are just normal Democratic politics.

NAFTA also convinced Clinton that he faced less resistance to his free-market worldview from Republicans than from the Democratic majorities in Congress, foreshadowing the sacramental status to which Democrats would elevate bipartisanship in the future. Too many Democrats were rooted in old paradigms. Some resisted the more conservative New Democrat approach as insufficiently liberal; others felt it was still too liberal. By 2000, though, a Washington Consensus embraced by Clinton would form around economic ideas Democrats had once resisted. After the booming dot-com economy of the 1990s, who could resist? Unions and protections for American workers *were* bad, outdated stuff. Budget deficits *were* a very serious thing, a political priority. Creative entrepreneurs *were* precious resources in need of careful collective nurturing and encouragement so they could address social and economic problems. It would be a seismic break from the past of Democratic politics—exactly what Bill Clinton wanted.

---

* Paleoconservatives like Pat Buchanan, a direct antecedent of Trump, seized on anti–free trade, antiglobalization sentiment—rhetorically if not in practice—as an effective pitch to Rust Belt voters.

THE DEFICIT, STUPID

The Clinton White House established unambiguously that deficits and reducing government spending were now key issues for Democrats. No longer the party that preached Keynesianism, widely shared prosperity, and the good that government could do, Democrats were eager to show that Republicans weren't the only ones who could advocate belt tightening and fiscal discipline. Deficit politics were not new in 1993; in fact, they had been a regular feature in political discourse since the economic downturns of the late 1960s and throughout the 1970s.[13] But the Ross Perot campaign, with its single-minded obsession with the deficit, heightened the deficit panic that prevailed in the collective political consciousness as Clinton entered the White House.*

New Democrats felt deficit reduction was not only good economic policy but also the best political medicine for Republican cries about liberals' profligate spending. If Democrats reduced the deficit, then Republicans would have to stop tarring them as tax-and-spend liberals, obviously.† Economic orthodoxy held, briefly, that the federal deficit‡ was inversely related to interest rates.§ High interest rates increased the cost of doing business and made borrowing more expensive. Lower deficits meant lower interest rates, at least according to everyone Bill Clinton listened to. Some observers in the Clinton orbit were amazed at how unanimously the professional, political, and financial classes agreed about deficit reduction as a priority.[14] No less an authority than Federal Reserve Chairman Alan Greenspan instructed Clinton that deficit reduction was not even a point of partisan debate; it was necessary to "improve the confidence" of the

---

* Perot's campaign also popularized the intentionally deceptive analogy of comparing the federal budget to household budgeting, a fallacy that continues to poison politics.

† The only alternative would be for the GOP to lie. Seems unlikely!

‡ Note that the national debt and the budget deficit are distinct but related concepts. The deficit is the difference between revenues and expenditures in a single budget year. The debt is the total amount borrowed by the federal government, an accumulation of deficits across years.

§ More recent developments have seriously called this into question, with low or even negative interest rates corresponding with exploding deficits and debt. As of 2021, the debt stands at an inconceivable $29 trillion while the Federal Reserve interest rate is 0.25 percent.

bond market* and only cranks and unserious people believed differently.[15] It was not difficult to convince Clinton, already predisposed to fiscal conservatism, that attacking the deficit was necessary. Wrote Woodward of the groups of educated elites—Wall Street financiers, prominent capitalists, Congress, academics, the media—that embraced neoliberalism without reservation: "Only steep deficit reduction would persuade [them] of the administration's seriousness."[16]

There were dissenters, even in Clinton's inner circle. When Clinton began sacrificing priorities—first his cherished middle-class tax cut, then investment in new technologies and education—to deficit reduction, Paul Begala, who had teamed successfully with James Carville to run Clinton's presidential campaign, noted that the idea "had become a religion."[17] It was bad politics, he said, because it was the consummate insider issue that "only propeller-heads cared about."[18] Whatever a propeller-head is, we can presume it isn't a normal voter. For most people, the deficit was at best poorly understood and certainly was less important than tangible issues like jobs, education, crime, and health care.

In its first two years, the Clinton administration sacrificed much to appeasing the deficit gods, often with little logic beyond fiat (Clinton himself once claimed the bond market wanted it, as if it were sentient).[19] Clinton struggled mightily to merge his commitment to deficit reduction with his campaign promises to do . . . anything other than reduce the deficit, really. It was, as Begala noted, a classic issue of elite consensus. It was not that "everyone" demanded it, but that everyone demanding it was influential.[20] Clinton's White House was lousy with elite experts—economists, financial industry gurus, academics—leading Carville to note, half in awe and half bitterly, that it was impossible to find anyone on the campaign or White House staff who had not spent time at Harvard.[21] In the world of highly educated elites, it was simply conventional wisdom that government spending was out of control and had to be tamed. When

---

*James Carville remarked (quoted in Woodward, B., *The Agenda* [New York: Simon and Schuster, 1994]) that if reincarnation were a possibility, he once "wanted to come back as the president or the pope or as a .400 baseball hitter. But now I want to come back as the bond market. You can intimidate everybody."

deficit reduction conflicted with anything, deficit reduction won. It became a sledgehammer in a game of rock paper scissors.

Two bad habits immediately developed in the Clinton White House as the difficulties in enacting the rest of his agenda mounted. First, communication and messaging became the solution for everything. Any outcome could be made to sound like a winner with the right framing.[22] The reality, you will be shocked to hear, was not quite so simple. Spin, a novel term at the time that gained mainstream currency thanks to the Clinton White House, quickly wore thin on the press corps and public who recognized it for the abstruse runaround it is.*

The second habit was to negotiate with all comers in the spirit of cooperation and bipartisanship, reflecting Clinton's powerful belief that the best solutions arise when smart people convene to hash things out. The practical result was that everyone in Congress quickly realized they could hold out and extract concessions from the White House. In the process of crafting their first budget, Clinton made concession after concession, displaying "the worst political management"[23] House members said they'd ever seen; one priority after another was lopped off in endless rounds of negotiations and deals.

In a tragicomic highlight that reveals how Clinton was the worst combination of an eager negotiator and a bad one, treasury secretary and former Texas senator Lloyd Bentsen—Michael Dukakis's 1988 running mate who is remembered, if at all, for his "You're no Jack Kennedy" rhetorical execution of Dan Quayle—exasperatedly took the phone from Clinton as the president was begging a House Democrat, another Texan, for a budget vote. "I expect you to remember what I did for you," said Bentsen in his best Don Corleone impression. "I am telling you: you're going to vote for this." Bentsen privately voiced disgust with how Clinton "made it too desirable" to challenge him and then "[paid] off the holdouts."[24] Lloyd Bentsen was by then an old man, an unremarkable senator best known as a reliable spokesman of the Texas banking industry. Quiet.

---

* The term *spin* and its negative connotations were also advanced by Howard Kurtz's bestselling *Spin Cycle: How the White House and the Media Manipulate the News* (New York: Simon and Schuster, 1998), which drew the overwhelming majority of its examples and discussion from the Clinton White House.

Dull. When he's disgusted that you are doing so much horse trading, you're doing too much horse trading. And when Lloyd Bentsen has to act as the heavyweight, things aren't going well.

Clinton's first budget negotiations were a process of constant bar lowering. Everything fell victim to the "victory" of achieving deficit reduction[25] or to the need to buy off some balky House member. As aides privately worried that "we have just gone too far. We're losing our soul," Clinton and his team "settled into a state of lessened expectations."[26] Eventually, the goal was redefined simply as producing a budget—any budget. The "details no longer mattered" as long as they could pass a budget and declare victory for having passed—something.[27]

In the end, they did. It showcased none of Clinton's priorities except deficit reduction, which only elites noticed or cared about, but it was a budget, and they passed it. Economic adviser Gene Sperling said, "I realize it's not the best of worlds; it's not even the second-best world. We are operating in the third-best world. This is what we're left with. We've got to get something through the Congress." That sounds an awful lot like the description of a defeat, not a victory. If that was how the architects of the policy felt, how could they expect voters to react with any more enthusiasm?

And remember, this is Bill Clinton, a Democrat with notable communication skills, plus 57 Democratic senators and 258 House Democrats at his disposal—huge majorities by modern standards. In the House, where Clinton played *Let's Make a Deal* with what seemed like everyone but the House pages, his party had an *eighty-two-seat* majority. Lyndon Johnson turned an eighty-two-seat House majority into the Civil Rights Act and Voting Rights Act. Bill Clinton had the same majority and struggled to get a shitty budget out. Of course, he was new to the job. There's a learning curve. There was room for improvement, and Clinton did figure some things out. Unfortunately, he learned mostly the wrong lessons from his early experiences.

OBAMACARE, THE PREQUEL

During the Reagan years, dissatisfaction with the American healthcare system rose considerably. That dissatisfaction, the reforms of 2009 notwithstanding, remains high—and uniquely high in the United States among peer nations.[28] In concert with the general diminishment of the power of workers that began in earnest in the 1970s, the 1980s saw employers increasingly shifting the cost of health insurance premiums onto employees. Meanwhile, health-care providers were experimenting with new ways to provide cheaper, faster service (managed care systems like HMOs, while not new, exploded in popularity) while for the majority of nonretired Americans, insurance was tied to employment.* Amid the general economic malaise leading up to Bill Clinton's election, support for a national health plan was at an all-time high.[29]

Clinton saw health care as a winning issue. He hoped health-care reform, whatever that might look like, would prove to be his signature legislation. Unfortunately, the reasons it failed became a template for later Democratic policy failures. High public dissatisfaction with health care did not readily translate into support for a specific set of changes, and reform fell victim to the Anna Karenina principle[†]—everyone was unhappy, each in their own way. In a quest for bipartisan support, consensus, and appeasement of the health-care and insurance industries, the White House couldn't even nail down what its proposal *was* let alone convince people to like it.

Clinton kicked off his push for health-care reform in a speech to Congress on September 23, 1993, referring to it as "Health Security" to liken it in magnitude to Social Security. In keeping with his need for elite consensus, Clinton insisted on bringing to the table organizations representing doctors, the insurance industry, drug companies, and other health-care insiders. He also appointed the First Lady to head the effort to craft legislation. Despite her professional qualifications, this had the

---

* COBRA (Consolidated Omnibus Budget Reconciliation Act of 1985) created an employer obligation to allow employees to continue to purchase insurance after termination of employment, ostensibly to address this problem. Anyone who has ever seen the cost of COBRA coverage understands why it didn't.

† "Happy families are all alike; every unhappy family is unhappy in its own way." This is used in economics to illustrate an endeavor in which any one deficiency dooms the whole to failure, so success requires the unlikely feat of avoiding every pitfall.

consequence of diverting some of the finite space for debate over health-care reform to defending against charges of nepotism.*

During and after the reform efforts, critics accused the Clintons of hatching a plan in secret and then springing it on Congress. What contemporary documents show instead was that, as with the 1993 budget, the White House was *too* solicitous of congressional input.[30] In particular, Bill Clinton quickly locked onto a group of centrists, including moderate Republicans led by John Chafee (R-RI), as the key to success. Given the large Democratic majorities at the time, the logic of this was and remains questionable. But both Clintons found it more palatable to make concessions to the ideological center than to Democrats further to the left whose interests veered toward a UK-style national health system. It wasn't the first or final time Clinton found that his goals simply aligned better with Republicans than with Democrats.[31]

While Clinton acted under the assumption that Republicans wanted to work with him in good faith (is any of this sounding familiar?), the reform effort coincided with increasing GOP emphasis on denying the White House any kind of win. Conservative brain Bill Kristol (last seen enchanting liberals as a Never Trump Republican) gave the GOP simple advice on responding to the Clinton proposal: "Sight unseen, oppose it."[32] Republicans did propose market-based reforms of one flavor or another, some sincerely and some as part of a strategy to muddy the waters with a confusing number of proposals. Most focused on funneling individuals into the private sector to buy insurance. This would later lead to accusations that Obama's Affordable Care Act was originally a Republican plan.†

The short version of a complex story is that "Hillarycare"—a moniker encouraged by Newt Gingrich—never even came to the House or Senate floor. It collapsed under the weight of its own efforts to appease everyone, along with an infamous ad campaign by the health insurance industry

---

* This was also the moment at which key GOP figures realized that for their base, attacking Hillary Clinton was like catnip.

† This is hard to adjudicate. Clinton's plans used a "managed competition" model that moved individuals into private insurance, so the idea was not originally Republican property. However, several important aspects of the ACA do resemble one or more Republican proposals floated in 1993–1994.

featuring middle American (read: white) ciphers "Harry and Louise" de-crying big government taking over health care. The for-profit health-care sector hammered exaggerated versions of the shortcomings of other na-tions' systems, with heavy emphasis on supposed rationing of care. The industry and the GOP quickly realized that describing the proposals—which were ultimately free market and, cynically, a giant handout to insurers—as big government was an effective scare tactic,[33] made possible by the fact that the White House could not even counter their rhetoric with a straightforward explanation of its plan.

Bill Clinton was consistent if unclear. He never promised government single payer as a solution during his campaign, and in office he defined his view as "competition within a budget"—a New Democrat solution that emphasized market forces. The problem was, nobody (perhaps in-cluding Clinton himself) knew what this meant or how to explain a sys-tem derived from that principle to voters. The plan that was supposed to appeal to everyone appealed to few. While political elites loved the smarts of the proposals, they defied explanation and were easy to depict as a bureaucratic leviathan.

Moderates were quick to point out during and after the debacle that single payer was not a realistic option.[34] But these voices from the cen-ter had no leg to stand on when it came to divining the possible. It may well have failed, but a push for single payer might at the least have given the White House a base of passionate supporters to equal the pas-sionate opponents of "big government" health care. As it was, Clinton found it impossible to generate enthusiastic support for a plan nobody understood.

The failure of health-care reform in 1993 is a sad story, not "defeated [but] compromised away piece by piece until there was nothing left."[35] They declared more ambitious plans nonstarters, then pursued the most implausible goal of all: satisfying everyone. Hillary Clinton, even more than Bill, was made deeply cynical by the experience. She would later write that "our most critical mistake was trying to do too much, too fast."[36] The experience inspired her to make ever-greater efforts to achieve consensus and work with Republicans.[37] How they repaid her is well known.

Above all, Hillarycare demonstrated the Democratic flaw of asking the wrong question and seeking the wrong attributes to sell policy while assuming that messaging could bear the weight of convincing voters to support whatever the policy would become. What if instead of *bipartisan*, the plan was *good*? What if instead of fiscally responsible, it was popular? What if instead of a complex culmination of think-tank brainpower, it was simple? If no plan more ambitious or more liberal could have succeeded, it is impossible to do worse than a proposal that failed even to reach the floor of Congress.

THE CRIME BILL

Heading into the midterm elections, Clinton and congressional Democrats needed a win to bump the health-care mess from voters' minds. They also saw a need to push back against what many Democrats considered the Republicans' most effective talking point: Democrats Are Soft on Crime.™ The early Clinton era was one in which crime was uniquely prominent as a political issue;* contemporary Gallup polling on the "most important issue" for American voters showed that crime had been in the single digits since 1970. But for one brief period between 1992 and 2000 (when the number returned to single digits), concern about crime exploded. Over 20 percent of Americans called it their biggest concern—briefly exceeding 50 percent in 1994.[38] For Democrats—for the entire political system, state, local, and national—flexing muscle with new tough-on-crime legislation seemed like good politics.

Michael Dukakis's 1988 presidential campaign convinced Democrats, especially moderates, that the party had an image problem regarding crime among mainstream (white) America when the campaign was damaged by two high-profile incidents. First, Dukakis gave what was panned as a robotic, uninspired answer to a (wildly inappropriate, for the record) debate question from CNN's Bernard Shaw about whether he

---

* Considerable research demonstrates that perceptions of crime and actual crime rates are separate phenomena. Media coverage impacts whether the public is likely to believe crime is high or increasing even when it is decreasing or at low levels. See, for example, Lowry, D., et al., "Setting the Public Fear Agenda: A Longitudinal Analysis of Network TV Crime Reporting, Public Perceptions of Crime, and FBI Crime Statistics," *Journal of Communication* 53, no. 1 (2003): 61–73.

would favor the death penalty in the case of the rape and murder of his own wife. The second was a GOP ad featuring a prison inmate, a Black man named Willie Horton, who had been given a weekend furlough under a program Dukakis oversaw as governor of Massachusetts, during which Horton committed rape and murder. These attacks, Democrats felt, fatally wounded Dukakis, whose record and quiet demeanor made him an easy target for the soft-on-crime attack Republicans deployed so effectively.

New Democrats like Clinton and then senator Joe Biden, author of what would become the 1994 Crime Bill, had little difficulty convincing their party that some tough anticrime posturing would help. Politically, however, the legislation's more promising components, like the Violence Against Women Act (VAWA) and Assault Weapons Ban (AWB),* were overwhelmed in the long term by its negatives. And as the midterms would show, Democrats failed to gain even a short-term boost from the new law. The long-term impact has been mass incarceration, disproportionately of people of color and particularly Black men.[39] The effort to woo white voters condemned another part of the electorate the Democrats relied (and still rely) heavily on to suffer generational consequences.

As federal law dealing only with federal crimes, the 1994 Crime Bill was *directly* responsible for comparatively little of the mass incarceration that grew out of that era. State prisons hold the vast majority of America's incarcerated. Yet state laws getting tough on crime were endemic in that era, imposing prison-filling measures like mandatory minimum sentences, three-strikes laws with mandatory life sentences, expanded death penalty offenses, and antidrug laws by the hundreds. The federal crime bill was more a reflection of the zeitgeist than the motive force behind it.

Undeniably, Biden, Clinton, and other Democrats sought to use the legislation to convince voters that their criminal-coddling reputation was undeserved. Whether the long-term consequences were foreseen (and the damage considered acceptable) or not, the intention to appeal to largely

---

* The AWB, which expired under George W. Bush, was limited in its effectiveness because of difficulty in defining what an assault weapon is.

white, middle-class ex-Democrats was clear. After Clinton obsequiously praised the legislation, calling it "the toughest, largest, and smartest attack on crime" in American history, Senator Biden noted:

> The liberal wing of the Democratic Party is now for 60 new death penalties. That is what is in this bill. . . . The liberal wing of the Democratic Party is for 100,000 cops. The liberal wing of the Democratic Party is for 125,000 new state prison cells.

Democrats, including then representative Bernie Sanders and even bill author Biden, criticized parts of the bill even as they voted for it. For example, Biden called three-strikes laws "wacko" but kept them in the bill. Whether the bill proves Biden was or is a "mass incarceration zealot" is debatable,[40] but there is no debating the role he, Bill Clinton, and other Democrats played in yielding to the right on the politics of crime. The aggressive right-wing approach that reduced the range of acceptable solutions to more cops, more laws, and more prisons became—and remains—the default position that all efforts at reform must overcome. The process of recognizing and addressing the damage done is only beginning.[41]

Even potentially useful parts of the 1994 Crime Bill like VAWA—included as a sop to Democrats who wanted something that reflected liberal priorities—were little more than sentencing enhancements that purported to reduce crime not with prevention but with punishment.[42] But if Democrats hoped the crime bill would boost their fortunes in 1994, they badly miscalculated. In the analogy of the Overton window,* the idea that disagreement between the parties is often lively but limited in range to elite consensus definitions of acceptable outcomes, the Democrats' evolution on crime under Clinton shifted the discourse considerably rightward. The debate was and remains largely a debate over how much money to shower upon law enforcement.

---

* This idea, popular on the Internet, ironically came from the libertarian think tank Mackinac Center for Public Policy but is essentially a light rebranding of Noam Chomsky's theories on discourse shifting as fleshed out, for example, in *The Common Good* (Berkeley, CA: Odonian Press, 1998).

IT GETS BETTER, RIGHT?

The beginning of the Clinton presidency, seen hopefully by New Democrats as their opportunity to take the reins of power and lead the party in a new direction, was not pretty. It combined successes that before Clinton were actually Republican priorities with failed attempts to secure Democratic priorities, and, in the process, demonstrated many of the bad habits that not only characterized his White House but have hamstrung the Democratic Party ever since: trying to please everyone (and ending up satisfying no one), negotiating with themselves, obsession with elite issues like the deficit that have political consequences but few benefits, and an inability to state directly, simply, and clearly what their policy proposals are. Fortunately, presidents do not have a mere two years to accomplish things. After the 1994 midterm elections there would surely be more opportunities for both Clinton and the Democratic Congress.

CHAPTER 6

RED TIDE

1994 and the Republican Revolution

On Election Day 1994, I clearly remember watching CNN coverage of the results—we were *basic cable* rich!*—with my father, who was born in 1951. By the time Democratic Alabama senator Richard Shelby punctuated the Republican landslide by announcing, in made-for-TV dramatic fashion, his switch to the GOP, the on-camera personalities agreed that we were indeed witnessing a historic change.

It wasn't immediately clear to me why that was true. I was sixteen at the time, and the events of that day seemed much weightier to my father than to me. As I saw it, parties pass power back and forth in elections. It happens. And nothing about the numbers in 1994 was unprecedented; the trusty *Congressional Quarterly Almanac* told me that a loss of ten Senate and fifty-four House seats was substantial but hardly record breaking. Republicans had, for example, gained twelve Senate seats in 1980 and lost eight in 1986; nobody proclaimed those elections epochal.

---

* Basic cable lay one social stratum above no cable, and one below pay cable (with HBO).

But the 1994 election shook the political system in a way that a young person couldn't appreciate: it gave the GOP unified control of Congress for nearly the first time in fifty-two years.* Since 1932 Democratic control of the House had been a fact of life, the political equivalent of the sunrise. It wasn't the number of seats the GOP won that night; it was the transfer of power that occurred in a way that didn't feel temporary or fluky. Older people who had lived through more political events understood that they were watching something change. Things henceforth were going to be different.

Boy were they.

Republicans were led to victory in 1994 by Newt Gingrich, a former small-school history professor with a yawning void where most people have a soul. Gingrich understood better than any of his contemporaries the weaknesses not only of the establishment Democratic Party but of the political culture of Washington, DC—especially the political media. He knew, in short, how to steer the narrative. And once in the Speaker's chair, he demonstrated that he was completely uninterested in doing things as the New Deal Democrats had done them. He changed the way Congress and American national politics work so comprehensively that the Democrats are still struggling to adjust decades later. McKay Coppins in 2018 called Newt Gingrich "the man who broke politics."[1] A statement like that usually prompts cries of bias and hyperbole. But in this case, it was too obviously true to dispute.

CHANGE AGENT

Newt Gingrich did not become a transformational figure in the modern Republican Party by accident; like Bill Clinton, he set out to change what his party stood for. Looking back on his career, he said his goal was to "drive the system as hard as I could, to reshape the way the system worked."[2] He entered politics during an era in which the GOP was a permanent minority. By the Reagan years its leaders, people like House Minority Leader Bob Michel (R-IL), pursued a "go along to get

---

* The GOP gained brief control of the House and Senate in the 1946 and 1952 elections. In both cases, they retained the majority for only two years. Republicans also held the Senate, while the minority in the House, from 1980 to 1986.

along" strategy that had proven politically expedient for them throughout the New Deal era. This approach saw winning the majority as an impossibility—the Democrats were the House majority, period. Hence, the best strategy was to make deals, to get what the GOP could from the Democrats by playing along and extracting periodic concessions. To Michel and other Republicans who had only ever known Democratic control of the House, developing a coping strategy made more sense than trying to defeat an invincible foe.

Gingrich was frustrated by his party's approach of "get as much as you can without being disruptive" and sought to replace it with "be as disruptive as necessary to get what we want."[3] He succeeded, and the ways in which he taught Republicans to be disruptive left the system of bipartisan congressional palm greasing in tatters. Republicans rallied behind Gingrich and adopted his approach for the simplest of reasons: they saw a chance to win if they tried his tactics, whereas they could not win if they continued to play the role of amiable doormat to the Democrats.

Newt Gingrich and Bill Clinton, as endless news features reminded us in the 1990s, had eerily similar backgrounds.[4] They were born in moderately humble circumstances, excelled academically, and entered politics with unsuccessful congressional campaigns in 1974. They also shared similar beliefs about the future of their respective parties, envisioning "revolutions" that weaved together a new postpartisan, beyond politics approach to winning voters.[5] In that sense, the Clinton-led shift toward the DLC's centrist, technocratic politics was the mirror opposite of Gingrich turning the GOP into an antigovernment party of cultural grievances waging endless war against the libertine 1960s.*

In his early political career, Gingrich confronted the central problem of a Republican attempting to win a House seat in the solidly Democratic New Deal South: Why do these voters loyally vote for Democrats who do not represent their beliefs? He saw Black voters voting for white segregationist Democrats, and white conservatives voting for Democrats even as the party embraced ideas most rural southerners abhorred like the gay rights and women's liberation movements. The solution Gingrich

---

* This strain already existed in American conservatism, of course, but Gingrich moved it from the fringes to the mainstream.

concocted was a scorched earth approach to politics that disdained party and presented voters with a stark choice of personalities and moral views between two candidates. At the subpresidential level, where voters are more open to casting votes across party lines, Gingrich felt that this could succeed if done properly.

Throughout his early failed forays into politics, Gingrich concluded that liberals were loyal Democrats and could not be won over. The opening for the GOP was with a hard right-wing message that appealed to the areas where liberals were perceived as weak: patriotism, hegemonic (as opposed to merely staunchly anticommunist) foreign policy, and traditional values wherever that frame could be applied. In an era when there were still conservative Democrats, Gingrich clearly saw a future in which all liberals became Democrats and therefore all conservatives must be won over by Republicans. New Deal lite, as previous generations of Republicans had accepted, would not cut it, nor would the GOP approach of salvaging some scraps as the permanent minority in Congress.[6]

The Clinton-Gingrich comparisons extend to Gingrich creating a Republican counterpart to the DLC, the Conservative Opportunity Society, to hone his new style outside the formal structure of the Republican Party.[7] Gingrich made many Republican enemies in an era when Ronald Reagan's cloyingly optimistic patriotism reigned, relegating to the margins the dark, confrontational politics of moral warfare Gingrich favored. But Gingrich slowly made himself into a force to be reckoned with in his party with the alluring promise that his way would bring the GOP into the majority. He identified the "liberal welfare state" as the common enemy that all conservatives could rally against—be they Bible Belt social reactionaries, quasi-libertarian New England antitaxers, or neoliberal deregulation enthusiasts. House Minority Leader Michel underscored Gingrich's point about feckless GOP leadership by urging Republicans to ignore Gingrich's "seductive" promises of winning and instead continue to work to cut deals with the Democrats. Then, as now, there was a self-defeating, even repellent, quality to the argument that winning is an unrealistic goal.

Though first elected to Congress in 1978, Gingrich made his first major mark on national politics in 1988 when he led a group of House

Republicans bringing ethics charges against heavyweight Democratic House Speaker Jim Wright.[8] Wright was, for the Republicans of his era, what Mitch McConnell represents to modern Democrats: a chamber tyrant, a win-at-all-costs leader who would bend, break, or change any rule necessary to get what he wanted. He was an aggressive partisan and a skilled legislator, a vote gatherer. Comity was not his priority. Wright, who became Speaker in 1986, mastered House rules and used them to crush opposition (from either party) without mercy, but he adhered to an older, more casual attitude toward rules of conduct outside the chamber. He was a throwback who learned politics in the era of cocktails at lunch, backroom dealing, and string pulling. And that ultimately gave Gingrich an opening to engineer Wright's downfall.

After Watergate, ethics and reform were the watchwords of the era, and sweeping rule changes were enacted throughout the federal government. No member scrupulously follows every single rule and regulation to the letter; violations can be found for anyone with enough searching.[9] But Wright made it easy for Gingrich, misreporting income from a book deal and pulling strings to maneuver Mrs. Wright into a perk-laden job. Many members of Congress were guilty of this kind of misconduct—Gingrich would soon attract notice for his own unusual book deal income. But Gingrich was aggressive where his colleagues hesitated. Other Republicans felt that as residents of glass houses, they should not lob stones at Wright. Gingrich believed that ethics and corruption could be a winning play for Republicans, even if they were guilty of the same.

Gingrich redefined scandal politics in two ways. First, he simply repeated the allegations against Wright incessantly. He knew that the more people heard it, the more "real" it became. When challenged or questioned by the media, he accused them of covering for Wright and demonstrating that old chestnut, liberal bias. Neither the media nor Congress—especially not the Democratic forever-majority Congress—were held in high regard by the kind of voters Gingrich sought. So he pursued a strategy of relentless attack with the assumption that neither the Democrats, who worried about their vulnerability to ethics charges, nor the media, who yearned to appear nonpartisan and balanced, would fight back. He was right.

Speaker Wright resigned in 1989, handing Gingrich a victory that made him a force in the GOP at a time when its leadership was in flux. Reagan was retired, George H. W. Bush was as inspirational as dry rot, Dan Quayle was a national punchline, and congressional leaders like Michel were nonentities preaching a strategy that promised permanent minority status. Many Republicans disliked or even detested Gingrich, but his secret was simple: he promised to fight—hard—and lead them to victory if they followed him. After decades in the minority, Republicans found that very persuasive. So the politics of scandal became central in the GOP playbook (not always successfully, as the Clinton presidency would demonstrate).[10]

The Gingrich strategy of using ethics charges to bring down Speaker Wright changed the tone of politics in the Capitol permanently.[11] When modern politicians of a certain age yearn for the good ol' days in Congress, they're referring to a period predating the Wright scandal. The subsequent rise of a "professionalized" Congress was an unintentional gift from Gingrich to the polished, successful young Democrats favored by the DLC. Men like Wright, with their cowboy hats, everyman personas, and power broker ways were out; the Gingriches and Clintons of the world—slick, clean-cut, smart, more like rising junior executives than politicians—became the norm. But Gingrich would change far more about politics in Congress than simply the esprit de corps and personal style preferences among members. If he could attain the Speaker's chair, he planned to run the place very differently.

THE NEW RULES

The 1994 midterms made everything Gingrich had hoped for a reality. His strategy of uniting conservatives, including ex-Democrats, around antigovernment, anti–welfare state, protraditional values messaging paid off. During midterms, presidents' parties all but inevitably lose seats in Congress.* Often those losses are significant.[12] The losses Democrats

---

* The midterm loss phenomenon holds for every midterm election in the two-party era except 1998 and 2002, which were affected by Clinton's impeachment and 9/11, respectively. The theory is that presidents pull some members of their party into Congress on the "coattail effect" in presidential election years but then inevitably lose some support

experienced in 1994, however, shook the party to its core and badly rattled the incumbent president.

But losing the majority was only the first blow. Gingrich, loudly supported by House Republicans, was preparing to make major changes to the way the House did business. He was able to do this for two reasons. One is that the Speaker position is a powerful one, with considerable control over internal House politics. The other is that the Republican caucus had a large group of freshmen legislators who gave Gingrich wide latitude. Because he was the architect of victory, they were willing to enable him even if they didn't like him.

Congressional scholars would soon argue that Gingrich was able to exercise something approaching "conditional party government" in the House. That is, with House Republicans in general agreement on what policy goals to pursue, the members consented to changing House rules and enhancing the power of the Speaker to facilitate passing legislation more efficiently.[13] If the House GOP had been ideologically divided—as the House Democrats had been during Clinton's first two years—such changes would not have been possible. But since the Republicans were able to agree on some core policy goals—lower taxes, deregulation, reduced government spending on social programs—they had an incentive to make it easier on themselves to pass legislation. Giving the Speaker more control over the agenda did that.

There are some notes of dissent about just how responsible Gingrich was for the changes that took place in the House during this era; one prominent scholar has argued that these changes were already happening and Gingrich came along at the crest of the wave.[14] But there is more evidence for the counterargument, that Gingrich himself was a driving force behind the changes.[15] Without his Sinatra Doctrine* approach to power and the trust of his GOP colleagues, much of what ensued would have been impossible. Gingrich didn't simply have some rule changes in mind. While other Speakers were legislative leaders, Gingrich wanted to

---

due to unfulfilled campaign promises, reduced voter turnout, and two years of the out party attacking the president.

* This was Mikhail Gorbachev's coinage for a policy of doing things "My Way."

be a political leader of similar standing as the president. The man never lacked for ambition.

Gingrich understood the value of party discipline, of members going along with what the Republican caucus in the House wanted to do even if they personally weren't eager to support it. By focusing the agenda on things conservatives could nearly all agree on (most memorably in the Contract with America that Gingrich flogged incessantly in 1994), he was able to maximize what the party could do with its time in power. Democrats, then and today, often struggle to press the advantage of having power precisely because they lack this kind of unity.

In theory, members of Congress don't have any reason to obey the leadership. If I can get reelected comfortably (in my safe, gerrymandered district) by doing whatever I want, the incentive to vote for something I don't like is small. But party leaders do have some carrots to offer. Foremost among these in the House are committee assignments. Committees are an infamously dull topic for nonpoliticos.* In Congress, though, a choice committee spot both enhances one's personal brand (lots of media attention is a prerequisite for higher political ambitions) and facilitates the delivery of benefits to the constituents back home.

This, Gingrich understood, was his best card to play. Ignoring the decades-long tradition of seniority determining committee assignments, he passed over older moderate Republicans he considered neither reliable nor loyal. Instead, prominent committee spots went to young or sometimes even freshmen members who were willing to follow orders. Rewarding members for simply punching the time clock year after year makes them more independent of the leadership, and over the long period of Democratic House majorities, committee chairs became powerful lords of their own fiefdoms. Some House power brokers were both ardent New Dealers and staunch segregationists, like fifty-four-year veteran Rep. Jamie Whitten (D-MS). This often stymied Democratic cohesion on noneconomic issues. With numerous ways for a committee to hamper or kill bills, Democratic House leaders were forced to tread lightly with these powerful senior figures. What Gingrich did, starting in 1995, likely

---

* Skeptics are welcome to try teaching college freshmen about the committee system at 9 a.m. and report back. Good luck.

would not have worked with the ideologically scattered House Democrats of earlier eras.[16]

Aside from ditching seniority, Gingrich also used the Speaker's power to alter and eliminate committees. He aggressively revised the mandate—the range of issues covered—of committees he perceived to be Democrat friendly or of committees led by Republicans he distrusted. It is false to say that Gingrich ruled with a strict iron fist; some Gingrich-endorsed legislation was chopped up and amended in committees and some bills failed altogether. But as Speaker, he was skilled at separating the central from the peripheral, bills on which he demanded control versus bills on less crucial issues, where members and committees had more leeway.* Interestingly, the Contract with America promised more open rules (House rules that allow members to propose amendments, giving them power to potentially alter a bill to enhance or reduce its chance of passing). Once in the majority, Gingrich quickly determined that voters neither care about nor understand legislative rules, and he could easily ignore that promise.[17] When all else failed, Gingrich circumvented the committee system if it suited his agenda. The leadership created task forces and other loosely defined groups of representatives to do some of the tasks traditionally given to committees. It all gave the Speaker more control, more power.

Gingrich simply felt no obligation to do things the way they had been done previously. His view of how the House should work was diametrically opposed to how Democrats had seen it for fifty-plus years. He "reject(ed) explicitly the Madisonian model of congressional politics based on bargaining, negotiation and compromise, and organized institutionally around the labyrinthine, cross-cutting committee system with its imprecise, subject-of-negotiation relationship with the majority party. Republicans . . . should be 'party activists' rather than 'district guys.'"[18]

At this point, I could say, "See? That's how to use power. Democrats should do what Newt did and stop worrying about decorum, norms, traditions, and hurt feelings." That would ignore some important context, though. The stars aligned for Gingrich when he became Speaker in a way they have not for Democratic leaders—although their own biases,

---

* *Leeway* originated as a nautical term for the sideways drifting off course of a ship to its lee (away from the wind).

preferences, and assumptions about the proper role of leadership have contributed to their comparative weakness. The GOP had been out of power for so long in 1994 that the leadership took over with what amounted to a clean slate, an opportunity to rewrite the rules from scratch. There were also decades of pent-up frustration at the petty slights and indignities of being in the minority, which reinforced a bunker mentality among Republicans.* Most importantly, though, Republicans took the majority nearly unified in the pursuit of a handful of key policy goals. They had a short, nonnegotiable list of demands. The Democrats did not and rarely have since. Just as a more ideologically coherent GOP was coming to power, the Democrats were actively splitting into Old and New Democrat factions, with white southern conservative Democrats all but disappearing.

POISONING THE WELL

The 1995 handover of congressional power was about far more than rule changes. It is not merely that the Republicans won, or that they won for the first time in a long time. The Republican Party that won in 1994 was different than the Republican Party that preceded it. Gingrich and the Class of '94 freshmen firebrands† represented a faction of the American right with deep roots. Now, however, they were in charge. They *were* the GOP, and for all the Democratic pining for the "good Republicans" of the olden days, they have been the GOP ever since, with one caveat: they've gotten much worse.

All this was intentional. Gingrich and other Republicans who came of political age during the waning years of Democratic dominance of national politics detested the argument that the Republicans needed to be accommodating because they could not win the majority. The point of politics, Gingrich thought, is not to play nice but to win. And to win, you must demonstrate to voters that you're willing to go to the mat—maybe

---

* For example, Republicans long complained bitterly of being given undesirable office spaces; see Fiore, F., and R. Trounson, "No Longer Capitol Doormats, Republicans Revel in Perks," *Los Angeles Times*, November 22, 1994.

† This is the word used in polite political reporting when someone is a prick and their colleagues hate them.

even fight dirty. In a now infamous 1978 speech (during his third, and first successful, run for Congress), he candidly diagnosed the GOP's problem: they were too nice, too willing to be second fiddles, too polite. They were accommodationists, and who wants to vote for a party that doesn't believe it can win and demand what it wants? "One of the great problems we have in the Republican Party is that we don't encourage you to be nasty. We encourage you to be neat, obedient, loyal and faithful and all those Boy Scout words, which would be great around a campfire but are lousy in politics."[19]

So at his core, Gingrich saw politics differently than Democrats *and Republicans* of his early political career. He had a clear sense of what goals he wanted to accomplish politically, and he accepted the price he might have to pay in the condemnations of the pre-1994 political establishment. Part of the reason he cared so little about how the media and official Washington thought of him was that he and the broader American conservative movement beyond the GOP were busy creating an alternate universe in which he would be lauded as a superstar.[20]

The rise of conservative AM talk radio shows in the early Clinton years and the launching of Fox News in February 1996 were the first tentative steps toward building the fortress of victimhood and distortion the conservative media inhabits today. The "liberal media" has inspired complaints on the right since time immemorial, and it rose to a position of prominence on the right's enemies list during the Nixon years. The otherwise forgettable Spiro Agnew, Nixon's vice president, was among the most important figures in turning this talking point into a core conservative belief. He realized how readily the media could be depicted as East Coast, Ivy League elites who presumed to know better than average Americans, and consequently conservatives could undermine trust in the very idea of news when it benefited them to do so.[21] It proved effective, and when conservatism moved beyond crude newsletters and the odd contrarian columnist in major newspapers to offering a polished product on TV, radio, and the nascent Internet, the audience was there, ready to be tapped.

The right also put considerable effort during the 1990s into building up the network of foundations and think tanks that play a crucial role in elite policy making. Deep-pocketed conservative activists spent lavishly to counter what they saw as the liberal bias in traditional sources of policy ideas, like academia.[22] Yet the amount they spent was not the reason they became so influential. Conservative think tanks were strengthening, becoming more openly partisan, and explicitly advocating for conservative policy solutions at the same time their prominent, well-funded, ostensibly liberal counterparts like the Brookings Institution were pivoting toward nonpartisan self-identification and shifting to solutions, full stop.[23] The difference was and is crucial. This dynamic, of Republicans going balls-out* to push policy as far to the right as possible while liberals seek good, moderate, nonpartisan governance, has tilted the policy universe considerably rightward since 1994.

The DLC and its affiliated think tank, the Progressive Policy Institute, proved within the Democratic Party that such groups are important sources of legitimacy and of steering elite political discourse. On education, for example, conservative think tanks turned the political right from an uncoordinated mass of people with disparate criticisms of the educational system to a well-organized heavyweight with policies that got taken seriously in Washington and in state capitols.[24] Right-wing media worked hand in hand with these elite institutions, taking their white paper policy messages and distilling them into talking points viewers could absorb and repeat. It very quickly became a well-oiled machine for providing a counternarrative to both the mainstream media and elected officials.

Gingrich both encouraged and used these resources at every turn. Conservative radio and TV fulfilled the demand for nastiness he had called for back in 1978, while the PhD-holding side of his personality understood the value of the pedigreed legitimacy that the very serious scholars of the Cato Institute, American Enterprise Institute, Heritage Foundation, and others lent his ideas. Rather than continuing to fight liberal institutions—as he saw them—for acknowledgment that conservative ideas were legitimate, the American right simply created its own parallel institutions. The aggression, rancor, and accusations lobbed at

---

* Technical term.

Democrats played an important role in the GOP's midterm victory in 1994, but Gingrich also extensively counseled Republicans on the importance of a positive agenda. Waging war against the 1960s, Bill Clinton, and McGovern liberalism could win the GOP some seats, Gingrich argued, but to get all the way there they needed a serious face too.[25] Hurling insults is easy and appealed to Rush Limbaugh fans. But obtaining real power necessitated winning some measure of approval, or at least recognition, within the establishment as well.[26]

Make no mistake, though: the insults were a huge part of it. Gingrich continually encouraged the right, particularly on talk radio, to get meaner. Democrats were not an opposition party with whom cooperation might be necessary; they were enemies at the gate of Western civilization coming to destroy the American way of life. In an infamous memo that predated the 1994 Republican Revolution, ominously titled "Language: A Key Mechanism of Control," Gingrich helpfully suggested some good words to use to describe Democrats including *sick, pathetic, lie, anti-flag, traitors, radical,* and *corrupt.*[27]

Overall, Gingrich convinced Republicans to stop working with Democrats to keep the business as usual of Congress puttering along. It is easy (and common) to bemoan this Gingrich effect on American politics, the replacing of collegiality with "a style of partisan combat—replete with name-calling, conspiracy theories, and strategic obstructionism—that poisoned America's political culture and plunged Washington into permanent dysfunction."[28] Lest we get carried away pining for polite Republicans devoted to the greater good, it is important to recognize the limits of that mythologized era of low partisan conflict. If comity was maintained by ignoring civil rights, women's rights, inequality, and other issues of importance outside the dominant white male Congresses of the era, was comity useful or good? Ignoring divisive but crucial issues is, after all, one way to make sure everyone gets along.

Rather than attempting to resolve the larger question of whether decorum, bipartisanship, and other warm congressional feelings are inherently good, what matters here is more straightforward: the Democrats have never managed to effectively counter the new GOP approach Gingrich introduced. As recently as the 2020 presidential election, when Joe Biden ran on a theme of unity and promised to work together with Republicans who clearly had no intention of ever doing so, Democrats seemed to think that they could bring back the kinder, gentler atmosphere unilaterally. And while the Democratic establishment has proven capable of fighting challengers from its left with limitless vigor and creativity, they constantly express unwillingness to fight the opposing party as vigorously as Gingrich taught the GOP to do.

In more elections than not, the moderate voters to whom this high road is supposed to appeal have failed to deliver wins to Democrats. Meanwhile, riled up to fever pitch, the conservative base of the Republican Party has shown up hopping mad like clockwork in every election since 1992. In the wake of the 1994 elections, Bill Clinton expressed amazement that the Gingrich-led Republicans "got away with" and weren't "punished" by voters for their "mean-spirited" rhetoric.[29] Nearly three decades later, some Democrats are still amazed, waiting for the decency of the electorate or a ruling from the decorum referee to deliver the success Democrats deserve for being good.

THE GINGRICH DEVOLUTION

Newt Gingrich and the 1994 Republican Revolution represented the first of two crucial steps in the transition of the GOP from a conservative political party broadly interested in governing into a nihilist cult. He encouraged his copartisans to abandon any ideas of accommodation in favor of fighting to delegitimize Democrats at every turn. However, the years that followed 1994 showed that Gingrich was more talk than action on that point. He did not wantonly obstruct Bill Clinton—so long as Clinton was offering to advance Republican policy priorities. The second step, as we will see later, was taken by Mitch McConnell and the Tea Party GOP under Obama, when the party's dedication to mindless obstruction became total. By 2010, Gingrich's generation, once the wild-eyed, extremist revolutionaries, had become the Republican moderates. Gingrich was long gone by that point, felled in 1998 by a grab bag of ethics scandals. The lurch to the right that began with his ideas became self-sustaining, fed by the endless feedback loop of the growing right-wing media universe. Given his later staunch support of Donald Trump, it's unlikely Gingrich regrets any of it. But it remains hilarious that one of the first prominent casualties of Newt Gingrich–style GOP politics was Newt Gingrich.

And how did Bill Clinton react to the historic transfer of congressional power that took place after the first two fitful years of his presidency? He was relieved not to have to deal with the congressional Democrats anymore; he figured the GOP would be more favorable to his agenda anyway. Besides, he had a plan. It worked in the short term and did incalculable damage in the long run. He boldly considered the possibility that he could redefine the Democratic brand as "the same things the GOP wants, but somewhat less extreme and crazy." Which is great—unless of course there's a downside to a party ceding the narrative on a bunch of key issues to its opponents.

CHAPTER 7

THE SENSELESS HABITS OF HIGHLY DEFECTIVE PEOPLE

There would never again be a doubt that he was a different kind of Democrat.

—DLC founder Al From after Bill Clinton signed the Personal Responsibility and Work Opportunity Reconciliation Act of 1996 (aka welfare reform)

The Republican Revolution of 1994 changed Bill Clinton. After being accused—implausibly, even ludicrously—of having governed too far to the left up to that point, he ran (ideologically) back into the arms of the DLC's brand of centrism. It makes no sense, obviously, to characterize as "too far left" a two-year span Clinton dedicated to NAFTA, a punitive crime bill, and sacrificing every campaign priority on the altar of deficit reduction. But as subsequent decades would prove, in elite Democratic circles the only acceptable response to failure was to move to the right. The insistence that everything bad that happened to Democrats was a consequence of excessive liberalism didn't need to be true to be accepted as an article of faith by Democrats increasingly obsessed with white suburban professionals who were seriously disinclined toward bolstering the social safety net or redistributive economic policies.

As Clinton saw it, the problem lay with perceptions of the Democratic Party. When voters told pollsters that Clinton raised their taxes—which he almost certainly didn't—they were basing that belief on their own stereotypes of liberalism. That he was paying for sins of others infuriated him. Changing a political party's image is not easy, but Clinton persisted. Faced with a hostile Republican Congress and a rudderless Democratic Party, he seized the opportunity to redefine what Democrat meant. Unfortunately, his changes were mostly for the worse. Clinton mortgaged the future we live in today for short-term success, redefining the Democratic brand in a way that made it nearly impossible for politicians without his charisma to make it sound appealing (Barack Obama could; John Kerry couldn't), and even then its appeal became increasingly specific to the degree-holding, successful HEPs who are now the backbone of the Democratic base. He taught Democrats to embrace ideological agnosticism, to recast the partisan political divide not as a competition between two parties with opposing ideologies but as one party that is crazy and one that is competent.

What could be wrong with that? Crazy is "bad" and competent is "good." But when success is defined in managerial terms, as getting something done while besieged by extremists on both sides, one of the fundamental truths of politics is ignored: politics is ideological. Not every voter has a coherent belief system, but many of the most important voters have at least vaguely coherent beliefs and specific demands. And you can only tell voters you didn't get what they wanted (and sometimes did the exact opposite of what they wanted) so many times before they succumb to cynicism and disillusionment. Some voters can be motivated with a promise to steer the ship responsibly without mentioning the destination or direction. Many cannot.

One baffling academic analysis of 1994 concluded that Clinton "campaigned in 1992 as a moderate Democrat, but then, once elected, proposed a legislative agenda that in many respects was on the left of the political spectrum, [exposing] the right-flank of his party to precisely this sort of ideologically directed challenge [from Republicans]." The paper continues:

"For many other Democrats, especially those representing more conservative districts, the choice was far more difficult; vote for a decidedly liberal legislative agenda . . . or vote against the party leadership."[1] The "decidedly liberal" agenda is not spelled out. It simply was. It's not like alternative explanations for the disaster in 1994 were difficult to imagine; even DLC-friendly researchers admit that, for example, low Black turnout—perhaps a consequence of Clinton's habit of taking stereotype-based potshots at people of color to curry favor with white voters—could have explained part of the drubbing. By reclaiming the political center, Clinton gave the GOP incentive to move to the right while resigning the left to political irrelevance except during elections (when they would be warned sternly that they had "nowhere else to go," a charming phrase that would by 2000 be central to the Democratic game plan).* As early as the 1992 Democratic National Convention—before Clinton won the White House—some core Democratic groups like Black Democrats and organized labor were getting the New Democrat message.

"We're ambivalent," said Julie Harris, an African-American delegate from Philadelphia. "They have decided they want to win and this is the way they had to go in order to do that. It's strictly political."

Some of the delegates said they are resigned to supporting the Democratic ticket because *they have nowhere else to go*. . . .

"There is a tremendous malaise in the black community, which we saw in the low (primary) turnout," said Ronald Walters, chairman of the political science department at Howard University in Washington. "Even the people who are coming here are not clear that any of the candidates, including the Democratic nominee, really represents their interests."[2] (emphasis added)

This now-familiar dynamic became the Democrats' preferred means for retaining the support of groups it nominally represents—anyone to

---

* On Election Night in 1994, as good news for the GOP flooded in, ABC newscaster Cokie Roberts's on-air response to a question about advice for President Clinton was "move to the right, which is the advice that somebody should have given him a long time ago," followed by an ominous, "you can get out the Democratic base if you need to."

the left of Mitt Romney, in theory—while pursuing an agenda that either yields to the Republicans or attempts to placate everyone with contorted compromises that satisfy few.

Bill Clinton and many Democrats like him moved to the center because, ideologically, *that is what they wanted to do*, not because an unbiased interpretation of the 1994 election results obligated them to do so. The argument of necessity is a canard, a way to defer responsibility and surrender agency by insisting there was no alternative. We must consider whether Clinton, and later Obama, did the things they did because they wanted to do them and omitted other things because they didn't want to do them. It is at least as compelling an explanation as, "the Democrats who gave us NAFTA and the 1994 Crime Bill were guilty of governing as radical leftists."

It is often noted that no Republican, not even Ronald Reagan, could bring the New Deal to an end. Only a Democrat could institutionalize that government is bad, that the social welfare state is an anachronism, and that free markets are the answer. Unsurprisingly, few Democrats at the time would take these positions. Clinton not only believed them sincerely, but his rise also coincided with one of the Democratic Party's familiar (and more or less permanent) identity crises. The identity, bolstered by the force of Clinton's charisma, was that Republicans were fundamentally correct about many things, and if Democrats didn't accept it, they'd be permanently marginalized.

It paid off for Clinton in the moment, aided by strong economic growth and America's end-of-history victory lap following the fall of the Soviet Union. But from the outset, cracks were evident in the new foundation. The "triangulation" process that delivered short-term benefits to Clinton convinced many voters over time that the Democrats and Republicans were too similar on too many issues. If the GOP represented free trade and the Democrats represented smarter, better, kinder free trade, the obvious question is: What happens to the voters who don't want free trade at all? And how will the voters explicitly harmed by free trade react when they realize nobody is on their side? As Clinton ally Bill Curry put it: "If that's [New Democrat ideology] then there's also a really useful name for the people who believe in it—Republicans."[3]

WELCOME BACK

All elections are followed by a scramble to diagnose what went wrong and what political response is required.* For Democrats, the inevitable conclusion that the party was too liberal and needed to move to the center became canon under Clinton, thanks in large part to his embrace of that interpretation of 1994 and his subsequent reelection in 1996. DLC cofounder Al From sternly warned Clinton in the wake of the midterm election to "get with the [New Democrat] program or you'll have to pay consequences."[4] Apparently even minor outbursts of center-left thinking, like the tentative, ill-considered "Don't Ask, Don't Tell" policy or a market-based health-care reform all but written by insurance companies were too much. He also failed to move fast enough for their liking on privatizing Social Security and reforming welfare. So get with the program he did. Chastened, in a speech at Georgetown University two days after the election Clinton promised that he would "work to pursue the New Democrat agenda," in the monotone of a Soviet show trial defendant confessing his ideological sins.[5] Within two months Clinton allowed From and a key DLC alum in the White House, Bruce Reed, to rewrite his State of the Union address to their liking.[6] DLC-affiliated columnist David Osborne thought Clinton's problem was simply that he didn't hire enough New Democrats.[7] Of course, the fine folks of the DLC were good examples of New Democrats prepared to accept White House jobs. At the highest levels, the Democratic interpretation of what happened in 1994 mirrored From's assertion that the "election said the New Deal coalition is Humpty Dumpty and it isn't going to get put back together again."[8]

Sensing an opportunity to steer Clinton during a period of uncertainty after the Republican takeover, the DLC not only scolded him but quickly moved to shape elite opinion and produce detailed policy alternatives—the group's strengths. In less than a month, it produced

---

* This "constructed explanation," the gradual coalescing around a broadly agreed-upon explanation for why X won or lost, is the work of Marjorie Randon Hershey, "Do Constructed Explanations Persist? Reframing of the 1994 Republican Takeover of Congress," *Congress and the Presidency* 38, no. 2 (2011). Aside from the brilliance of the work, she was my dissertation adviser in grad school and has the patience of several monasteries' worth of monks. Thank you for everything, Margie.

a response to the Republican Contract with America, the unsubtly and derivatively named Mainstream Contract. They bombarded the world of Democratic politics with white papers, manifestos, and policy agendas. In *The New Progressive Declaration* (1995)[9] they openly advocated the death of the New Deal conception of government in favor of a tech-fueled future where entrepreneurialism, not government, solved social problems and provided public goods.

The metaphor of running government like a business, long a conservative talking point, was embraced wholeheartedly in the White House. Al Gore was tasked with a National Performance Review[10] (renamed in 1998 the National Partnership for Reinventing Government) aimed at divining the "secrets" of big, successful companies. It was such a sensation among some people, presumably, that it was released to the public with illustrations by *Dilbert* creator Scott Adams* (whose cubicle-parodying comic was then a sensation) as *Businesslike Government: Lessons Learned from America's BEST Companies.* It is an invaluable time capsule of the era in which many Americans believed big corporations were well run or had some secret other than avoiding taxes and squeezing labor costs to the greatest extent the government would allow.

By June of 1995, Clinton was producing a budget loaded with DLC themes and priorities that promised not just to cut but to eliminate the deficit without raising taxes. That budget, with Clinton in his new role as the guardian of the center fighting both the right and the left, prompted perhaps the most Bill Clinton headline of all time: "Clinton Infuriates Almost Everyone."[11] While deficit reduction pleased Wall Street, Clinton needed to attack the very core of liberalism: the welfare state. That, he would come to believe, was a necessary precondition for his reelection in 1996—and for the long-term future of his party.

SELLING THE SURRENDER

How did Bill Clinton and the Democratic Leadership Council turn the middle-against-both-sides center position into a political winner—at least

---

* Adams has since gone full Trumper, so perhaps his royalty checks didn't clear.

in 1992 and 1996—barely a decade after Jimmy Carter tried it and failed? Superficially, maybe they found a more appealing messenger. Charisma matters in politics, and charmers like Clinton have a marked advantage. But simply swapping Carter the sourpuss for Clinton the ebullient orator oversimplifies why centrism worked on the second try.

Clinton and the DLC came up with a formula to fix what ailed Carter's brand of moderate liberalism. That formula, in the years after Clinton's presidency, cemented Democratic loyalty among a core group of HEP liberals while simultaneously making it more difficult for Democrats to appeal to voters outside that demographic. Over time, Clinton's "winning formula" has proven a lot less winning than it appeared during his presidency. An unlikely commentator, conservative columnist David Frum, offered a useful reduction:

> Clinton has offered the Democratic Party a devilish bargain: Accept and defend policies you hate (welfare reform, the Defense of Marriage Act) . . . and I'll deliver you the executive branch of government. . . . He has assuaged the Left by continually proposing bold new programs. . . . And he has placated the Right by dropping every one of these programs as soon as he proposed it. Clinton makes speeches, [Treasury Secretary Robert] Rubin and [Federal Reserve Chair Alan] Greenspan make policy, *the Left gets words, the Right gets deeds.*[12] (emphasis added)

For Democrats, this became more than the timeless political struggle between idealism and pragmatism. Two complicating factors emerged after the Clinton years. One is that the kind of technocratic, everyone-wins solutions advocated by New Democrats' managerial liberalism did not work. Too many voters were promised outcomes that never materialized. The second is that the Clintonian approach of sacrificing principle for electoral success hasn't won nearly enough elections. The only response to lost political ground has been to insist that the same strategy—move to the center, embrace decidedly unliberal policies, tone down anything that might offend a hypothetical white suburbanite—must be tried again, but harder.

MAKING CENTRISM WORK

Three different governing strategies get lumped together under labels like "moderate" or "centrist." Political scientists Paul Quirk and William Cunion summarize these as "splitting the difference," "principled centrism," and "opportunistic centrism."[13] *Splitting the difference* is a simple strategy wherein a politician adopts a position between two points. It works well, for instance, on a debate between two dollar amounts, but it is infeasible on many issues. What is the center point, for example, between capital punishment and no capital punishment?*

Principled centrism attempts to combine policy goals and methods in a way that satisfies everyone. An example is market-based incentives to reduce pollution, which theoretically placates environmentalists without upsetting free-market enthusiasts by imposing the heavy hand of government. This, as Jimmy Carter discovered, can put a politician in the position of advocating something whose only natural constituency is a temporary coalition of traditional political opponents. That is a difficult trick to pull off, let alone repeatedly.

Finally, there is *opportunistic centrism*. Bill Clinton dabbled in the principled variety and accepted a split-the-difference approach when no alternatives seemed viable. But in his heart, he was an opportunistic centrist. This approach adopts whatever issue position has the most public support. It's buffet ideology, poll reading as a belief system. It requires a skilled politician who can keep his own party from revolting when he adopts a position that conflicts with their core ideology—or a voter base without a core ideology. With a demoralized base like the Democratic Party had in the early 1990s, the argument that liberal ideology must be sacrificed to win elections found a receptive (or at least not vehemently opposed) audience. Democrats wanted to win. It had been a while.

Under the banner of electoral necessity, Clinton argued that Republican positions on many issues—crime, poverty and welfare, taxes, small government, foreign policy—were more popular, and Democrats' expectations had to be adjusted accordingly. Tellingly, the list of issues on

---

* A prominent example of a failed middle ground was the Democratic promotion of civil unions as the halfway point on same-sex marriage. Ultimately, neither side was satisfied, so the issue persisted.

which the existing Democratic position was deemed acceptable is much shorter—essentially the environment (provided the free market replaced the government as change agent), Social Security, and Medicare. Rather than continuing to fight for the rightness of seemingly unpopular positions, Clinton urged ceding ideological ground to conservatives. To avoid the appearance of conceding to the GOP on the issue, however, Clinton would "moderate" the GOP position.

Clinton succeeded in appealing to suburban HEPs and white Reagan Democrats with this approach. He gambled, correctly, in 1992 and 1996 that Democrats could win over the growing professional middle class with neoliberalism and regain some portion of the white working class by taking a hard line on welfare, crime, and other things that dog-whistled the politics of race.* After Clinton's defeat of Bob Dole in 1996, Republicans seethed at how effectively the president had stolen their thunder. "President Clinton only won because he made people think he thought like a Republican," whined Governor John Engler (R-MI), seconded by New Jersey Republican governor Christine Todd Whitman,† who observed that "Republican ideology won the election."[14]

As with Carter, contemporary liberals saw the pitfalls in Clinton's approach. George McGovern resurfaced in 1994 to criticize that Americans had lost faith in liberalism not because it was wrong but because Democrats stopped aggressively defending liberal positions before the public.[15] If Democrats would not stand up to say government is good and markets often fail, voters would inevitably hear only variations on the theme that government is bad and markets are good. House mainstay Dick Gephardt, once a core DLC member, was by 1997 openly critical of Clinton's opportunism, which he characterized as "set[ting] [one's] compass only off the direction of others," a strategy that suggested Democrats "lack core values."[16] Gephardt's comments prompted blasts of criticism

---

* After the Republican wins in 1994, Al From recommended—seriously—that Clinton crack down on unwed mothers and "deadbeat dads," in case the socioracial coding in "crime and welfare" was too subtle. Quoted in Drew, E., *On the Edge: The Clinton Presidency* (New York: Touchstone, 1994), 129.

† As if to underscore the extent to which Republican ideology would conquer the Democratic Party, in 2020 Whitman was a featured speaker in prime-time on the opening night of the Democratic National Convention.

from House New Democrats, one of whom refused to be named while fuming, perhaps a tad melodramatically, "for Dick Gephardt to seek to emphasize differences within the Democratic Party is criminal." Meanwhile, liberals like David Obey (D-WI) applauded, arguing: "Our party cannot win by being bloodless, our party cannot win by being tactical."[17] Historian Arthur Schlesinger Jr. bemoaned the growing Democratic belief that "fidelity to convictions is politically suicidal."[18] There is always room for ideological flexibility, he felt, but surrendering core principles threatened to set the party dangerously adrift. The risk Clinton's strategy ran was clear: voters could rebel against Democrats who seemed to stand for nothing and everything, for whatever some focus group of fickle, minimally informed, suggestible yahoos wants at a given moment, and see virtue in a Republican Party with total, unwavering confidence in its own lamentable convictions. Democrats have struggled ever since to repeat that success, with 2008 as an exception that proves the rule.*

WITCH DOCTORS

On December 30, 1994, seven weeks after the big GOP win, Bill Clinton was at Camp David meeting with celebrity self-help gurus Tony Robbins, Stephen Covey, and, no kidding, Marianne Williamson (a minor contender for the Democratic nomination in 2020). The midterm loss was such a blow to Clinton's psyche that political advice wasn't enough; he needed healing on the level of spiritual crystals and *The 7 Habits of Highly Effective People*. Although none of these authors became close Clinton allies, that he had them flown to Camp David underscores just how adrift, wounded, and embattled he felt after the midterms.

It might have been better in the long run had he chosen Williamson or Robbins to whisper in his ear. Instead, he gravitated toward Republican consultant Dick Morris and polling guru Mark Penn to help him define his twin strategies for governing and winning reelection in 1996. Morris

---

* This phrase is almost universally misinterpreted to mean "the existence of this exception proves that the rule is correct." In this context *prove* has the archaic English meaning of *test*, which also survives in the use of proofing dough in baking. The implication of the phrase, then, is actually that the rule should be reevaluated in light of an example that disconfirms it.

is often credited with creating the presidential strategy of triangulation, but elements of the idea were already part of the New Democrat schema by the time he entered the picture. Triangulation was a strategy aimed at saving Clinton's prospects for reelection in 1996, period—a "classic statement of a cynical and manipulative version of pre-emptive politics which did not look to innovate but simply to find an electoral formula which would win."[19]

The theory is simple enough: the president might benefit from depicting himself as the lone voice of reason beset by extremists in both parties. Then Clinton could claim to be the last trustworthy man in Washington, the dealmaker, the man who forced the Democrats to accept that the GOP worldview on many issues is fundamentally correct while reminding people that they needed someone like him as a bulwark against the loony Republicans. Implicit in the theory is that the GOP will get what it wants, which suited Clinton. Ideologically, he had far more common ground with Gingrich than their hostile public political relationship implied.[20] He had, after all, campaigned in 1992 on a promise to "end welfare as we know it" and approvingly declared that "the era of big government is over" in his 1996 State of the Union address.

Reaching out to Dick Morris was the classic devil's bargain, and Clinton knew it; Morris "represented a side of Clinton that the president disliked in himself."[21] For all his contradictions and lukewarm centrist ideology, Clinton was an idealist, and he recognized Morris as the kind of sleaze whose assistance would require, frankly, some moral compromises. Although following Morris's advice would increase Clinton's chances at reelection, it would involve scapegoating the Democrats as well as the Republicans and would cede ground to the GOP in ways that made even some centrist Democrats blanch. In the wake of 1994, Morris reinforced a point Clinton had already concluded, though: that he was not getting credit for things he had done (like cut the deficit) and was blamed for things he did not do (like raise taxes) because of the Democrats' reputation.* To succeed, Clinton needed not only to present himself as the lone voice of reason but to redefine the Democratic Party in the eyes of voters.

---

* Never was it considered that Americans outside elite circles simply do not care about deficit reduction.

Not all Democrats objected to such changes. Younger, successful boomer liberals (not unlike the Clintons and Gores) were sympathetic. While identifying solidly as liberals and as Democrats, these voters concurred with Clinton's view of government and bureaucracy as inefficient, the poor as coddled, organized labor and unions as fossils, and educated creatives (like themselves!) as the problem-solvers of the future. NAFTA may have been the final nail in the coffin of the working class and labor unions in the United States, but it is false to cast Clinton as entirely unrepresentative of evolving liberal thought on free trade. Many liberals shared, or were easily convinced of, the fundamental New Democrat economic worldview that free trade, deregulation, retraining of the working classes, and other Clinton policies promising growth were the way to the go-go tech economy of tomorrow, even if it decimated blue-collar America. As a 2005 hagiography of the Clinton years noted, "[Clinton's economic policy] was regarded by the nation's financial elite as the essential catalyst to a decade of remarkable prosperity."[22] The idea of a winners-and-losers economy, unsurprisingly, suited the winners just fine. That the prosperity left so many people behind was considered acceptable collateral damage by those benefiting.

Morris and Clinton wagered that victory could be achieved in 1996 by growing the Clintonian appeal among HEPs faster than driving away traditional (at the time) Democratic voters. It worked. What the two men cared much less about was the potential long-term damage the shift could do. After all, only in the heady dot-com economy days could anyone imagine a future in which well-paid, expensively educated managers outnumbered working-class people just hoping to get by.

Morris's guidance, which reinforced Clinton's own instincts, quickly raised the president's standing from its post-midterm doldrums.* Riding the high of the Republican takeover, Gingrich initiated an ill-advised, poorly considered showdown with Clinton over the federal budget in 1995. Morris relished the chance to show Clinton standing firm against

---

* *Doldrums* originated as a nautical term for the area near the equator where ships floundered due to lack of wind. An appropriate metaphor for the Democrats' last half century if ever there was one.

the extremist GOP. The ensuing shutdown of the federal government* (and eventual Republican capitulation) was almost universally seen as an embarrassing defeat for Gingrich. Welfare reform in 1996 fit the template even better, with Clinton firmly standing between the extremes of the GOP (which wanted deeper cuts) and the old Democrats, who objected to reimagining an antipoverty program as a limited and heavily qualified benefit. Clinton vetoed two GOP welfare reform bills† before signing a third that excluded measures he had criticized as too harsh. It remains a classic of the triangulation genre: reconcile Democrats to a Republican priority but declare victory by forcing the GOP to back down from its most extreme demands.

Mark Penn was a less objectionable figure than Morris during the Clinton era. While contemporaries and Clinton allies accurately saw Morris as a moral Three Mile Island, Penn was a bland Democratic operative in good standing. His influence on liberals' core ideas about electoral politics has been immense. Penn was a pollster, a believer in using data to inform political decision-making. Clinton's 1992 campaign embraced public opinion data, particularly from small focus groups, to an unprecedented extent. Insiders and political operatives like James Carville, Paul Begala, Dee Dee Myers,‡ Stan Greenberg, and George Stephanopoulos were depicted not merely as the political hired hands behind Clinton's rise but as experts dealing in objective, fact-based analysis. The idea of professionals with proven strategies in place of the traditional political soothsayer—half wizard, half ward heeler§—appealed to the image of managerial competence Clinton

---

* This and all subsequent "government shutdowns" are Kabuki theater, with numerous exceptions made for government operations and services deemed essential. This insulates both elected officials and the public from having to feel the effects of a real shutdown.

† The bills were designed to be unpalatable to Clinton so the GOP could accuse him of reneging on welfare reform in 1996. The bill Clinton signed was intended to include cuts to Social Security to force a third veto, but the GOP caucus could not reach consensus on such a dangerous ploy.

‡ She later served as Aaron Sorkin's on-set consultant for White House realism on *The West Wing*.

§ In the era of machine politics, a ward heeler was an on-the-ground campaign worker who went door to door to turn out reliable Democratic votes. As a *heeler* dog excels at herding livestock, a ward heeler herds voters.

projected. This was a scientific, not instinctive, politics. What was in reality the New Democrats expressing their own ideological preferences was depicted as an unbiased response to political reality, with objective analysts simply responding to the facts and data.

Penn was an outlier even in that universe of political wonkery. He saw the electorate divided into voters and nonvoters. One or the other. Voters tend to have firm preferences for one party; nonvoters are very difficult to turn into voters. So elections are a competition for a very small number of votes that are up for grabs: reliable voters without an ironclad allegiance to one party. They're often politically moderate or indecisive, susceptible to campaigns' efforts to woo them, and— crucially—members of definable, hyperspecific demographic cohorts to which political messaging can be targeted. Penn, in this way, was the godfather of "soccer moms" and other attempts to identify subpopu- lations perceived as particularly important.* Penn argued the need to target not merely broad groups like women but a certain *kind* of woman. Focus groups were a tool to help the Clinton team—campaign and White House—understand the needs, wants, and concerns of these vi- tal swing voters.

Penn was telling many Democrats what they wanted to hear anyway: you've got it right, now just tweak it a little to make it appealing to differ- ent market segments. The approach was a political application of an idea with a long history in marketing, one in which the marketer (or candi- date, in this case) is playing an active role in creating the market segment they plan to target. As the business historian Richard Tedlow noted in describing the cola wars between Coke and Pepsi, companies used the term *segment* "as a verb rather than a noun."[23] Just as the Pepsi generation didn't exist until Pepsi created it, Penn's theory both gave Democrats a target to aim at and played a role in creating new political group identities into which voters could be shoehorned. Tedlow's theory of *psychographics*, the profiling of consumers not only by demographics but also by world- view, was well established in his field. Penn merely applied it to a new type of consumer.

---

* Pennisms that never quite caught on included "office park dads," "wired workers," and "success-oriented Latinos," which excludes the failure-oriented Latinos, I guess.

These Pennographic groups* were always in the political center and hated economic populism.† The left and groups like labor and people of color would have no choice but to vote for the Democrats, he concluded, since Republicans were worse and third parties are not viable alternatives. The Democrats' task, then, was to move to the middle in a way that appealed to these microconstituencies that—surprise!—were generally middle class, white, and distinctly Reagan Democrat in temperament. Politically, Clinton's job became giving these groups what they wanted, often by trial and error. Despite his short-term success, this turned Clinton from the leader of a political party with a core ideology to a nervous caterer trying to win a wedding gig: Do you like this? What if I add a side of parsnips in a nice red wine reduction? You don't like red wine? Then I meant white wine! Or no wine at all! Wait, where are you going? You don't like parsnips? A parsnip is basically just a carrot. What if we called them white carrots?[24] It was Clinton's commitment to postideological politics taken to their logical extreme, where nothing is sacred compared to the shifting, inscrutable wants of the most mercurial part of the white, middle-class demographic. In time, and with political actors less talented than Bill Clinton, it would prove disastrous.

Both Mark Penn and Dick Morris encouraged Clinton to live for the political now without regard for long-term consequences. In the liberal worldview, this is easily justified by the alarming prospect of Republicans in power: that the GOP is so crazy that defeating them right now is more important than any ideological disagreements. Polling was an integral part of that narrative, providing the clearest window into what the public wanted at present. The art of polling was regarded with something approaching awe by the kind of data-driven, scientifically inclined, and very smart people who coalesced in the New Democrat universe. At one point, Penn commissioned a poll to find out where Americans wanted

---

* Get it? Like demographics? Eh.

† In 2002, Penn's colleagues at the New Democrat Network—an influential centrist election advocacy group—noted that "office park dads" are "not anti-corporate, because [they] work for a corporation—or [they] know [they'll] be working for one again. So the 'people versus the powerful' is not the world they live in." Quoted in Marinucci, C., "Move Over Soccer Moms—Here Come 'Office Park Dads,'" *San Francisco Chronicle*, August 13, 2002.

the Clinton family to *go on vacation*. The 1995 poll asked what married people with kids approved of, vacation-wise. Camping won, and off went the dutiful Clintons to Grand Teton (including one night spent in a tent, which created a nightmare for the Secret Service).[25] Morris called the exercise "idiotic," and then told Clinton to do it anyway. Taking a position about anything without first taking the public's temperature became unthinkable.

WINNING THE WRONG WAY

Even when Bill Clinton got things right, the long-term political consequences left Democratic candidates with more baggage to lug around. The Earned Income Tax Credit (EITC) offers a case study in why even successful policies didn't produce political rewards for Democrats.

In 1993, Clinton tripled the EITC by executive order, making it among the biggest and most effective federal antipoverty programs. Millions of Americans benefit from it. How much political credit and goodwill have Democrats wrung from the EITC since this historic expansion? Remarkably little; like most of the tax code, voters tend either to be unaware of it or to misunderstand it. Taxes are a black box for the individual. It is all but impossible to parse which deduction, which credit, which income source, which IRS incantation is responsible for adding x to one's tax refund or subtracting y from the amount owed. Annual pleas for tax literacy do little to change the reality that not only do Americans fail to understand the effects of specific tax policies, they also fail to understand the broad strokes.[26] Why should they? The process is overwhelmingly complicated by design, and the widespread use of software or tax preparers obscures the occult tax magic behind a curtain.

This matters because Clinton established a Democratic habit of using the tax code as a politically expedient backdoor for social welfare policy. Tax cuts are an easier sell, especially to moderates, than a social welfare program that could be depicted as big government or a handout to the poor. It's not welfare, you see; it's just one of the millions of bits and bobs in the tax code that entitles specific taxpayers to certain benefits. Perfect!

Perfect, except for the fact that a Democratic policy gives billions of dollars to millions of voters who fail to realize that they are receiving a windfall from a Democratic policy. When people file tax returns and get a refund, the assumption is simply that we must have paid too much in taxes already and the government is just returning some of our money to us. This kind of logic also enables millions of better-off Americans to pretend, for example, that they have not received a huge handout in the form of the home mortgage interest deduction.*

While an old-fashioned social welfare policy is an unambiguous exchange between society and the individual—a check one receives monthly, for example—a benefit like the EITC is invisible. Worse, Democrats cannot straightforwardly tell voters what the EITC puts in their pocket because the amount varies for every taxpayer. They end up having to message a truly baffling, complex benefit formula that varies on marital status, income, income type, dependents, and more. Consider this attempt to explain to a general audience—not accountants or legislators, but ordinary taxpayers—EITC benefits in 2018 based on IRS guidelines:

> A married couple in 2018, whose total income was just shy of $24,350, of which exactly $3,500 was investment income, would receive the maximum credit for their number of qualifying children (i.e. $6,431 with 3 kids). But if this couple instead had $3,501 of investment income, then—because of the rule that for any claimant, whether single or married, with or without children, investment income cannot be greater than $3,500—they will instead receive zero EIC. This is a loss of up to $6,431 due to one extra dollar of investment income, and the loss is nearly twice the entire amount of the couple's investment income. (Instead of $24,350, the phaseout for Single, Head of Household, and Qualifying Widow(er) begins at $18,700.)[27]

That may be a description of a good program, but good luck making it *sound* like a good program. In the post-Reagan era, though, Democrats have shown a strong and consistent preference for engineering social welfare policy this way because it is politically safer and the complexity purports to weed out the undeserving so only the deserving benefit.

---

* GOP changes to the tax code under Trump largely eliminated this deduction in exchange for an increase to the standard deduction.

The policy looks great in a white paper and is incomprehensible on the campaign trail. The penalty they pay for this is that no one outside the Beltway, or perhaps obsessive readers of Nate Silver's statistical musings, understands it.

BAD ACTORS

Bringing new voices into his inner circle in 1995 was an understandable move for Bill Clinton, given doubts about his prospects for reelection following the midterms. But the people he chose to bring in were, in the long term, of the kind that undermined the Democratic Party. Post-Clinton, Morris reverted to his previous career as a right-wing bile merchant, while Penn would go on to play a leading role in the 2008 Hillary Clinton campaign. After that disaster, he slunk ever rightward until he found himself on Fox News in the Trump years, feeding its audience red meat about the liberals.

Clinton's second term was a personal vindication for him and of the people he chose to turn to for advice after the midterms. Despite the embarrassment of his sex scandals, impeachment backfired on the GOP spectacularly, and by 1998, Newt Gingrich was ousted from a leadership role he had assumed only four years earlier. Clinton's approval ratings at the height of impeachment were among the strongest of his eight years in office. Yet the policy record of the second Clinton term was, in the cold light of history, nothing short of abysmal.

Mychal Denzel Smith has described the Democratic embrace of symbolism over policy as the embrace of seductive distractions that "allow us to pretend things are better than they are." They mollify (or are intended to mollify) while taking the country further from "a noble vision of freedom, justice, and equality."[28] Clinton understood intuitively that, as a talented communicator, he could resolve the tension between the interests of power and the demands of the powerless by giving the former what they want and trying to keep the latter satisfied with gestures.

Perhaps the best illustration of the problems with the New Democrat approach was his double cross of organized labor shortly after reelection. Unions pulled out all the stops for Clinton in 1996, seething over NAFTA but convinced that a Dole-Gingrich government in DC would offer even worse. Despite the sense that Clinton's track record on labor didn't merit their support, union money and volunteer work poured into the campaign as other traditionally Democratic groups remained wary of the New Democrat changes. As with organized labor's failed efforts to rescue Hubert Humphrey's campaign in 1968, the 1996 Clinton campaign relied on organized labor to the point that the campaign could not have survived without it.

In 1997, Clinton repaid them by proposing fast-track authority for trade agreements—essentially the power to negotiate mini-NAFTAs with trading partners with only an up-or-down vote in Congress to follow. Unions were vociferously opposed to this obvious threat to domestic blue-collar jobs, and Clinton knew it. He simply didn't care. As a lame duck, he no longer needed their support, and besides, the Republicans would always be a worse deal for them than the Democrats.[29] So, the cynical pattern of soliciting from core constituencies during election years and then actively working against their interests while governing took shape. The Clintonian view was that the Democratic base—labor, people of color, social activists, the left, and so on—were morally obligated to vote Democratic with the understanding that, to win theoretical moderate votes in the center, Democrats would not actually deliver on any of their policy demands. Sounds like a healthy and sustainable relationship!

Fast track was but one example. Even more damaging were the banking and telecommunications deregulations Clinton championed. It was Clinton's repeal of key portions of the Glass-Steagall Act (which separated commercial and investment banking)* that initiated the tidal wave of complex derivatives and mortgage-backed securities that cratered the global economy in 2008–2009—but hey, the financial industry was all for it, and it theoretically would contribute to all-important economic growth. And that ultimately was the point in Clinton's political theology. It doesn't necessarily matter if something is popular with the little people

---

* Carter Glass (D-VA) was a Senate conservative and New Deal opponent who introduced the bill that bears his name in the hopes of preventing a permanent federal takeover of failing banks. Like much of the New Deal, what looks like enlightened progressive legislation in hindsight was calculated at the time to protect capitalism from more aggressive reforms.

if it is consensus wisdom among the right people—the Harvard-degreed experts, the wealthy entrepreneurs and CEOs, the upwardly mobile professional class. They saw banking regulations as an obstacle to making even more money, so the regulations had to go. They saw tariffs and trade barriers as an obstacle to profit, so free trade had to happen. The social consciences of our business leaders are all the regulations America needs.

Unions weren't the only constituency Clinton alternately placated and attacked. Black voters maintained—and maintain—extremely high levels of support for Bill Clinton, not because his policies addressed structural inequalities but because, as political scientist Sharon D. Wright explained, Clinton was uncommonly skilled at symbolic representation (centering Black people in his campaign and administration) and speaking familiarly, comfortably, and sincerely to Black audiences. One pair of scholars credited Clinton for appealing to Black voters in ways previous campaigns did not, not as a special interest but with symbolic actions, diverse appointments, and personal connections in the Black community.[30] Another scholar assessed Clinton's appeal to Black voters less charitably, noting that Clinton reasoned "black voters would have nowhere else to go" given the state of the GOP and then threw Black voters' interests under the bus in pursuit of white votes.[31] The pithiest reduction came from Clinton ally Congressman Charles Rangel (D-NY) who likened his relationship with Black voters to a tryst: "Meet me in the hotel room; I don't want to be seen with you in the lobby."[32]

What promised to be all things to all people turned out to be all things to certain people and a ration of absolute shit for the poor and working class. If you're an architect, a college professor,* a mortgage analyst, a consultant, or in any of the other highly skilled, highly credentialed professions that exploded in the postindustrial economy, Clinton's middle path has produced rewards. The 1990s were a banner decade for knowledge economy workers, and the two decades since haven't been half bad either (check your retirement account balance if you're one of the about 40 percent of working adults who have a 401(k) or similar).[33] Many other once-loyal groups of Democrats learned that their support was expected

---

* Tenured, of course.

every two years even as the party jettisoned their interests: labor, Black voters, the working class, the poor, environmentalists. "Nowhere else to turn" became a blank check to move to the right to solicit moderate votes, and the Democrats found themselves practicing political contortionism, trying to hold on to those whose economic and social policy preferences are effectively Republican and win back the people those policies screw directly and enthusiastically. As one well-known Clinton critic put it, "rich people will *not* work unless they are given money, poor people will *only* work if they are not. . . . Once the Democratic Party had adopted this theology, the poor had no one to whom they could turn."* What are they gonna do, vote Republican on the assumption that neither party represents their financial interests but the right can offer them endless grievance and illusory cultural superiority? Or simply stop voting altogether?

Imagine if either of those things happened. You'd really have a Democratic Party in trouble, in that case.

---

* I am truly sorry for quoting Christopher Hitchens, *No One Left to Lie to: The Triangulations of William Jefferson Clinton* (London: Verso, 1999), 60.

CHAPTER 8

THE MYSTERIOUS WORLD OUTSIDE WASHINGTON, DC

So far, this story has focused heavily on domestic American politics at the national level. Before wading into the Bush* years, let's pause for two frequently neglected topics: the decline of Democratic strength in state politics and the meanderings of Democratic foreign policy. Neglecting state politics is a key problem for Democrats, albeit one the party establishment makes periodic, unconvincing noises about addressing.[1] American liberalism is an overwhelmingly DC-centric world; that's where the glamor resides, where the only careers worth a damn are made. Given Democrats' tendency to equate control of the White House with success writ large, they managed to waltz into 2016 feeling like things were going well despite having lost hundreds of state legislative seats between 2009 and 2016.

Foreign policy is an issue where little has changed yet everything has changed since 1990. During the Cold War the Democrats held a safe position: anticommunist but not to the obsessive, occasionally deranged extent many Republicans were anticommunist. When the Soviet Union

---

* As with "Clinton," context should clarify that "Bush" is George W. Bush rather than his father unless otherwise noted.

and the global communist boogeyman disappeared, Democrats continued to adhere to Washington Consensus foreign policy—interventionist
and favoring military over diplomatic solutions—as it shed the Cold War
paradigm and pivoted to terrorism and "rise of China" posturing. In practice, Democratic politics back-burner foreign policy, correctly identifying
it as a tertiary issue for most voters. But when it comes to the forefront, as
it did after 9/11, Democrats struggle mightily to develop a brand that is
both convincing to voters and sufficiently distinct from the GOP.

IT'S A MAD, MAD, MAD, MAD WORLD

It would be glib and unsatisfying to whip through fifty years of American
foreign policy in a few paragraphs. Instead, let's consider one major paradigm shift that took place around 1990, with the end of the Cold War
and collapse of the Soviet Union. Both before and since, American foreign policy has been defined by elite consensus on goals but partisan disagreement on methods and intensity. During the Cold War, both parties'
foreign policy was anticommunist; the difference was of degrees, with
Republicans tending toward the General Ripper from *Dr. Strangelove*
variety while Democrats advocated a somewhat cooler-headed approach
that remained tough on communism. The Democratic position is exemplified by the Kennedy White House during the Cuban Missile Crisis
of 1962, when their posture was resolutely anti-Soviet and anticommunist but also adamantly opposed to demands from the Pentagon and the
American right to resolve the conflict with an invasion of Cuba or even
nuclear war with the USSR.[2]

The Clinton years marked a period of confusion in foreign policy, the
era of Francis Fukuyama's *The End of History and the Last Man* in which
liberal democracy and capitalism vanquished all alternative ideologies.*
In the 1990s, the foreign policy industry—including the military, defense contractors, NatSec (National Security) professionals—faced the
dilemma of writing a Superman story without Lex Luthor to serve as
the villain. It was challenged either to find a new permanent enemy
or to wither away. With time, terrorism emerged as an alternative that

---

* What is often called the West but mostly meant the United States won. U-S-A! U-S-A!

justified the continuation of a permanently aggressive military posture. Rather than halving the Pentagon's budget and refocusing spending elsewhere, the argument was to maintain but update the machinery of national defense to face new threats. The focus moved away from nation-states, armies, and formal warfare to nonstate actors and low-intensity, unconventional wars.

Suffice it to say that it happened, and there was no serious objection from within the Democratic Party to maintaining a hegemonic military, intelligence, and defense apparatus but redirecting it toward fanatics with suicide bombs instead of East German tank divisions poised to rampage through the Fulda Gap. What separates the parties on foreign policy continues to be their relative zeal for military adventurism and disagreement over best practices, over the proper *management* of war. The continued necessity to fight, to intervene abroad, and to spend lavishly has not been seriously challenged. The antiwar movement has been confined to the left, never seriously considered by establishment Democrats who see peaceniks as unsavory, vote-repelling reminders of McGovern-era protest politics.

As with crime and welfare, Clinton-era Democrats sought a position that undermined Republican accusations of weakness while maintaining some distinct identity. The solution as they saw it was to paint the GOP as hawkish and crazy while Democrats were hawkish and *smart*. So Clinton sent the American military into Somalia but in a "limited" fashion that avoided the optics of a big military invasion, with no armor or heavy air power for the TV cameras to capture. He intervened in the civil wars of the disintegrating Balkans, in Kosovo and the genocidal war between Croats and Serbs, but he did so under the auspices of transnational organizations like the United Nations and NATO. American involvement during this period lacked clearly defined goals and objectives other than to stop the fighting, and the Democratic Party never successfully conveyed the reasons for intervention to the public.

Then 9/11 came along, this time with Republicans in charge, and the Democrats needed a tough-but-smart retort to George W. Bush's swaggering aggression. At the moment of crisis, few Democratic elected officials were heavily focused on foreign policy. The case for or against going to war in Iraq was improvised on the fly, not guided by any established consensus within the Democratic Party on a specific theoretical approach to foreign policy. The decision-making and strategy were farmed out to the world of liberal- or center-left think tanks in the foreign policy and national security spheres. By their nature, inhabitants of that world see military solutions to problems and conceive of military action as fundamentally legitimate. They imagine an active, not passive, role for the American defense machinery that, directly or indirectly, gives people like foreign policy consultants and think tanks a reason to exist (not to mention a great deal of money).

After 9/11, Democrats defaulted in confusion to a hawkish, neoconservative foreign policy that was aggressive (please don't call us wimps!) but with the New Democrat trappings of efficiency, good management, and putting very smart people in charge. That Democrats believed in interventionism and strong defense was nothing new to anyone who could recall FDR, Truman, JFK, and LBJ. But outside the Cold War framework with its haunting, existential threat of global nuclear annihilation, they struggled to define goals and differentiate their position from Republicans'.

It was a Democratic Party remarkably ill prepared to deal with a political scenario in which foreign policy became the dominant issue. The Republicans' natural advantage (with both mass and elite political cultures that tend to be obsequiously deferential to the military) was pronounced. Bush was at his "let's go kick some ass!" best while Democrats sputtered about UN votes, inspections, Hans Blix, rules, and the minutiae of various military spending bills. The scenario recalled a famous formulation in political science of the two majorities in American politics, favoring Democrats when the focus is purely on domestic political issues and Republicans when it shifts to defense and foreign policy.[3] Democrats' strategy on Iraq, as demonstrated by their congressional votes and maladroit attempt to defeat Bush in 2004, was to support going to war but criticize how Bush conducted it, devolving to the Clintonesque argument that they could achieve what Republicans wanted in a better, smarter, less costly, less belligerent way. Voters appeared not to be impressed by a promise to make warfare 31 percent more efficient with this one weird trick.

Foreign policy continues to be largely a nonissue issue for Democrats. Barack Obama continued many Bush-era policies (Guantanamo Bay is still open and full of "detainees" at this writing), and both the Hillary Clinton and Joe Biden campaigns de-emphasized foreign policy. The welcome surprise of Biden following through on promises to withdraw the military from Afghanistan was the first Democratic foreign policy stance to seriously clash with the Washington Consensus in living memory; hysterical antiwithdrawal media coverage from outlets ordinarily sympathetic to Biden underscored the extent to which a taboo had been violated. Yet Biden has embraced other elements of established interventionist policy, like the controversial use of drone airstrikes.[*] And unless the Biden administration's insistence on withdrawal from Afghanistan signals a profound shift to a new, more limited foreign policy, what most distinguishes Democratic and Republican foreign policy is that Democrats accuse the GOP of being bellicose morons (an irrefutable charge, certainly) who do war and foreign policy wrong, while Democrats are thoughtful, smart administrators who do it right. The Pentagon's budget certainly isn't receding under Biden, even as some commitments are wound down.[†]

Crucially, foreign policy continues to do a poor job of holding voters' and the media's attention. After a few years of primacy during the Bush presidency, it has once again fallen deep into the background of American politics. Attempts to saber-rattle at Russia, China, North Korea, and Iran struggle for visibility in the news cycle. Even the contentious 2021 withdrawal from Afghanistan received a week of overwrought, saturation media coverage and then disappeared without a trace.

Ask yourself what the biggest foreign policy issue was in the elections of 2012, 2016, 2018, or 2020, or what role foreign policy will play in

---

[*] At writing, the Biden administration shows signs of finally winding down the American reliance on drone warfare; although typically, perhaps stung by the wild overreaction to the Afghan withdrawal, the White House is failing to capitalize on this significant accomplishment. See Cooper, R., "Biden Nearly Ended the Drone War, and Nobody Noticed," *Week*, December 1, 2021.

[†] For FY2022, Biden requested $715B while congressional Democrats joined with Republicans in insisting on $739B. See Edmondson, K., "Congress Moves to Increase Pentagon Budget, Defying Biden and Liberals," *New York Times*, September 2, 2021.

2022. If you can figure it out without resorting to immigration (a distinct question) or a general sense that the rest of the world was laughing at Donald Trump (who seemed dangerously casual about the potential to get us all killed), you're a bigger foreign policy aficionado than most of us. What exactly constitutes "Democratic foreign policy" today remains a mystery.

THE STATEHOUSE PROBLEM

It is an exaggeration to claim that the Democratic establishment only discovered state politics after Donald Trump's 2016 victory shook the "atmosphere of complacency and overconfidence" that defined the final years of the Obama presidency.* But the exaggeration is based on a pair of very real problems: Democrats have floundered at the state level since 1994, and Washington-focused party elites have been unwilling or unable to do something about it.

In 1994, the GOP takeover of Congress overshadowed simultaneous Republican gains in state legislatures and governors' mansions. In 1982, there were just ten state legislatures under unified GOP control; by 1995, there were seventeen. In 2021, there are *thirty*. At the time of writing, Republicans control sixty-one of the country's ninety-eight partisan legislative chambers.† From 2010 to 2018, Democrats lost nearly a thousand state legislative seats nationwide. With governorships, the GOP had twenty-one in 1990 and peaked at thirty-three in 2018 before Democrats wrested six back in that year's midterms. Republican dominance in state capitols has been "an issue" for Democrats the way reactor four was "an issue" at Chernobyl.

One factor is the different political cultures among liberals and conservatives. State senate races in rural Missouri or the political intrigue of state capitals like Augusta, Maine, and Pierre, South Dakota,‡ simply do not grip the most powerful and ambitious actors in the universe of

---

* Matt Yglesias wrote presciently in the aftermath of the 2014 midterms on the inability of Democratic elites to recognize the serious problem the party had at the state level, even before Trump. See Yglesias, "Democrats Are in Denial. Their Party Is Actually in Deep Trouble," Vox, October 19, 2015.
† Nebraska has a unicameral nonpartisan legislature.
‡ It's pronounced "peer," and its residents *will* correct you.

liberal politics, no matter how important those battlefields might be in practice. Conservatives, conversely, are more likely to define success in exactly those terms—every round of redistricting gamed in their favor, every state law against abortion or gun control passed, and every voting restriction is acclaimed a huge victory for the movement.

Alexander Hertel-Fernandez's magisterial *State Capture: How Conservative Activists, Big Businesses, and Wealthy Donors Reshaped the American States—and the Nation* chronicles the completeness of the conservative and Republican defeat of liberals and Democrats in this arena since 1990. There are myriad reasons for the state-level Democratic drubbing, but two stand out for how often they have been repeated. One is the jerky, uncoordinated, inconsistent character of Democratic efforts ("efforts") to improve state political fortunes. When Democrats experience a jarring defeat in Washington politics like in 1994 or in 2016, they rediscover state politics, and a mad scramble ensues to form organizations purporting to address the problem. When Democratic national-political fortunes rebound, as in 2008 or 2018, money, enthusiasm, support, and attention for the state-level efforts dissolve into mist. Things are once again "fine," and the feeling of crisis that is essential to any real effort toward political change dissipates. More frustratingly, liberal think tanks and organizations don't see themselves as partisan counterweights to conservative think tanks and activist groups. Their goal, Hertel-Fernandez explains, is to promote neutral, nonpartisan, good-government ideas, while their conservative counterparts pursue nothing less than driving policy as far to the right as possible. This shift, like so much that ails Democratic politics, accelerated in the 1990s. Hertel-Fernandez quotes a powerful liberal foundation chair explaining, "The way to make good local government is to clean up the political process, not try to skew things from a particular point of view," while another notes that liberal donors are not "comfortable with an agenda that often can be quite partisan."[4] Amazingly, this nonpartisan approach has not translated into success in *partisan fucking politics*.

A second problem is ideological. Republicans' calls for reduced federal power naturally elevate the importance of state and local governments in the conservative cosmology, whereas liberals believe that the federal government is the proper venue for the kind of policy change they want to see. They focus on uniform, national solutions that emanate from the White House, Congress, and the Supreme Court; their goal is "a society built on one unified vision of policy and culture, rather than a diverse array of policies and cultures."[5] Diversity in that context is a negative, as in the "diversity" of state laws that permitted legal segregation prior to the civil rights era. After the disaster of 2016, Obama aide David Axelrod mused at a conference: "I wonder, sometimes, whether the Democratic Party has contributed to [losses at the state and local levels] by making the president and the federal government the fulcrum of so much and [believing] we can solve these problems from the top down."[6] Good question. The heavy-handed approach from the White House during the Trump presidency has spurred a greater embrace (or at least encouragement) of federalism among Democrats. If the GOP intends to govern as an autocracy when it holds the White House, the best counterweight will be power wielded at the state and local levels. That requires a greater devotion of resources, attention, and energy to winning power down ballot; as usual, Democrats will say the right things about doing this but have yet to follow through.

Loss of control of state legislatures and governorships has hurt Democrats even more than losing the White House to Donald Trump in 2016 or control of the Senate to Mitch McConnell in 2014. The reason is simple: Republicans use control of those institutions as an opportunity to tilt the political playing field in their favor. They pass ludicrously partisan redistricting maps that make it harder for Democrats to regain power, and increasingly, they pass laws aimed at restricting voting access in ways clearly intended to have partisan benefits. Republican control also gives conservatives the power to set the tone and agenda of state-level politics, inundating voters with a steady stream of the kind of antieducation, antigovernment, culture war offal that fuels the right, all while Democrats refuse to respond by enacting popular policies or making structural changes to negate the GOP's democracy-eroding wins.

The behemoth conservative think tank American Legislative Exchange Council (ALEC) coordinates and pushes a coherent policy agenda by writing bills, networking legislators across state lines, providing legal and logistical support, and generally giving Republican state legislators what they need to do what conservative donors want.[7] ALEC is the motive force behind the proliferation of "stand your ground" gun laws, voter ID requirements, heartbeat abortion bills, and other right-wing fantasy fodder. The Democrats simply have no counterpart, nothing even approaching the resources, influence, or organization of ALEC. Like the think-tank world at the elite level of national politics, this is an area in which the right has unquestionably and consistently trounced Democrats for decades.

What do Democrats do when they have unified control of a state government? Well, in New York, disgraced former Democratic governor Andrew Cuomo helped convince a splinter group of "independent" Democrats in the state senate to partner with the GOP to give them the chamber majority. Sure, that's only one example,* but think about that—they used their majority to *give the other party the majority*. In 2021, Democrats in Illinois used their legislative supermajority not to squeeze more competitive districts out of an already Democrat-friendly state map but to punish Rep. Marie Newman for defeating right-wing Democrat Dan Lipinski in a 2020 primary.[8] Given a rare chance to push back against the national trend of hypergerrymandered Republican maps, Illinois Democrats instead prioritized screwing a reliable Democrat for having the temerity to challenge an incumbent whose idea of good politics was to ape conservative culture war talking points.[9] This is not merely anecdotal; research shows that Republican control, whether by one seat or a supermajority, is maxed out in redistricting to benefit Republicans, while Democratic control by any margin is seldom used to similar partisan effect.[10] The result is that the GOP constantly strengthens its position while Democrats, rather than responding in kind, wag their finger and try to shame them for being such nasty partisans. Long gone is the spirit of the Democratic legislator memorably quoted by redistricting scholar Jonathan Winburn: "We are going to shove [the district map] up your [redacted modifier] ass and you're going to like it, and I'll [redacted verb]

---

* The same thing happened in Washington state, where two Democratic state senators joined with the twenty-three-member GOP caucus to give Republicans control of the forty-nine-seat chamber from 2012 to 2017.

any Republican I can."[11] A bit uncalled for, yes, but . . . can someone find this guy and put him in charge?

In recent decades, state political parties have lost power relative to national party organizations and independent groups like PACs, a phenomenon that has affected Republicans too.[12] Yet Democratic state parties have given over to a "politics of listlessness,"[13] a zombie state that makes it unclear what role they ought to be—let alone are—serving. On-the-ground ward heeling—once a core party function—has disappeared from both parties. Republicans replaced it with a network of organizations that keep activists primed and engaged (read: worked up to a lather, usually over an imaginary threat). Democrats have replaced it with temporary organizations that fan out from the coasts and then disappear after Election Day. State parties have become vestigial, their purpose rendered unclear by a "mercenary, money-driven, candidate-led, nationalized, and deinstitutionalized [electoral process]. . . . [Even] as parties in service, state parties have been supplanted; in off years, many 'barely even have anyone around to answer the phone.'"[14] The potential for building an activist network has been there; Obama for America (OFA), which existed in 2008 and 2012 but not otherwise, is a good example of a large grassroots-focused group built rapidly and then forgotten postelection.[15] Rather than try to convert voter enthusiasm into a durable movement or organization after 2008, Democrats decided that enthusiasm from demanding, inflexible young activists would only get in the way of the plan to sacrifice most of Obama's soaring progressive rhetoric to the gods of compromise and bipartisanship. One journalist described Obama's desire to "muzzle" the activists, whose expectations he had no desire to try to meet.[16] Old-fashioned ineptness played a role as well: after 2008, OFA moved its entire operation into the Democratic National Committee, and perceptive readers may reliably guess what happened next.

This strategy showed its clear limitations in 2020. The Democratic Senatorial Campaign Committee's plan, aligned with the Biden-Harris campaign's eschewing of groundwork in favor of a virtual campaign, was to support the nomination of centrist candidates who had the potential to raise huge amounts of money from out-of-state liberals eager to see the Senate retaken. Then these races, notably Sara Gideon's challenge to Susan

Collins in Maine, were bombarded with out-of-state ad buys that produced nothing except windfall profits for well-connected liberal campaign professionals. Local activity was left up to the campaigns, which did what they could and in some cases bucked the Biden-Harris campaign's virtual emphasis.[17] State parties were nearly nonentities.

Contrary to the perception that Republicans succeed by bluntly outspending Democrats, there is ample money circulating among liberal actors. But too often it is misspent. Hertel-Fernandez describes numerous attempts to found organizations to rival ALEC's influence in state-level policy failing due to the absence of two or three million dollars to fund operations while ridiculous, kamikaze Senate campaigns easily raise eight-figure war chests. No efforts are made to coordinate or plan where money is directed and spent. Predictably bad results flow from the confusion.

After the disaster of 2016, a spate of liberal groups purporting to focus on rebuilding at the state and local levels emerged. With youthful names like Future Now, Flippable, Sister District, Run for Something, and Forward Majority, these groups appeared or expanded with the stated goal of doing what the Democratic Party wasn't: rebuild electoral strength from the ground up.[18] It's not a great sign, of course, that it took 2016 to convince Democrats that there were some problems down ballot. But the Democratic establishment may at last be waking up to the need for state-level action—better late than never, right? The 2018 midterms, a chance for liberals to vent disgust with the Trump administration, offered the first positive signs down ballot since 2006 (more on that later). Hopes rose momentarily that the plan was working. Then in 2020, matters regressed, with Democrats losing House seats (but retaining the majority) and losing even more ground in state legislatures at the worst time, with postcensus 2020 redistricting looming.*

The lesson is not to give up; indeed, persisting with a strategy even when it does not pay off immediately is something Democrats badly need to internalize. Yet it is appropriate to question methods and to look honestly at what worked in 2018. It is both easy and tempting to overinterpret

---

* Hence Russell Berman's accurate assessment of the 2020 election in his article "The Failure That Could Haunt Democrats for a Decade," *Atlantic*, November 10, 2020.

victories in a two-party system as the logical product of whatever strategy is employed in a given election. After a sufficient length of time in power, a majority party inevitably loses some of its marginal seats, and the voting public naturally grows weary. Democrats saw the downside of this in 2010, when they lost many seats they had won in wave elections in 2006 and 2008, seats they would inevitably lose in anything but a wave year. In 2006 and 2018, Republicans felt the same pinch. An overall shift in attitude and political culture needs to take place in American liberalism to stop focusing on the nation's capital to the exclusion of politics closer to voters' homes. Legislation in states and at the local level has the most direct impact on our lives, and Democratic electoral and practical politics simply do not reflect that reality right now. They seem to get it and, after 2016, said many times that they get it. Whether they actually do and have a strategy that will succeed remains to be seen.

CHAPTER 9

THE BUSH YEARS

B ob Woodward's chronicles of the Clinton era, *The Agenda* and *The Choice*, signaled the author's transition from muckraker to storyteller, from exposés to access journalism offering the masses a peek behind the curtains of power. During a long slog through his nearly dozen books on the Clinton, George W. Bush, and Obama presidencies, a curious pattern emerged. For Obama and especially Clinton, the Republicans are always present. They're part of the story—an important part. Newt Gingrich and Bob Dole, John Boehner and Mitch McConnell, they're always there. Involved. Relevant. The tale of Obama's or Clinton's presidencies cannot be told without them.

By contrast, in three books about George W. Bush, the Democrats barely register.* They aren't there. The story doesn't require them; when they do appear, they're inconsequential. The GOP governed to the greatest practicable extent as though the Democrats were a nonfactor. In *State of Denial*, the Democratic nonexistence is almost literal; the book makes one mention of them in the context of Bush appointing a committee to

---

* *Plan of Attack* does discuss the 2004 election and John Kerry, but outside the specific electoral context, in the great bulk of Woodward's writing on Bush the president (not Bush the candidate), the Democratic Party disappears.

study prewar Iraq intelligence. He needed to involve Democrats in the investigation to make his bureaucratic whitewash look good. That's it.

The Democrats' role in five hundred pages of *Plan of Attack* (2004) is to express "concern" and "misgivings" (307–308) about Iraq War resolutions and budgets—budgets Democrats ended up supporting, of course. Even "vocal critics" (204) got on board. But the comic masterpiece of the series is *The War Within* (2008). Sen. Barack Obama makes a brief cameo to mildly criticize Bush after the president's approval had tanked so badly that even Senate Republicans were scoring points off their lame duck president (316).* Senate Democratic leader Harry Reid criticizes Bush's "surge" proposal for Iraq—and is attacked by other Democrats for "demoralizing" the troops (Sen. Carl Levin is noted to have really "chewed his ass," 346). And finally, after the Democratic Congress passed $124 billion in supplemental war spending in the spirit of supporting the troops—Bush vetoed the bill for being too small and for suggesting a specific date that a troop withdrawal must begin—Speaker Pelosi called him "obstinate" and promised to pray for him (349).

That's it. That's how the Democrats feature in the presidency of George W. Bush. Liberals derided him as the buffoon, failson, and bagman he was (and remains, character rehabilitation aside) but could not defeat him in two tries.† They hated him but became so enamored of the Clintonian method of accepting the premise and criticizing the details that they couldn't successfully attack him directly. They had to nitpick, to argue managerial competence without exposing themselves to mockery as McGoverniks waving peace symbols and trying to surrender American sovereignty to the nearest convenient one-world government. We know how well "support the troops but oppose the war" or in some cases "support the troops and the war even more than Bush" worked.

THE CLINTON CONTINUATION

Since Bill Clinton left office popular, having overseen what were by consensus eight good years of peace and prosperity, the ascension of his

---

* Obama called an increase in troop levels "a mistake." Scathing stuff.
† The year 2000 gets an asterisk, of course, with the Supreme Court pushing Bush over the Electoral College finish line.

vice president to the White House seemed likely. Al Gore was, unfortunately, a mediocre candidate with none of Clinton's charisma but all of his wonkiness. Gore would talk policy, most of it laced with gee-whiz techno idealism, until the heat death of the universe. Liberal elites love that stuff; voters, conversely, tended to find him ponderous and confusing. Meanwhile, with the assistance of deferential media coverage, Bush was able to sell himself as a "compassionate conservative," which sounds nice but isn't a real thing. It was a two-bad-candidates election: the tedium of Gore the technocrat versus the inanity of Bush the regular fella.* The razor-close finish underscored the oh-well-whatever dynamic of the moment.

Predictably, Democrats leapt upon two aspects of the loss that absolved Gore (and running mate Joe Lieberman), the Democratic Party, and its ideas: the Supreme Court and Nader voters. It is a fact that had every Nader voter instead voted for Gore, he would have won (although this argument conveniently ignores that third-party paleoconservative Pat Buchanan "stole" more votes from Bush than Nader did from Gore.)[1] The inconvenient question is: If Bush is the total dipshit liberals claimed (spoiler: he was!), why couldn't Gore score a win regardless of the usual smattering of votes to minor candidates? Why did a Gore victory require the same helping hand from the Supreme Court that Bush needed to reach the White House? Reasonable political actors might consider what they did wrong and learn something from it. Instead, 2000 was a prominent example of the new thinking in the New Democrat era. It's never our fault. We do not fail, but other people fail us.

So, fault ultimately landed upon the voters (idiots who fell for Bush's regular guy act, or who recognized a fellow idiot and embraced him), Nader voters and the left who stabbed the Democrats in the back,[†] and institutions (Florida elected officials and courts, the federal courts) who refused to step in and award the Democrats a deserved win. To this day,

---

* The rebranding of a man who was virtually a parody of elites—son of a president and grandson of a congressman, a *cheerleader at Andover* for Christ's sake—as a Texas cowboy remains a feat suffused with mystery and awe.

† I wonder if there is any relevant historical precedent for centering a stab-in-the-back myth in one's worldview.

the lack of clarity about what happened in Florida in 2000 reigns. Various studies of ballots and recount methods tend to confirm the official tabulation that put Bush very slightly ahead; although it has been argued cogently that with better balloting and counting techniques less prone to overvotes (ballots disqualified for multiple votes for one office), Gore won comfortably. Alas, those better ballots and techniques were not what was used in 2000.[2]

Too infrequently was it asked in good faith why Al Gore couldn't match Bill Clinton's 1992 and 1996 performances, even against a candidate who was demonstrably a dolt. It was and remains easier to scold Nader voters and remind them of their moral obligation to vote for Democrats (who openly disdain them) than to ask the Occam's razor question of why Gore couldn't achieve the simplest path to victory: convincing just a few more people in a few more places to vote for him. No one asks why or how Gore's poll numbers, at one point solidly over 50 percent, fell steadily, and why it seemed like the more voters saw of him the less they liked him.[3]

In a postelection analysis by venerable political scientist Gerald Pomper, Gore's campaign and personal performance were found badly lacking. Gore "did little to focus voters' attention on the Democratic achievements," "neglected to put the election into a broader context" of Republicans' dismal record at the helm of Congress, and "made the election a contest between two individuals and their personal programs" by "eschewing" partisanship.[4] Another established scholar tellingly titled a retrospective "Ideology in the 2000 Elections: A Study in Ambivalence."[5] I'm no venerable scholar, but it sounds like there may have been some pretty serious shortcomings in the Gore campaign. The written history matches the lived experience of 2000, a campaign in which a robotic Gore did little but argue that he would be the better manager of what was essentially a mutually understood agenda. He told voters he would better administer the legacy of Clintonian prosperity without actually talking about or claiming credit for the prosperity.*

---

* "In an apparent effort to distance himself from [Clinton] . . . Gore appeared to run from rather than on the administration's economic record." in Holbrook, T., "Forecasting with

Yes, the Supreme Court could have decided differently. Florida elected officials could have been something other than hysterical, blindly pro-Bush partisans. Nader voters could have all woken up on Election Day to realize they owe their vote to a candidate representing a faction dragging the Democratic Party rightward. Everyone could have recognized what was right in front of them, that Bush was a store-brand Gerald Ford fronting a cabal of Nixon-era psychopaths. But it is ludicrous to ignore that Al Gore could have done a lot of things better and given people a reason to vote for him. It is telling—and unbelievable in hindsight—that a campaign that chose Joe Lieberman as the running mate has not prompted more soul searching and more consideration of its self-inflicted wounds. Maybe a powerful explanation for the debacle of 2000 was that Al Gore did almost everything badly. Instead, Democrats faced down the question of why they lost by blaming everyone except themselves.

9/11, IRAQ, AND ABB (ANYONE BUT BUSH)

Imagine a George W. Bush presidency without 9/11. Remember what the first nine months of his presidency were like, before 9/11? Of course you don't! Nobody does. He was a guy who barely squeaked into office and whose defenders—mind you, *his defenders*—argued that he was probably an idiot but would appoint competent people to run things. The terrorist attacks and subsequent (putatively but not actually related) wars in Iraq and Afghanistan gave the Bush presidency a sense of focus, purpose, and mission that it would not otherwise have found. It also played to his strengths (posturing, bombast, a third-rate John Wayne impression) and those of his administration (warmongering, profiting from warmongering). Even with the boost he received as a wartime president, Bush entered 2004 with uncertain prospects for reelection.

Democrats, who loathed Bush passionately and rightly considered him a nitwit, created their own uncertainty with an uninspiring field of candidates that included attempted Clinton impersonator John Edwards and alleged (but not actual) populist Howard Dean. Longtime senator John Kerry was essentially the default choice, a known name perceived

Mixed Economic Signals: A Cautionary Tale," *PS: Political Science and Politics* 34, no. 1 (2001): 40.

as steady, stately, and competent—the perfect anti-Bush. His military service would also project strength and gravitas, tapping into the post-9/11 emphasis on terrorism and reminding Americans that Democrats liked war too. Ultimately Kerry was shrugged into the nomination without passionate supporters.[6] He'd do. Besides, the election would be about "anyone but Bush."[7] Americans could see clearly that Bush was an idiot, a liar, a buffoon. All Democrats felt they needed to do was present a determined visage to contrast with Bush's impish smirk. Surely wisdom and steady leadership would win over dick-waving bravado and faith-based foreign policy. Not for the last time, Democrats bet big on a consummate establishment candidate and assumed that the Republican candidate being a moron would win the election for them.

Bush-era politics linger. A White House aide at the time coined the phrase "reality-based community" in an interview with Ron Suskind to denigrate liberals during the run-up to the Iraq War. Marvel at the sheer balls of the full quote:

> The aide said that guys like me were "in what we call the reality-based community," which he defined as people who "believe that solutions emerge from your judicious study of discernible reality. . . . That's not the way the world really works anymore," he continued. "We're an empire now, and when we act, we create our own reality. And while you're studying that reality—judiciously, as you will—we'll act again, creating other new realities, which you can study too, and that's how things will sort out. We're history's actors . . . and you, all of you, will be left to just study what we do."

Democrats, the label implies, place their faith in rules, facts, and projecting an image as the adults in the room. It was up to the voters, aided by a media that cherished those values, to recognize and appreciate those qualities. Bush's cadre created its own reality by repeating lies until they became recognized truth and acting without concern for the constraints that were supposed to limit their actions. Liberals wore the intended insult as a badge of honor, proudly proclaiming their allegiance to reality, truth, fair play, and following the rules. That position appealed strongly—and if this sounds familiar, it's because the exact same dynamic played out in 2016 and 2020—to the highly educated people for whom America's social and economic systems seemed to be working fine and for whom conforming to the demands of the meritocracy had panned out. But like Reagan, Bush found that the public reacted well to pro-America rhetoric that came without a side of scolding and caveats. Bushism was, in every sense, "America, fuck yeah!" elevated to a political worldview. Instead of trying to offer voters an alternative, Kerry and most Democrats endorsed the basics of Bushism and its global war on terror—the 2004 Democratic convention used the slogan "Strong at Home, Respected in the World"—but argued that they would do it better. To this day, Democrats have not resolved the contradiction of supporting institutions at the core of the reactionary worldview like the military and law enforcement while simultaneously attempting to be the party for people who are skeptical (or worse) of those institutions.

The core message the Kerry campaign sought to project at the 2004 Democratic convention was the candidate's record of military service.[8] "I'm John Kerry, and I'm reporting for duty" is about all anyone remembers from the otherwise bland convention.* The intent was straight from the New Democrat playbook: to neutralize GOP attacks on Democrats as soft on foreign policy. Of course, those attacks came anyway, irrespective of Kerry's veteran status. The counterproductive pattern played out: Democrats recognized that, of course, everyone knows we need to drop a lot of bombs, but we can't trust George W. Bush's judgment; Kerry's is sound. The military emphasis during the campaign repeatedly "lost [opportunities] to present a compelling reason to voters to cast their ballots for Kerry."[9] With no substantially different foreign policy and with broad agreement on core economic ideas continuing from the Clinton years, there simply was no fulcrum for pushing back against the post-9/11 Bush position.[10] Democrats were convinced that crucial, persuadable voters shared Republicans' promilitary, proaggression worldview and thus they could not attack it directly.

---

* The other moment of that convention was the debut on the national stage of a Senate candidate named Barack Obama.

Worse, the GOP refused to play by the tacit understanding that certain things like the service record of a war hero could not become fodder for attacks and conspiracy theories. At a historical moment of performative patriotism, the GOP nonetheless deftly undermined what was supposed to be Kerry's strength. Kerry's record of criticizing and questioning US military involvement in atrocities in Vietnam left a substantial portion of the usually proveteran, promilitary voting bloc feeling chilly toward him. When the GOP attacks came, amplified by the growing sophistication of right-wing media messaging, they unleashed an avalanche of hit pieces with sinister titles like "Unfit for Command." The "swiftboating" of Kerry was done largely through surrogates rather than by the Bush campaign, but it was clearly signaled to the rank and file that Kerry's war record was fair game. Memorably, 2004 Republican convention attendees wore Band-Aids with fake Purple Hearts to mock Kerry's medals.* The indignity didn't stop there, though. Kerry wasn't just stripped of the political benefits of military service; he was emasculated through rhetoric designed to depict him as "French and feminine."[11] Every benefit Democrats expected to accrue from Kerry's status as a veteran, a stern leader, and a serious person seemed to be parried effortlessly by the GOP. Everything Democrats believed would work failed to work.

No doubt it would have been difficult for a Democratic nominee to chart out a different course for the nation in 2004. It was an era of jingoism, of fear, of the Hummer H2, of "with us or with the terrorists." Yet with previously supportive Americans beginning to sour on the wars in Iraq and Afghanistan, Bush was hardly on firm ground. It turned out that Americans love the troops, kicking ass, bombing bad guys, and the kind of war that asks no sacrifices of the public and has no negative externalities. What they love less are wars that drag on after a promise of quick victory, are costly in terms of blood and money, and lack clear objectives. In a futile effort to preclude Republicans from calling them weaklings on terrorism, congressional Democrats overwhelmingly supported the Iraq

---

* Democrats were reduced to sputtering back that the GOP was "mocking our troops," even though it was clear the GOP had the votes of support-the-troops enthusiasts well in hand. See "Delegates Mock Kerry with 'Purple Heart' Bandages," CNN, September 1, 2004.

War and then tried to carve out middle positions later; "We took Bush at his word and he disappointed us" was not the definitive riposte they thought it was. Questioning—and opposing through actions as well as words—the fundamental premise of the wars appears not to have been seriously considered. Afraid of the old charges of mealy-mouthed cowardice, Democrats offered war on terror lite to the GOP's full-strength formula.

Alas, Mark Penn's beloved swing voters must have trusted Bush to kick more ass and blow up more things. "Security moms" terrified of terrorism are hard to discern in survey data, but Bush won by 11 percent among married women.[12] All the equivocating, the protroops folderol, and surrender to the surging nationalism of the era accomplished nothing. The strategy to beat the GOP by conceding that we needed to do a lot of war stuff, only better, failed. Bush not only won, but the GOP also increased its margins in the House, Senate, and in state capitals. The GOP emerged from that election "in its strongest position since Herbert Hoover was elected" in 1928.[13]

RAHM-ING DOWN THE DOOR

Like the hangover from 2016, the period after the 2004 election was a dark one for liberals. Recriminations and finger-pointing abounded. They had made what to them was a rock-solid case—George W. Bush is a lying, evil moron and John Kerry is a man with a great résumé and integrity—and Americans didn't respond. It is hard not to cringe looking back at the liberalism of the Bush era, to see what passed for a coordinated response to the protoauthoritarianism of a GOP that claimed to represent the only America that mattered. Satirical comedy became unusually central as a source of comfort, entertainment, catharsis, and truth to power for liberals,* as though if the ascendant right could be made to look sufficiently silly it would crumble. George Lakoff's *Don't Think of an Elephant!* (2004) was a sensation because it suggested that the problem wasn't Democrats' message or ideology but simply the words they used to describe these things. The still-nascent Internet produced liberal bloggers

---

* Go ahead, do a Google Scholar search for research and hot takes on the phenomenon of Stephen Colbert, Jon Stewart, and *The Daily Show* between 2002 and 2012.

offering fresher, cooler, less buttoned-down takes than the legacy media focused on aggressively hitting back at conservative outlets. The overwhelming emphasis was not on what Democrats wanted to do—that was negotiable, provided Democrats were in power—but on how outrageously *bad* Republicans are. The argument was simultaneously irrefutable and unpersuasive to American voters.

The reelection of Bush also introduced politically attentive Americans to a phenomenon that was already being noted in political science: the growth of partisan polarization. Polarization is the idea that the parties are becoming more internally consistent and thus more likely to oppose one another on a given issue. There is great complexity to this concept, its many causes and consequences being beyond us here.[14] In his retrospective on the 2004 elections, Gary Jacobson apparently used a crystal ball to write:

> In future contests for control of [Congress], a continuation of the current era of relatively high partisan loyalty and sharp partisan polarization would appear to serve congressional Republicans well. As long as voters in an evenly divided electorate stick to their parties, the Republicans' structural advantage will keep the party on top. Republican leaders, then, have little electoral incentive to accommodate congressional Democrats.[15]

Because Democrats had moved toward the center in response to the Gingrich revolution and made no moves to pull leftward in the post-Clinton era, polarization was almost entirely driven by Republicans veering hard to the right since Nixon.[16] It is no wonder that some Democrats (including prominent voices in the DLC's offshoot, the Progressive Policy Institute) believed that the answer lay—you won't believe this—in the tremendous political potential of occupying the ideological center.

That narrative fueled the Democrats' approach to the 2006 midterms led by archetypical opportunistic centrist Rahm Emanuel, an Illinois representative heading the Democratic Congressional Campaign Committee (DCCC). The role of groups like the DCCC and its Senate counterpart can be overstated; after all, candidates in every House and Senate race run their own campaigns independently. Yet the DCCC and other national party organs are influential as kingmakers, tipping the balance in primaries by directing money, resources, and attention toward favored candidates. Emanuel, who would later serve as Obama's White House chief of staff, firmly believed the center was the place to be. His commitment to neoliberal economic ideas, in fact, stood out even among business-friendly New Democrats.[17] His midterm strategy was straightforward: run conservative Democrats in all but Democratic strongholds and shower them with money. Liberals couldn't win in those areas, and with the Democrats needing only seventeen more seats to end the Republican majority, flipping the chamber was tantalizingly close. Taking risks made no sense to Emanuel. That it would be next to impossible for a majority built on conservatives to fulfill Democratic campaign promises once in power was fine with him. The preference for conservative candidates was not a distasteful bit of pragmatism for Emanuel but an ideological "remaking [of] the Democratic Party in his own image."[18]

The crucial backdrop to the 2006 midterms, though, was the plummeting stock of George W. Bush. On Election Day in 2004, Bush clung to an approval rating of barely 50 percent. Throughout 2006, it rarely exceeded 40 percent and sunk as low as 31 percent. What changed? Two key factors were Iraq's descent into a violent quagmire without an end in sight and the president's bumbling, inept reaction to Hurricane Katrina. While his swaggering response to 9/11 made his presidency, he was all thumbs in 2005.[19] His approval never recovered and fell even further by the time he left office.

After twelve years in power in Congress, the GOP had not only grown stale but had overextended its majority in an unprecedentedly strong 2002 midterm and on the tails of Bush's win in 2004.* The Bush presidency had certainly lost its charms by 2006, and the strutting leadership of Newt Gingrich in the House was a distant memory, replaced by the bland visage of GOP Speaker Dennis Hastert (soon to be outed as a pedophile). House Republicans were weathering the Jack Abramoff lobbying scandal, the indictment of Majority Leader Tom DeLay, the sex scandal involving Rep. Mark Foley, and the sentencing of Rep. Randy Cunningham to

---

* Historically, the president's party loses seats in the first term midterm; 2002 and the post-9/11 environment allowed Republicans to avoid this.

prison in a corruption case. Democratic messaging focused on the powerful feculent odor wafting off the congressional GOP and on Iraq, about which, thanks to public discontent with the war by 2006, they weren't obligated to detail an alternate strategy. Anticorruption measures and a minimum wage increase—an important piece of economic populism they actually followed through with—rounded out the message. Democrats saw their first big collective win since the disaster of 1994: five Senate pickups, six governorships, and thirty-one House seats. Not the stuff of legends and folk songs, but a good year.

As if to highlight their tendency to pinball wildly between catastrophic depression and exuberant triumphalism, the post-2006 narrative declared the Democrats "Back, Baby!" Sure they had floundered a bit after 1994, but now they had found their way. Fawning postelection pieces with titles like "The House That Rahm Built" heaped credit upon Emanuel, who touted his own centrist vision as the driver of victory: "Democrats across the country owe a big chunk of their new electoral success to a nine-fingered,* ballet-dancing inspiration for a *West Wing* character with a reputation as a jerk."[20] This conveniently ignored the role of the GOP's self-immolation, the catastrophe in Iraq (which Democrats had abetted on multiple votes in Congress), Bush's dismal performance during Hurricane Katrina, and the old Democrat issue of low wages. Instead, Emanuel and liberal analysts declared the key to victory was phenomena like "pro-gun, anti-abortion, fiscally conservative" Democratic candidates.[21] *What?*

Here Emanuel made the mistake of concluding that because those were the candidates he personally selected, candidates of different ideological stripes could not have won. By insisting on centrists (although progun, antiabortion, and fiscally conservative sure sounds like the right, not the center!) what Emanuel's brilliant strategy did was ensure that when Democrats retook the White House, Congress would have a sizeable contingent of class of 2006 representatives who wouldn't support an agenda they defined as too liberal. The limits this would impose in 2009 were not counterbalanced by long-term electoral benefits; fourteen members of the Democrats' thirty-one-person freshman House class were

---

* In high school he cut one off—I kid you not—on an Arby's meat slicer.

gone by the end of 2010. Twelve remain as of 2021, most in safely blue seats in places like Vermont, New York, and New Jersey, where more liberal candidates would be electable.

Interpreting election outcomes is a form of soothsaying; poll data helps (and told us Iraq was the most important issue in 2006), but the oracle never speaks as clearly as we might wish. In postelection interviews, however, Emanuel just seems confused. When notoriously brutal questioner Meredith Vieira (of cheerful morning show *The View* fame) asked him how Democrats planned to take Iraq in "a new direction"—a softball question offering Emanuel an opportunity to rattle off a loosely defined contrasting vision—he said they were waiting for something called "the Baker-Hamilton Report" (ordinary voters *love* Blue Ribbon panels of DC insiders!) before reminding her that Democrats agreed with Bush on the fundamentals: "[Bush] has Democrats who are eager to work with him because we think Iraq is the single greatest national security challenge in over two generations. And we know this can't be solved by trying to politicize this." Perhaps such wisdom as "we shouldn't politicize politics" is the reason Emanuel was touted, likely via inside sources like Rahm Emanuel, as being "in line for a big promotion."[22]

There was a contradiction in the Democrats' attempt to please everyone with their Iraq messaging, one that would reappear under Trump. On the one hand, the president, Bush or Trump, was a duplicitous, evil figurehead of all that was wrong with American politics, but on the other, they were happy to reach out and work with him. If the Republican president is a deceitful, brainless monster, why would Democrats be happy to work with him? Are they admitting that they share some of the monster's goals or are willing to help it do monster stuff? That's kind of weird! Emanuel hid behind the inability of Congress to do anything without the president being on board, which simply is not true given Congress's grip on the checkbook that funds military adventures. A policy of "he's terrible, just terrible, and we want to work with him to advance some of his agenda" might appeal to consensus-seeking elites who want the status quo to roll forward unimpeded while everybody gets along, but it's decidedly strange messaging if, for example, voters explicitly unhappy with the Iraq War pushed one's party into the majority.

So the good news was that the Democrats won in 2006. The bad news is that none of the most powerful or visible figures in the party on the national stage elucidated a plan for doing something differently in Iraq. This left them unable to capitalize in the long term on the antiwar sentiment that had arisen five years into what would become a decade-long conflict. Nobody made a compelling argument that the Democratic Party had distinctly different ideas or what those ideas were; an important exception was the New Deal throwback of increasing the minimum wage, which Democrats did over GOP opposition. It was the first ominous sign of what was to come under Obama.

CHAPTER 10

OBAMA COMETH

I n 2008, Barack Obama won Indiana.

Indiana. The Mississippi of the North. That potpourri of empty rural and decaying urban landscapes. Its big city approximates the experience of being in a coma without the associated medical costs. It produced Mike Pence and Dan Quayle. It was run by the Klan until almost 1930. That Indiana.

I lived in Indiana when it happened, and any suspense over the outcome that night was ruined when the nation's earliest election results—from rural Indiana*—showed Obama neck and neck with opponent John McCain. When the Democrat is splitting the vote in rural Indiana, it is going to be a very bad night for Republicans.

By historical standards, Obama won by a pedestrian margin but by a landslide in the context of modern elections. To win a red state like Indiana, Obama must have really tapped into something with his campaign.

Obama ran in 2008 as the candidate of soaring optimism, the man who would change an economic order that so inarguably had failed

---

* Back when nearly all voting was done at polling places on Election Day, states with the earliest poll closing times reported results first. Generally, rural counties with the fewest ballots to count reported first within those states. Hence, rural Indiana, which closed at 6 p.m. EST in 2008, returned the first official election results in the country.

working people. You remember it. Hope. Change. Yes We Can. He not only won; he got people fired up. A new generation of voters practically worshipped him. Many people who had wandered away from the Democratic Party—some white Rust Belt Indianans, for example—returned to the fold in 2008. In the moment, it looked like nothing less than a miracle, like Barack Obama was (or embodied) the solution to the Democrats' post–New Deal dilemma.

Yet his presidency was defined not by lofty ambition but by its commitment to the status quo and a belief that a nation weary from the long George W. Bush experience would find normalcy revolutionary. It was defined less by what it was than by what it was not, not by what it did but by what it consciously chose not to do. People saw what they wanted to see of Obama during his transcendent campaign; progressives thought he was progressive, moderates thought he was moderate. What he was, though, was a masterful electoral politician and rhetorician who always found the right words—and then let his devotion to consensus, bipartisan cooperation, and the rightness of the most idealistic version of the liberal worldview doom any hope for major change. He wasn't a progressive change agent occasionally mouthing banal platitudes to appease the center; the platitudes were his true preferences, and the hopeful rhetoric was for show. Barack Obama was the man who had an opportunity—not a guarantee of course, but a chance—to be FDR and instead set out to be a less horny Bill Clinton. No matter what Republicans did to try to destroy him and undermine his legitimacy as an elected official and even as an American, Obama persisted in believing that the GOP's lurch to the right was merely a fever that inevitably would break as Republicans returned to their senses.* It was a disastrous miscalculation.

So what happened in his first two years that the result in 2010—what he called a Republican "shellacking"—was so different from 2008? The answer was simple: Obama and his Democratic congressional majority acted. In that sense, liberals saw great success. He got some things done! The problem was, what he got done alienated many of his more hopeful

---

* This metaphor is made explicit in quotes in Tau, B., "Obama: Republican 'Fever' Will Break After Election," Politico, June 1, 2012.

supporters and represented a serious miscalculation of what had attracted them in the first place. As Ezra Klein would say in an autopsy written in 2011, while unemployment was in many areas stuck in double digits, "the promised recovery was always just around the corner, but it never quite came. Eventually, the American people stopped listening."[1] Somehow, a Democratic president failed to internalize "it's the economy, stupid!" and to recognize how badly many voters wanted a president to take their side against an economic order that ruined their lives and left them feeling powerless to fight back.

Just two weeks after he was elected, the tone for Barack Obama's presidency was set when Senate Democrats followed the encouragement of the president-elect (and Majority Leader Harry Reid) by allowing Joe Lieberman to keep his chairmanship of the Homeland Security and Government Reform committees. Lieberman, who shared the 2000 Democratic ticket with Al Gore but later switched his affiliation to independent, actively campaigned for John McCain, spoke at the Republican National Convention (where, I shit you not, he criticized Obama sharply for failure to reach across the aisle to work with Republicans), and did all in his mediocre power to see that Obama lost. Harry Reid commented, "I would defy anyone to be more angry than I was [over Lieberman's actions]. But I also believe that if you look at the problems we face as a nation, is this a time we walk out of here saying, 'Boy, did we get even'?"[2] That Reid could not conceive of any reason to withhold rewards from Lieberman beyond playground-style "getting even" speaks in hindsight to how spectacularly the Democrats of that period misunderstood the basic point of politics. By establishing that Lieberman would pay no price for working overtime to see Obama defeated, every member of Congress was incentivized to defy the president and hold out for endless concessions, just as House Democrats had done to Bill Clinton in 1993 and 1994.

The overwhelming underwhelmingness of Obama's eight years looks worse today at a considerably direr political moment. He spoke in the grandiose language of transformation and rebirth, of peaceful revolution even, but governed as a technocrat with no inclination to inconvenience the powerful. He was less interested in remaking institutions than in remaking the soul of the political process, a noble but utterly misguided goal. He represented a liberalism happy to sacrifice the contents of policy to creating policy *the right way*. Obama's White House was staffed with exactly the kind of young, idealistic liberals who believed unironically that *The West Wing* was a template for how real-life politics and governing worked (or could work.)* The Democrats' increasingly well-off, professional liberal base was starry eyed in love with this and with Obama; the rest of the electorate either hated Obama (and would never be convinced to do otherwise) or just wanted health care and under 10 percent unemployment rates and could care less about bipartisanship.

That is Obama's legacy. He refused to see his mandate as that of a change agent, of our last real chance to attack the festering problems that Reaganomics, neoliberalism, and neoconservativism had inflicted upon the country, culminating in the Great Recession of 2008 and 2009.[3] Now all the same problems have metastasized, and we find ourselves on the verge of democratic backsliding without any meaningful attempt being made to prevent it. It might not have worked had Obama gone bigger, pushed harder, and tried to be the transformative leader the system and the country so badly needed in 2009. He might have gone down in flames. But he should have tried. His philosophy of "radical incrementalism" is summed up by one of his favorite analogies: "Sometimes the task of government is to make incremental improvements or try to steer the ocean liner two degrees north or south so that, ten years from now, suddenly we're in a very different place than we were."[4]

Here we are ten years later. Certainly in a very different place.

---

*In a mass review of Obama alum memoirs, Corey Robin noted that all but one explicitly mentioned the show and the Obama White House's collective fondness for it. Obama alum Gautam Raghavan not only entitled his recollections *West Wingers: Stories from the Dream Chasers, Change Makers, and Hope Creators Inside the Obama White House,* but he noted, "Working in Barack Obama's White House was like watching Aaron Sorkin's *The West Wing* brought to life. It had all the necessary elements: the brilliant, articulate professor in chief with an unapologetically progressive vision of America; a narrative arc rooted in ongoing themes of idealism and public service; but most importantly, a cast of patriotic Americans who labored every day, as members of the President's staff, to serve the country they loved." Unfortunately, the GOP missed the memo and did not behave as Sorkin Republicans always do, left speechless and defeated when liberals hit them with the truth in the climactic scene.

NUDGE NOT LEST YE BE NUDGED

In 2011, with little fanfare and even less mourning, the Democratic Leadership Council disbanded. It was both a victim of its success—Bill Clinton had so completely redefined the party in the postideological, moderate image the DLC championed that the organization became superfluous—and a reflection of the changing tenor of aughts liberalism. Al From made two fatally poor choices when preparing for the DLC's post-Clinton era. First, he hitched his wagon to Joe Lieberman (DLC chair, 1995–2001) in the belief that the Connecticut senator's brand of condescending, sanctimonious conservatism represented the future of liberalism. Then the DLC, like Lieberman, went all in supporting the Iraq War. By the time Obama took office, it was painfully obvious that the DLC had misread the pulse of Democratic activists in the George W. Bush era. The group's credibility was shot, even in the elite circles where its strength once lay. It was by Obama's election an anachronism, a factoid for VH1's *I Love the '90s* and nothing more.

Yet Obama, who explicitly refused any affiliation with the DLC (going so far as to request removal from a DLC list of promising young politicos), proved to be sympathetic to its worldview. For all the differences in rhetoric and presentation, Obama was as devoted to Clintonian neoliberalism as any avowed centrist. The DLC was gone, but the Democrats continued to center the same kind of voter who was central to the New Democrat worldview. The grand theory of progressive liberalism that Obama championed proved, in practice, little different from Clintonian triangulation. In the wake of the disastrous 2010 midterms, Obama was already inviting "triangulation 2.0" comparisons.[5] Mark Penn asked rhetorically: "In 1994, [Clinton] navigated his way out of danger by working with Republicans while simultaneously holding his base. Can President Obama master the same lessons?"[6] The second time around, the GOP wasn't remotely interested in "working with" Obama even on Republican priorities, while the base had grown restive, emerging from fifteen years of seeing liberal priorities not only disregarded but actively rejected by Democratic leaders who seemed positively obsessed with getting Republican buy-in rather than pushing their own agenda.

Liberal commentators Franklin Foer and Noam Scheiber wrote early in the Obama presidency of the administration's grand theory for bridging the gap between progressive goals and New Democrat–style neoliberalism.[7] Obama and his inner circle were enthralled by behavioral theories popularized in the bestselling *Nudge* (2008) by Cass Sunstein and Richard Thaler, a classic text of the era in which things like TED Talks and *Freakonomics* had great cultural currency. New Deal interventions in the economy and government-oriented solutions were not the answer, the authors argued, but by 2008 fatal flaws had been recognized in the New Democrat faith in markets to solve problems if government simply got out of its way. Instead, Obama grew to believe that government could best solve problems by incentivizing individual actors to change their behavior. More invasive than the invisible hand of the market but less stultifying than bureaucracy, these gentle nudges would encourage relevant economic actors to do the right thing. This approach, Foer and Scheiber admit, "makes enormous political sense" but "also represents a huge gamble" due to the unprecedented scope on which Obama intended to apply this principle and "heroic assumptions about how people respond to new incentives."[8]

The ideology espoused by New Democrats had, by 2008, run into two serious problems that Obama's near-messianic campaign proposed to resolve. One was the direct, causal link between the 1990s deregulation spree and the financial crisis that emerged in 2008. Deregulation, once the New Democrats' most prized all-purpose solution, had failed catastrophically. The second was the irrefutable evidence that the New Democrat theory of economic growth as panacea—making the pie bigger instead of squabbling over who got which slice—precipitated an explosion in income inequality. The rich and successful, if you can believe it, were treating themselves to all the rewards of economic growth rather than sharing it with labor. Clinton's economic nostrums were in practice little different from Reaganite trickle-down economics, and predictably, nothing trickled.

The joys of hindsight make clear what, amazingly, was not obvious contemporaneously: that Obama's embrace of nudge theories was the intellectual justification for refusing to tackle the problems exposed by the Great Recession directly. While bolder observers proposed nation-alizing failing banks and purging them of toxic assets before returning them to private ownership, "the prospect of something so heavy-handed offends the administration's sensibilities. Instead, Treasury has chosen to partner with hedge funds and private equity firms to relieve the banks of their toxic assets." Instead of giving distressed homeowners money to stay afloat while going through a process to renegotiate better mortgage loan terms, Obama's Home Affordable Modification Program (HAMP) gave the money *to lenders* to "encourage" them to modify bad loans. It comes as no surprise that some voters who expected "change" felt cheated.

Foer and Scheiber obviously saw in real time what is insane about this approach, the maintenance of loathsome actors with miserable track rec-ords in positions of great economic and political power but with some gentle encouragement to elicit better behavior from them. After recount-ing the myriad failures of the banking and insurance industries, the authors allow that "in light of these industries' track records, Obama's solicitousness might seem puzzling." Indeed. But fear not: "Except that it may well work."

That's it. That's the crux of an argument of how best to respond to a global financial collapse directly caused by deregulation and the run-ning amok of rapacious plutocrats at the highest levels of the economy: give them a lecture and another chance and maybe this time they will do better. Asking them nicely and laying out some incentives to stop do-ing robber baron stuff might work. What neither Obama nor his circle appear to have asked is, What happens if it doesn't work? Because from the vantage point of 2009, at the depths of a recession and with sky-rocketing income inequality contributing to growing rage and alienation among working-class voters, Obama and the Democratic Party would be *enormously* fucked, hypothetically, if this approach failed and voters interpreted it as Democrats choosing to coddle elite bad actors instead of pursuing an economic recovery that benefited ordinary Americans.

Since the costs and consequences of the Great Recession were borne by the working class, the benefits of any recovery needed to accrue to the same. The political moment for which Democrats seemed to be waiting for decades was at hand: an opportunity to reassert themselves as the one and only party of the social safety net, the robust welfare state, the equitable and rising standard of living, and defending the powerless against the powerful. Instead, they considered that option and decided that there was little wrong with the status quo that old-fashioned compromise couldn't fix.

This was the legacy of New Democrat thinking under Obama. Not only did a Democratic Congress balk at change, but its conclusion that government or regulatory solutions "offend[ed] the administration's sensibilities" reflects the successful internalization of Clinton's boast about the demise of big government, of unconditional surrender to conservatives' antigovernment message. Using such a light hand to regulate gargantuan economic bad actors is a recipe for failure on par with using an ordinary dog leash to restrain a fully grown lion. It is a strategy so obviously bound to fail that a cynic, and not even an especially cynical cynic, might wonder whether you ever intended to restrain the lion in the first place.

Conveniently, of course, nudge-ism absolved Obama and congressional Democrats of having to do anything hard.* Certainly implementing big government solutions would have exacted a high political cost. The right would have been apoplectic, and a generation of Democrats running away from the New Deal would have needed regular pep talks to steady their nerves. Electoral consequences in the short term might follow, with benefits becoming apparent only over time. But the right was apoplectic anyway, the electoral consequences came anyway, the high political costs were extracted anyway. Americans saw an administration that seemed more worried about upsetting economic elites than about upsetting regular people because that is exactly what was happening. The theoretical approach was tweaked, but fundamentally it was New Democrat redux: Fix the economy from the top down, not the bottom up. Government isn't the answer. Rely on the economically powerful to do the right things. Pander to moderates. Bipartisan solutions are more

---

* As Foer and Scheiber admit, "Sure, the Obama program makes some big assumptions. Yes, there may be more direct routes to universal health care or a solvent banking system. On the other hand, it's easy to underestimate the challenges of the more statist alternatives." Oh no, not challenges!

important than effective solutions. When in doubt, satisfy the elites and use messaging to spin it to voters as a victory.

That is the crux of why Obama failed, as alluring as it is to choose from the smorgasbord of villains available to heap with blame: the GOP, racist voters, Blue Dog Democrats, the media, George W. Bush, and so on. Obama's failures were his own because he bought into the same deluded beliefs that undermined Bill Clinton—that he could have it both ways, that he could please moderates and conservatives by avoiding big government solutions while also satisfying liberals and progressives by addressing problems they prioritized. As ever, trying to please everyone pleased no one; when interests inevitably conflicted, the right got deeds and the left got words. What began with even stolid middlebrow opinion, like *Newsweek* declaring early in 2009 that "we are all socialists now," ended up looking little different than the openly conservative approach of the previous Democratic president.[9] As a typically tactful academic analysis of Obama's approach noted in 2010: "Certain Democratic policy choices appear to perpetuate rather than break with those of the recent past."[10] To fail to see the connection between this approach and voter disillusionment with a candidate who promised change requires willful ignorance, which abounds among Obama loyalists desperate not to reckon with what his presidency was: a historical pivot point where, confronted with two paths to choose from, he took the one that enabled him to avoid confronting the rigged economy head-on.

The question naturally follows why Barack Obama remains so popular. Even more so than Bill Clinton, infatuation with Obama depended on whether voters embraced him as a solution to problems or as a talisman of an elite liberal understanding of how the world should work. If outcomes are irrelevant or if political compromises (or flat-out failures) end up benefiting the better-off and hurting invisible poor and working-class people, it is nearly impossible to find fault with Obama's presidency. His cosmopolitanism, intellect, personality, professional and educational credentials, poignant life story, beautiful family, and easy projection of all the right liberal values made him irresistible. His political worldview, which placed ultimate faith to solve problems in others like himself, all but guaranteed that he could not fail in HEP eyes, and his high-minded progressive rhetoric, distilled to yet another round of antiredistribution, incremental, neoliberal, winners-and-losers outcomes, did nothing to hurt his standing among the winners.

The people Michael Lind classifies as the managerial elite saw in Obama everything they ever wanted,[11] and they struggled mightily to understand what became of those big crowds of riffraff who gushed with enthusiasm for Obama back in 2008. A 2011 headline of unintentional hilarity accentuated the growing divide between elite and mass support: "Obama Reps Woo Liberal Elite at Aspen Ideas Festival but Face Angry, Disappointed Supporters."[12] For some, it was enough simply for Obama to exist, to be in power, and to be one of them. For the small matter of supporters—the amorphous mass of little people not invited to Aspen or Davos—the lack of results built discontent. This remains incomprehensible to many liberals. Look at how much worse the GOP is! Look at what Obama did and stop complaining about what he didn't do! Would you rather have Trump? All these sentiments, common as they are, presume one is insulated from Obama's failures; they are, at most, conceptual failures (or, more commonly, victories you people aren't smart enough to recognize). For the people who experienced them directly—the Rust Belt denizens who saw bad places get even worse, for underwater homeowners who saw banks get paid and evict them anyway—the Obama years look much different. Everyone at the Aspen Ideas Festival, after all, goes home to the same upper-class lifestyle irrespective of the outcomes of the eternal political battles in Washington, and the consequences of the trends gaining currency among thought leaders fall elsewhere.

PRAGMATISM: THE GOD THAT SUCKED*

In the fall of 2015, Barack Obama visited Alaska during a late-presidency push to draw attention to climate change and solidify support for the Paris Climate Agreement, which ranked high on his list of second-term achievements (Trump would unilaterally withdraw the United States from the agreement in 2017).† He was in peak form during his public

---

* This phrase first appeared in Frank, T., "The God That Sucked," *Baffler*, April 2001.
† Trump announced the withdrawal on August 4, 2017, but for fine-print reasons, the official US withdrawal did not occur until 2020.

appearances, radiating a sense of purpose that most presidencies have lost by year seven. Warning of "condemn[ing] our children to a planet beyond their capacity to repair," he hectored oil-dependent Alaskans: "We're not acting fast enough." Climate change was urgent, not "some far-off problem."[13]

Environmental journalist Jeff Goodell found Obama even more strident in private during the trip. The president sought to make climate change "visceral" for Americans and impress upon them the urgency of taking action.[14] Yet Obama the pragmatist was never far away. What Obama described and clearly recognized as an existential crisis (mass extinctions "have happened before; they can happen again") was beyond his power to do more about than he was already doing. When Goodell pressed him on the gap between his urgent words and his incremental actions, he replied, "If I howl at the moon without [building] a political consensus behind me, nothing's going to get done."[15] Americans, even putting aside the prevalence of climate skepticism, simply didn't think the issue was very important: "[Despite] the office [of the presidency], you don't do things alone. I continually go back to the notion that the American people have to feel the same urgency that I do."[16]

It's a telling interview, a case study in Obama's progressive worldview colliding with a generation of moderate Democrats' deeply internalized, self-limiting understanding of power. Climate change is simultaneously an immediate crisis that threatens the habitability of the planet *and* something that must be addressed incrementally because that's all the political process will tolerate. That the damage might be irreparable by the time political elites are willing to start taking solutions seriously does not appear to faze Obama. This is it; this is the best we can do. Our only hope is to nudge and wait until individuals solve the problem on their own. If it never gets solved, it will be your fault. You should have switched to metal straws sooner.

Obama offered the clearest examples of the tendency of Democratic leaders to talk about problems as if they are powerless to do something about them. Follow Nancy Pelosi or Chuck Schumer on social media, for example, and you'll regularly see statements that speak to the urgent need to *do something* that would be understandable from, say, some random powerless individual. But such statements are bizarre bordering on deluded coming from the highest-ranking Democrats in the House and Senate. This messaging has the profoundly alienating tendency to redirect responsibility away from elected officials and back toward ordinary people who may have worked very hard to elect those officials with the reasonable expectation that they would address important issues. "Can't you people do something about this? My hands are tied!" is a bad attitude in the best case but outright poisonous when the obvious answers are, no, *we* cannot fix this, and no, *your hands* are not, in any sense, tied.

MSNBC host Chris Hayes noted in a preinauguration musing on Obama's ideological underpinnings that "if 'pragmatic' is the highest praise one can offer in DC these days, 'ideological' is perhaps the sharpest slur."[17] Hayes, unusually astute among cable news pundits, warned of the flaws inherent in pragmatic approaches to political questions that in reality require principled stands to produce useful solutions. Pragmatism inherently respects the limitations imposed by the existing hierarchy of power, institutions, and rules; any solutions that emerge from it will perpetuate the same power relationships. The fatal flaw of pragmatism as a guiding approach to politics and governing* is that it requires, if it is to work as proponents intend, a dispassionate, accurate, and unbiased determination of the possible. If I become convinced that it is impossible for me to finish this sentence, the pragmatic thing to do is to stop trying and use my time more productively doing something else. But the only limitation on my ability to finish the sentence is in my head (that the sentence has been finished proves I was wrong). The Democratic Party in the post–New Deal era has been nothing less than obsessed with the idea of defining the limits of its own scope of action and making a virtue out of a defeatist belief that better things are not possible because pursuing them would undermine the Democratic Party's ability to decline to do better things in the future. The party faction that pitches itself as the technocrats who know how to get things done gets elected and then spends a disturbing amount of time explaining why it can't do anything.

---

* Note here and throughout that the philosophical tradition of pragmatism is separate from (and only tangentially related to) the common use of the term *pragmatism* in politics.

But Obama's appeals to pragmatism as the only way forward were hardly novel. Jimmy Carter's disastrous neoliberal turn is lauded as "evidence-based pragmatism" by biographer Daniel Sargent, a sharp contrast with the "nostalgic" and "quixotic" Ted Kennedy.[18] Walter Mondale's historically bad 1984 campaign was noted for its "cautious, pragmatic approach."[19] Michael Dukakis rose to the 1988 nomination after using his second term as governor of Massachusetts to prove that he could reject liberalism in favor of "caution and pragmatism."[20] In 1992, Jesse Jackson's decision not to run against Bill Clinton (himself an uber-pragmatist) led prominent Black Democrats to adopt a "new pragmatism" in throwing their weight behind a candidate who seemed unusually eager to take cracks at people of color to win the approval of recalcitrant white voters.[21] Clinton's 1996 welfare reform, per Hillary Clinton's memoir, was necessitated by "pragmatic politics. . . . If he vetoed welfare reform a third time, Bill would be handing the Republicans a potential political windfall."[22] (Thanks for taking one for the team, poor people!) And Al Gore's 2000 campaign revealed a "pragmatic politician" (but also, forebodingly, a "panicky panderer" who lacked conviction) who co-stewarded eight years of economic prosperity.[23] Barack Obama in 2008 was the Democrat who could finally "synthesize idealism with pragmatism" and won the highest plaudit in the pantheon of liberalism from Democratic Senate leader Tom Daschle: "Those who accomplish the most are those who don't make the perfect the enemy of the good. Barack is a pragmatist." Cass Sunstein (of the aforementioned nudging, later an official in Obama's Office of Management and Budget) stressed: "Above all, Obama's form of pragmatism is heavily empirical; he wants to know what will work."[24]

But wait; there's more. The Sanders-Clinton nomination contest of 2016 opened a new gulf in the Democratic camp with the pragmatists on one side and starry-eyed, unserious people in opposition. Clinton's task in 2016 was "peddling pragmatism," and her ascent to the nomination was a victory for "pragmatism over flair."[25] After the cataclysm of Trump's victory, Democrats needed to find a "pragmatic progressivism" to return to power, identifying a just-right combination of the visionary and the realistic.[26] Democrats retook the House in 2018 not because Trump had governed for two years like a combination of Ceauşescu and Yosemite Sam but because they were "willing to check progressive purity at the door in favor of progressive pragmatism."[27] And was Joe Biden a pragmatic choice in 2020? You bet your ass he was! He understood nothing less than "the arc of history" as "[coming] down to pragmatism" in his frank assessment of "the art of the possible" during his presidency.[28] As events stand as of this writing, the art of the possible has not included following through on a number of campaign promises the executive branch could address unilaterally, like relieving student loan debt.

I could cite examples until you fling the book in frustration: every policy, every defeat, every retreat, every political battle invoking pragmatism as a guiding principle at some point. It suffices to say that pragmatism has been something of an obsession among Democrats since their coalition began crumbling in the 1960s. This is in stark contrast to Republicans, whose path to power involved focusing ever more intensely on ideological language and goals to be achieved by whatever means necessary. (When was the last time you heard Mitch McConnell ask if something is "realistic" or a GOP presidential contender polling above 3 percent described as "pragmatic"?) What is the Democratic love affair, which bloomed so elaborately under Obama, with pragmatism? Who are the voters that demand it? And most crucially, what has all this pragmatism accomplished?

Pragmatism's starring role in the Democratic worldview stems from its ability to justify whatever course of action (or inaction) political actors choose to take in the eyes of people with little stake in outcomes. Like its cousin "electability," pragmatism is the art of what is possible, and what is possible happens to be whatever Democrats in positions of power want to do. Joe Lieberman (a legendary "pragmatic centrist in debt to JFK" as the title of an embarrassing 2003 *Washington Post* piece put it[29]) refused to allow a public option in the Affordable Care Act on grounds of pragmatism—certainly not because Joe Lieberman himself did not want it in there or that he had spent his entire career as a lickspittle for the medical insurance industry. No, it had to be removed because with it the ACA would lose votes. It would lose, more specifically, Joe Lieberman's vote. Isn't pragmatism great? The shape of the ACA was also dictated heavily by pragmatic concerns about its effects on the

2010 midterms. Strangely, every sacrifice to that end made the policy worse without compensating electoral benefits.

Over and over we went through wash cycles of Obama the progressive becoming Obama the pragmatist, the man who had to make compromise after compromise because reality simply left no alternative. The economic stimulus his White House pushed through Congress in 2009 had to be insufficiently large for practical reasons—not because Obama filled his team of advisers with well-known neoliberal ghouls like Timothy Geithner, Larry Summers, and Rahm Emanuel (who insisted, based on research pulled from his own ass, that the stimulus could not exceed $1 trillion because reasons). He had to bow to reality and keep Guantanamo Bay open and troops in Iraq and Afghanistan not because he wanted to—heavens, no!—but because political reality so dictated. His signature health-care plan had to go through dozens of rounds of reworking, never to make it better but to take out something else in the fruitless quest to appease Republican faux moderates and Blue Dog Democrats. Like his fervent wish that something could be done about climate change if only it were possible, this powerlessness afflicted many issues during his presidency. *I want to do something, but you must understand that I can't.*

If that doesn't sound much like a winning message for a political party, we may be getting somewhere toward understanding the electoral fortunes of Democrats in the past half century. The cult of pragmatism among Democratic elites and elected officials trying desperately to appeal to two very different constituencies, one oriented toward outcomes and prone to alienation and disengagement when those outcomes are disappointing, the other happy to settle for "we tried" and other symbolic stabs at progressive goals because they neither feel the effects of failure nor ideologically desire the party to be any more liberal than it presently is. After hearing it for decades, "I share your progressive goals, but you have to be realistic about what we can accomplish" starts to sound less like an intelligent assessment of the world and more like an elaborate justification. It begins to sound, in fact, like the people preaching pragmatism are trying to convince themselves more than they're trying to convince voters who are demonstrably sick of hearing that better things aren't possible.

AFFORDABLE PARED ACT

Postmortems abound on the policy choices of the Obama administration, blessedly obviating a need for an eight-year play-by-play rehashing here. Because it is so closely intertwined with Obama's legacy and was his signature legislation, though, a closer look at the Affordable Care Act (ACA) is warranted. Long after everything else from the Obama years is forgotten, Obamacare will persist—if not as policy then at least as a showcase for the flaws in Democrats' approach to legislating. I will not, as leftists are so often accused of doing, use a "magic wand" theory to claim Obama could have gotten single-payer health care had only he tried harder. Obama could have pushed for a better bill and told Americans why it was a great idea, though, and he may even have succeeded given his strong political position in 2009.*

Instead, they chose not to try in favor of an approach based on three fundamental miscalculations. One was their obliviousness to the ways the program could be undermined at the state level. Another was that crafting a sufficiently moderate policy could save Democratic congressional majorities in 2010 (it didn't). And the lingering problem is their failure to recognize that, far from being the kind of generational social welfare policy that people get fired up to defend à la Social Security, the ACA is *at its best* a stopgap solution that has gotten worse, not better, over time. It was sold to the Democratic base as a stepping-stone toward truly universal health care, yet that goal has receded into the distance as the right chips away at the ACA and satisfied liberals declare the problem they call "access to" health care solved.

The ACA was complex to the point of self-parody. Liberal policy wonks don't believe policy can be good unless it shows off their enormous cleverness, manifesting as convoluted amalgams of flowcharts, formulas, and ten-dollar words. It is one reason why simple ideas like "if people are poor, give them some money" are so often dismissed out of hand. Proponents of the ACA—*proponents*—beamingly described it as the most complex piece of legislation ever passed by Congress.[30] What an accomplishment! To ordinary voters, complexity produces policy that is neither

---

* Or maybe not. Hypotheticals are fun, but they will have to wait for my forthcoming speculative fiction *What if Things Were Actually Good Sometimes*.

understood nor trusted and gives political opponents an easy opening to muddy the waters with disinformation. What is hard to understand is easy to undermine. As with Hillarycare in 1994, a major challenge for the White House was simply explaining what the proposal was. Unlike the Clinton plan, Obama and congressional Democrats did successfully communicate the basic idea. The use of words like *exchanges* helped many Americans grasp that a website would let users shop insurance plans, and the cost of those plans would be subsidized by the government for some buyers.*

All the flowcharts and rules aside, that was the crux. The ACA would funnel both private and public money to for-profit health insurance companies—which Obama and Democrats felt was necessary to prevent industry opposition from sinking the legislation—and previously uninsured people would have access to a website where they could buy insurance. Crucially, the plan assumed states (who would administer these online exchanges) would automatically accept the offer to expand Medicaid eligibility to 138 percent of the federal poverty level.†

When in 2012 the Supreme Court ruled that states were not obligated to accept Medicaid expansion, Democrats still didn't panic. After all, Medicaid expansion meant the federal government would hand states a substantial amount of money. Nobody would turn down money! Many Republican-led states, however, turned out to be so willing.[31] To Obama's policy architects, this was inconceivable. Incentivizing budget-squeezed states with money *had* to work. But partisanship is a hell of a drug, as the White House should have foreseen. During the pre–civil rights era, the New Deal regularly incentivized states to accept federal money with the caveat that programs paid for with those funds must be race neutral. And Jim Crow states sometimes rejected the money or threatened to do so if they could not administer the programs

---

* The maze of rules and regulations cannot be summed up easily, so from the consumer's perspective, this is as succinctly as I can put it. Please do not contact me with things I left out.

† Medicaid expansion was a trade-off intended to make the ACA more palatable to the left in the absence of a public option.

with racial preference.* It was more important to them to maintain the racial hierarchy of segregation than to get money from Uncle Sam.

Without Medicaid expansion, large populations of people who cannot afford ACA insurance even with subsidies (or are not eligible to receive subsidies for one of a cornucopia of reasons) remain uncovered. No-expansion states have nearly twice as many uninsured adults as states with expansion.[32] Disproportionately, these uninsured are Black and Hispanic. Republicans don't seem too bothered by it. A Vox piece in 2021—Democrats are *still* trying to fix this—succinctly summarizes the problem: "Republican governors." The fanatical GOP reaction in 2009 when the bill was being debated should have been all the warning needed that Republicans would gladly shoot themselves in the foot to undermine the plan. It was all part of a total war strategy to deny any victories to Obama, a strategy it took the White House years to grasp.

Democrats contemporaneously justified the play-it-safe approach to the ACA, which avoided potential lightning rods like single payer, by arguing the electoral necessity of creating something moderate Democrats in Congress could support without enraging their constituents. As usual, congressional Democrats failed to approach their majority—an unusually large one by modern standards—as an opportunity to enact an agenda before inevitably returning to the minority. They convinced themselves that with the right moves they could save seats that they only held because 2006 and 2008 had been anti-Republican wave years.

Cynically, perhaps the leadership catered to moderates because nobody in the Democratic caucus really wanted to pass a bill more liberal than what moderates wanted. In that view, the Blue Dogs simply provided the cover influential Democrats needed to move the legislation to the right to reflect their own preferences. If not, then Democrats spectacularly misread the electoral tea leaves. We were assured in 2009 that pushing for

---

* FDR and the New Deal itself also exacerbated and perpetuated racial inequality by agreeing to various cutouts that exempted Blacks from many programs and benefits as a political expedient for southern support. FDR was hardly blameless on this point. For an elaboration on states, race, and New Deal policy, see Brown, M. K., "Race in the American Welfare State: The Ambiguities of 'Universalistic' Social Policy Since the New Deal," in ed. A. Reed, *Without Justice for All* (Boulder, CO: Westview Press, 1999), 93–122.

anything more liberal than what was on the table would result in Democrats losing their majorities in 2010. Then they lost the majority anyway. No matter how much progressivism was stripped from the ACA, the reaction from the right never changed pitch. For all the difference the efforts at appeasement made, the Democrats might as well have enacted fully automated luxury space communism.

Throughout the process, Democratic power players seemed almost comically eager to steer the bill to the right. In 2010, a special election was held in Massachusetts to replace deceased Senate fixture Ted Kennedy. When Republican Scott Brown defeated inept Democratic challenger Martha Coakley,* Washington Democrats became apoplectic. Evan Bayh, soon to leave Congress to become a lobbyist for the Chamber of Commerce, warned his party that it was a wake-up call. Anthony Weiner† declared that health-care reform might be dead. Virginia senator Jim Webb called it "a referendum not only on health-care reform but also on the openness and integrity of our government process." Even famously liberal Rep. Barney Frank of Massachusetts rushed to declare that *everything* had changed overnight.[33]

Golly. It's worth noting that after Brown's fluky win (he was soundly defeated in 2012), the Democratic Senate majority shrank to—fifty-nine. Oddly, the GOP manages to enact parts of its agenda with the slimmest of majorities in either chamber, but for Democrats, a supermajority is the bare minimum. The White House ended up having to lean on congressional Democrats with the argument that it would be disastrous to pass nothing after all the energy devoted to health care. The Senate version of the bill already passed (and awaiting House passage) was better than nothing. However milquetoast its critics believe the ACA is, Democrats almost talked themselves out of passing anything at all.

Say that the worrywarts were right in 2010, though, and that passage cost Democrats that year's midterms. Democrats today describe the ACA as their most significant policy achievement of the twenty-first century. Wasn't it worth it? In 2018, Republicans looked at the Trump tax cuts and their success in confirming federal judges as such

---

* Brown served only two years before losing in 2012 to Elizabeth Warren.
† LOL "wiener."

important accomplishments that their loss of the House majority led to little hand-wringing and certainly no grand reassessments of their fundamental ideology. Of course they'd rather have held the House. But the point of having the majority is to do something with it. They pursued their goals, accomplished some of them, and were confident that they would regain the majority before long.

The difference is that Democrats have the tendency to see holding power as the end, not a means to an end. They believe that voting just so on just the right bills will enable a permanent blue majority. This is patently silly, since gaining majorities depends on parties' success, often fluky, in winning the relatively small number of competitive seats or lucking into improbable wins due to unique circumstances.* In an election year where everything goes one's way, seats are won in unlikely places. Those seats, once the extraordinary circumstances that enabled winning are gone, will swing inevitably back to the other party.[34] Tailoring policy toward saving the electoral fortunes of members in tenuous districts is folly, but folly that Democrats heavy on strategy and light on concrete ideological goals engage in too often.

Now that the ACA is law,† liberals defend it vociferously, with a passion that derives from the conflation of the ACA with Barack Obama himself. Given the assurances to skeptics from the left, including Democratic progressives, that the ACA was an important but incremental step toward universal health care, the legislation is by definition an incomplete solution, a half measure. It has helped. More people are insured, and some provisions, like requiring insurers to cover people with preexisting

---

* For example, in 2012 Clare McCaskill (D-MO) and Joe Donnelly (D-IN) won Senate races they were initially favored to lose because their opponents (Todd Akin and Richard Mourdock, respectively) made comments about rape and abortion so horrific that even red state voters recoiled. Absent those unforced errors, Democrats winning Senate races in such states is improbable.

† We will skip here the disastrous rollout of the ACA, featuring a website that didn't work for the first month or so, but it was important to fueling opposition and public skepticism. See Scheuer, F., and K. Smetters, "Could a Website Really Have Doomed the Health Exchanges? Multiple Equilibria, Initial Conditions and the Construction of the Fine," National Bureau of Economic Research working paper series, Working Paper 19835, January 2014.

conditions, have been literal lifesavers.* But the progress that was supposed to follow has not materialized, creating an untenable situation in which voters who raise legitimate complaints about the cost, quality, and clunkiness of the system hear only how thankful they should be for it.

Polling shows slight majorities of the public have favorable views of the ACA, a figure that has changed little over time.[35] It is hardly an albatross for Democrats. But neither is it the milestone in human history that some liberal rhetoric has tried to make it. It's an expensive, confusing, complicated, modestly successful policy that incompletely addressed the underlying problem and left millions uninsured. Not every piece of policy can be monumental and revolutionary. Some of it can be just OK. But perspective is necessary. As the centerpiece of one's policy pitch to voters, as an example of what your party can do at its top-dollar best, the ACA has proven ineffective. It is neither the political poison Republicans claim nor the generational accomplishment Democrats wish it was.† One look at our still-broken (and eye-wateringly expensive) health-care system is proof that the ACA, whatever its merits, was not the solution.

OBAMA AND RACE

Ignoring race would make any reflection on Obama's presidency seriously deficient. Fortunately, the topic has been covered extensively by people who are more expert in this area, so this section relies heavily on the work of others, particularly that of Black scholars and commentators.‡

Viewed through the lens of race, the election of Barack Obama was a pivotal moment in American politics. Obama's approach in government to the politics of racial issues, though, *did not deviate significantly from*

---

* A clear pattern in public opinion data on the ACA is that rule changes such as allowing dependent children to be insured by a parent to age twenty-six or the ban on insurers denying coverage to individuals for preexisting conditions are generally popular, while the mechanics of the ACA—the exchanges where individuals go to pay for an insurance plan—are unpopular.

† Interestingly, at some time points the survey data shows that high-income respondents are more favorable than people under $40,000 in income—the people purportedly helped most by the ACA.

‡ The best single-piece, highly readable, rigorous summary of Obama-era racial politics is Tillery Jr., A. B., "Obama's Legacy for Race Relations," in ed. B. A. Rockman and A. Rudalevige, *The Obama Legacy* (Lawrence: University Press of Kansas, 2019).

his approach to any other political issue. He sought consensus, not radical change; he appealed to the better angels of Americans' nature, not the heavy hand of federal policy. As a result, many of the institutionalized forms of racism in the United States either failed to improve or worsened under Obama. Tavis Smiley said of the Obama presidency that "black folk have lost ground in every single leading economic indicator category over the past eight years."[36] Even adulatory Obama retrospectives have chapters with titles like "Unfinished Business (and Failures)" that cite race relations as a major area in which Obama fell short.[37]

As Bill Clinton did, Obama sought to demonstrate a reformist approach to racial politics largely through his appointments; by any measure, Obama made more diverse appointments than presidents before or since. Cornel West has referred to this approach (*descriptive representation* in academic lingo) as "Black faces in high places." Descriptive representation is important.* Without a concurrent commitment to a strong policy response, though, its success in ameliorating racial inequality has proven limited.† After all, George W. Bush scored high on the racial diversity of his appointments too.[38] Diverse appointees enacting racially discriminatory policy or maintaining racist institutions do not address the underlying issues. As the activist and journalist Bree Newsome Bass put it: "Modern structural racism operates by pretending the presence of Black officials in what remains a racially oppressive system is somehow a form of anti-racism [and] a measure of progress for all Black [people]."[39]

Obama did push some policy changes that positively addressed institutional racism in the justice system, such as the Fair Sentencing Act of 2010. However, "neither candidate Obama nor President Obama made solving America's race problems a priority."[40] Obama spoke often of race, more than any predecessor. But his efforts to effect change were largely rhetorical. It is important, essential even, for presidents to use their bully

---

* A thorough overview doubling as a readable introduction to the topic: Phillips, A., "Descriptive Representation Revisited," in ed. R. Rohrschneider and J. Thomassen, *The Oxford Handbook of Political Representation in Liberal Democracies* (Oxford, UK: Oxford University Press, 2020), 176–191.

† For a broad discussion focusing on Obama and the nascent Biden administration, see Bhattacharya, S., "The Limits of Descriptive Representation," *Current Affairs*, February 11, 2021.

pulpit. Notable examples of Obama attempting to shape the discourse on race include his speaking forcefully on the Supreme Court's decision to defang the Voting Rights Act in *Shelby Co. v. Holder* (2013) and his public comments, some of which were deeply personal, on the killing of Trayvon Martin. But rhetoric alone is insufficient. It summed to the unsatisfying pastiche of "lots of dialogue, but (insufficient) action" endemic to Democratic politics.[41]

The value of Obama's racial-political rhetoric was limited by two factors explained by Melanye Price in *The Race Whisperer: Barack Obama and the Political Uses of Race* (2016). First, with a lifetime of experience carefully editing himself to avoid frightening white voters, Obama always positioned himself as the intergroup "racial interlocutor" who would translate, negotiate, and ultimately resolve through compromise the problems of race. But often no real middle ground exists. What is the compromise point, for example, on police killing Black men in appalling numbers? Killing some, but not as many? Beating instead of killing? Second and more troublingly, he regularly resorted to endorsing or validating stereotypes "based in beliefs about African-American cultural pathology." In this sense, the politics of race for Obama were consistent with his broader politics, settling on "the neoliberal view that African Americans had to draw on their own resources and initiatives to complete the work of the civil rights movement and guarantee full racial equality."[42]

One incident stands out as an exemplar of the Obama approach that these scholars have described: the July 16, 2009, arrest of Harvard professor Henry Louis Gates Jr. Gates, who is Black, locked himself out of his own home, and a neighbor called the police to report him as a potential burglar. Obama's reaction, highly publicized, was to invite Dr. Gates and the (white) officer involved to the White House to have a beer. This "beer summit" made a good visual and tapped into the liberal hope that racial discrimination can be swept away with a cold drink and a friendly chat.*

---

* Notably, Obama in his 2020 memoir *A Promised Land* attributed the largest single drop in approval during his presidency to this incident. That interpretation is not definitive, though; presidents regularly enter office with their highest approval rating and experience a notable decline during their first spring and summer. First-year drops of 10–20 points in approval are historically common.

Yet the response was also troubling; it put the onus on Gates, the victim of racial profiling, to help resolve a problem he should not have faced in the first place. Each Black person treated unfairly is not obligated to have beers with and "fix" the perceptions of others—particularly when those others are state actors from institutions like the police with deeply ingrained racial biases. The three men may have had a pleasant chat, but little was accomplished toward solving the ongoing problem of racial profiling by law enforcement.

This approach was further reflected in Obama's forays into increasing racial diversity in employment, particularly on the upper rungs of the economic ladder. He believed that the key to progress was not legal mandates but an awakening, a racial epiphany, by CEOs and corporate hiring departments.[43] His faith in the fundamental goodness of Americans reflected in this example resonated and resonates still with many people. We—the predominantly white American "we"—badly want to believe that racism can be "solved" in this way too. The problem is it can't. If the private sector could of its own accord solve their own problems with racial inequality (to say nothing of the broader social problems of racism), it would have happened by now.

After the murders of Michael Brown and Freddie Gray by police, Obama's Justice Department in 2016 issued "scathing" rebukes after investigations into policing in Ferguson, Missouri, and Baltimore, Maryland. The impact and value of rebukes are questionable, though. It is hopefully clear to readers that, since 2016, the problem of excessive force paired with little accountability for police has *not* been resolved. It has gotten worse. Whatever value there is in a scathing rebuke, we are surrounded daily by evidence that it is not enough. Obama spoke about race often and occasionally with great power. Yet his approach to the institutionalized racial problems in our political system and society mirrored his approach to other issues: encouragement but not action, as if exhorting all of us to solve the problem on our own. It is hard to look around today and believe that this approach accomplished much.

CHAPTER 11

DR. NO

B ill Clinton's presidency can only make sense in the context of changes in the Republican Party highlighted by the 1994 midterm elections. Likewise, Obama's presidency took place in the context of changes on the right that many Democrats were slow to recognize. The Tea Party–led Republican resurgence in 2010 reflected more than indifferent voters initially drawn into Obamamania quickly getting bored and abandoning the Democrats. It represented a new, dark turn in Republican strategy, even if the seeds—white nationalism, phony right-wing populism, inchoate antigovernment rage—had been a part of conservative politics since time immemorial.

Despite massive attention paid to the Tea Party—a heavily Astro-Turfed, carefully orchestrated "movement" directed by billionaires and enabled by an increasingly sophisticated (at disseminating nativist dreck, that is) right-wing media machine*—the ascension of Mitch

---

* Journalist Kate Zernike, author of *Boiling Mad* and a correspondent covering the Tea Party from 2009 to 2012, notes that the supposedly grassroots movement had "a real conservative media structure promoting it." Though sometimes still described as populist, there is overwhelming evidence that powerful right-wing organizations orchestrated and redirected the movement toward preexisting goals. As Jeffrey A. Nesbit wrote in *Poison Tea* (New York: Thomas Dunne Books, 2016): "The long rise of the Tea Party Movement was orchestrated, well funded, and deliberate. Its aim was to break

McConnell to a leadership position in the Senate GOP was the most important development of the era.* The Tea Party's role as an insurgent faction was to enforce right-wing discipline from elected officials who feared primary challengers from the right.† Though it lacked numbers to dictate Republican politics by fiat, it was a substantial (and active) enough minority to scare incumbents. McConnell, as his entire career demonstrates, was more than willing to satisfy the nihilist impulses of the far right in service of the long-standing right-wing movement goal of reorienting the entire political-economic structure of society to the liking of the ultrawealthy. This meant not merely winning elections but establishing right-wing dominance of undemocratic institutions like the courts and the Senate to ensure that nothing so insubstantial as an election could undo it.

The fault of Obama and the Democrats was not to cause the rightward lurch of the GOP but to fail through a combination of overconfidence, naïveté, fear, and ambivalence to recognize how the Republicans had changed. In 2021, Barack Obama admitted to CNN's Anderson Cooper that he never foresaw the GOP getting "this dark," believing there were "enough guardrails institutionally" to prevent many of the events of the Trump presidency. Optimism is a good trait, but there is a line between optimism and stupidity. Long before Americans had to seriously consider the possibility of a Trump White House, the Republican Party had signaled that democratic governance was not a cherished principle or an end goal but an obstacle standing in the way of its vision of the future.

Washington. And it has nearly succeeded" by holding hostage the debt ceiling in Congress in 2011 (page 9). See also Lo, C. Y., "Astroturf Versus Grass Roots: Scenes from Early Tea Party Mobilization," in *Steep* (Berkeley: University of California Press, 2012), 98–130; and Mayer, J., *Dark Money: The Hidden History of the Billionaires Behind the Rise of the Radical Right* (New York: Anchor Books, 2017).

* He became minority leader in January 2007, after the Republicans lost power in the midterms.

† This role is detailed in Blum, R., *How the Tea Party Captured the GOP* (Chicago: University of Chicago Press, 2020). See also Cohen, M., "The Future of the Tea Party: Scoring an Invitation to the Republican Party," in *Steep* (Berkeley: University of California Press, 2012), 212–241.

MITCH

At the 2016 Republican National Convention, Mitch McConnell was booed.

Yes, as he was pulling off nothing less than the theft of a cherished Supreme Court seat—McConnell was denying a vote on Obama's wet-blanket nominee Merrick Garland until after the election—Republicans *booed him*. Why? Because they understand that McConnell is not a true believer. He isn't one of them in any meaningful sense, especially when the Republican "them" is of the Trumpist variety. They know he doesn't care about them; they can see that, at his core, the man believes in nothing but power.

He began his political career as a moderate Republican. His evolution has been a case study in an insider's ability to sense changing winds and move with them in service of the only thing that approximates a belief in his withered soul: raising and spending money to achieve the power needed to remake the system to benefit plutocrats. That's McConnell's true political talent, the ability to identify where the real power on the right lies. The culture war issues come and go, and he is adept at using them to further his goals. Popular figures like Donald Trump or Newt Gingrich are clowns he's happy to tolerate when their goals overlap with his. But he has never lost sight of who writes the checks and what those people want. It ain't Benghazi hearings and outrage about critical race theory; these merely keep the base mad and therefore engaged. McConnell and his ilk want money and power, preferably institutionalized and unchallenged.

McConnell understood perhaps better than any contemporary that the judiciary was the key to remaking the country to conservatives' liking. Taking careful note of the important role the Earl Warren Supreme Court played in institutionalizing the New Deal after both FDR and the Great Depression were dead and gone,[1] McConnell grasped that every goal of the conservative movement had to be secondary to the goal of refining the raw material of donor money into a steady stream of confirmed judicial appointees.[2] Congress and state legislatures could pass laws, sure, but only filling the courts with conservative fellow travelers would keep those laws in force.

McConnell became Senate minority leader amid the wreckage of the Bush administration, the Iraq War, and everything that had looked like an ascendant GOP as recently as 2004. His colleagues did not turn to him as the 1994 GOP had Gingrich, admiring his winning ways and eager for his leadership even if they disliked him personally. No, McConnell was simply the guy who wanted the job most. His elevation to the position brought no ominous warnings from or to Democrats that McConnell was a juggernaut to be spoken of in hushed tones of awe. He was just a guy who had been around forever. Nobody predicted a sea change.

While the colorful circus of the Tea Party swirled and entertained the political class—the racism, the grammatically haphazard protest signs, the rank ignorance, the "get your government hands off my Medicaid" inanity, all of it perfect for educated liberals to laugh at dismissively—McConnell set to work changing forever the way Republicans would operate in the Senate (and, to a lesser extent, in the House, where a large, vocal Tea Party contingent was elected in 2010 and advocated a similar hostage-taking approach in that chamber). Republicans would no longer legitimize anything—*anything*—a Democratic president or Congress did.* Norms of how Congress operated would be discarded when they did not advance Republican goals, and Mitch McConnell would be the man who decided what those goals would be. Even the most basic Senate procedure, thanks to a new, wanton approach of threatening to filibuster everything, would require concessions to King Mitch. Minority or majority, it didn't matter. No matter how simple, everything would now go through him, and Democrats would pay dearly for every bit of it.

Rather than play good governance as the New Deal–era Republicans had done in Congress, the GOP in the Obama years became a machine for saying no. They would block, delay, obstruct, undermine, prevent, criticize, and contradict everything that came out of Obama's mouth. Democratic leaders like Harry Reid, Nancy Pelosi, and Chuck Schumer

---

* As noted in Chapter 5, Republicans were encouraged to adopt this approach early in the Clinton presidency in response to health-care reform. They deferred, instead choosing to let Clinton help them pass Republican policy priorities.

were almost beneath McConnell's contempt, and he credited Obama only slightly more as an opponent. He recognized the collective weakness on which he could break them: for Democrats, but not Republicans, bipartisanship was not a means to an end. It had become an important end in itself under Bill Clinton. The serious, professional, educated liberals who came to dominate the party demanded it. The leaders and long-standing incumbents in Congress expected it. There would be posturing and political point scoring, but ultimately the two parties would produce an outcome. Even Newt Gingrich, the consummate venom-spitting hyperconservative, gladly worked closely with Bill Clinton when it suited Republican purposes.

Now no matter what concession Obama made to win GOP support—even if he all but let them write a piece of legislation—the party denied him any legitimacy, any victory, any complicity in any Democratic goal. If he wanted Pepsi, the GOP would demand Coke. If he agreed to Coke, the GOP would switch its demand to sulfuric acid and call him a communist if he refused to drink it on camera. Unbelievably, many Democrats still haven't figured this out.*

McConnell did not have magic powers, but more than any of his Democratic contemporaries, he had the ability to hold together his coalition and limit defections. As Gingrich had once done as Speaker, McConnell used his position to demand loyalty, punishing colleagues who strayed from the flock. Since his rise to leadership coincided with the rise of the Tea Party, he could credibly threaten his Senate colleagues with the specter of primary challengers. McConnell controlled access to big money without which any Republican incumbent could be electorally vulnerable—not to Democrats but to the mob of right-wing loons. They all watched in 2010 as Delaware incumbent Mike Castle, a Republican moderate, was beaten in the Senate primary by the lobotomized Christine O'Donnell, whose campaign against eventual winner Chris Coons (D-DE) prominently featured her renouncing charges of witchcraft. That the Democrat won the seat did not matter to Tea Party activists; they

---

* As I write, Joe Manchin is loudly if pathetically insisting that "ten good, solid patriots" in the Senate GOP will vote to investigate the events of January 6, 2021. Spoiler alert.

were plenty willing to lose seats to make their point, rattle the GOP establishment, and enhance their intraparty power.[3]

To Democrats, McConnell is an all-purpose and mighty villain, a mastermind with control over his caucus that borders on mesmerism.* He encourages this mythical sense of his power, especially since it overlooks high-profile instances in which some Senate Republicans have defied him.[4] What he has, however, is an effective sense of what issues allow him to hold his caucus together. Like Gingrich, he recognizes that the uniting issues on the right are tax cuts, deregulation, privatization, and, his own hobby horse, stuffing the courts with right-wingers. On, for example, the legislative efforts to repeal the ACA (which failed by a single Republican vote in 2017, owing largely to John McCain's terminal illness and mutual personal loathing for Donald Trump), McConnell looks less powerful. Yet Obamacare is useful to him as a boogeyman, and he seemingly cares little if it continues or is repealed. It means only as much to him as it is worth in advancing his real goals. Show McConnell a Supreme Court vacancy, and nothing will stop him from filling it. Show him a plutocratic tax cut package, and he might even tolerate the staggering idiocy of Donald Trump to secure it.

Like Jim Wright—the dictatorial Democratic Speaker toppled by an upstart Newt Gingrich—McConnell is a master of his chamber's rules. He will use, alter, or ignore them to his advantage, always. Democrats are particularly ill suited to fight back on these grounds because the norms— the unwritten rules and customs—are treasured. The process itself is important. McConnell grasps that a Republican base that rejects the legitimacy of election outcomes if Democrats win is not at all interested in cooperation, rules, or compromise. To those voters, no tactics are off the table. It's war, and they cheer when McConnell treats it as such.

The nuclear option of eliminating the Senate filibuster is exemplary.[5] In 2005, George W. Bush departed from Washington norms by refusing to back down on any of his judicial appointees in the face of Senate resistance. Usually a handful (perhaps five out of over a hundred) would be

---

* Derived from the eighteenth-century German physician Franz Mesmer, who became convinced that people are connected by a powerful magnetic force that can be manipulated.

deemed too extreme by the opposing party, filibustered, and withdrawn. Bush, the "unitary executive," decided that he would tolerate no attrition. Every single appointee would be confirmed without exception. Republican leaders were dying for an excuse to eliminate the filibuster and stood on the verge of doing so. This would have allowed Senate Republicans to confirm every Bush appointee but would have also opened the door for Democrats in the future to do the same.

In stepped the kind of "compromise" political elites love: the so-called Gang of Fourteen Senate moderates, featuring Sunday show favorites like Susan Collins, John McCain, and Joe Lieberman. They reached an agreement that kept the filibuster—Democrats for some reason insisted it was a hallowed institution that needed saving when in fact the modern filibuster dates only to 1975—but limited its use to "extreme" circumstances. Never mind that Senate Democrats under Harry Reid were already limiting its use to the most extreme nominees, five right-wing ideologues* (two of whom voluntarily withdrew their nominations) out of over one hundred appointees. Mitch McConnell and other Senate Republicans simply convinced the Democrats that no Bush nominee met the standard—always behind the threat of going nuclear and eliminating the filibuster entirely. When the White House passed to Barack Obama, of course, the extreme standard was applied by Senate Republicans to nearly everyone he nominated.

Take stock of who got what in this deal. Bush got every judicial nominee confirmed. Republicans kept the filibuster so they could wield it later from the minority. Democrats got literally nothing. It took six long years under Obama before the Senate finally threw up its hands and eliminated the filibuster for most judicial nominations in 2013. It was the only way to get any Obama appointees confirmed. And it only took them a little under a decade to figure that out.

Tricks of this kind are McConnell's stock-in-trade.† It takes the acquiescence of Democrats willing to fall for it to upgrade it from a trick to a superpower.

---

* One was named Brett Kavanaugh.

† Note that in 2005, McConnell was the majority whip; Bill Frist of Tennessee was in his final Congress as leader, McConnell's later role under Obama.

DELEGITIMIZING OBAMA

Barack Obama was fortuitous for Mitch McConnell. He set out to deny any legitimacy to Democrats at the moment that a large part of the American right was eager to do so. The Tea Party movement, in fact, seems to have agreed initially on few issues other than that Barack Obama was illegitimate.* His birth, his citizenship, his college grades, his election, his very existence—all illegitimate. Racism—plain, simple, old-fashioned racism, the original sin of the American right—was a motivating factor for much of it. For all the Tea Party's ideological incoherence and ignorance, there was no ambiguity on this point: Obama is not one of us.

McConnell's infamous vow to make Obama a one-term president was interpreted within the White House as Gingrichian political bluster. Windbags always made similar proclamations, but when it came time to cut a budget deal, the Republicans would be at the table. Except something had changed, not simply in Republican leadership but on the American right overall.

The Tea Party brought what was once the far-right fringe of American conservatism into the Republican mainstream. Establishment Republicans had long winked at and played footsie with the more unbalanced elements of the far right, keeping them safely at arms' length but happily courting their votes. When the image Republicans wished to project was of stolid, prudent governance, fringe voters who dressed in camo and fancied themselves a militia were an embarrassment. But over time, the GOP establishment lost control;† social media and the extreme messaging of right-wing radio and TV amplified, legitimized, and solidified the farthest-out belief systems. The GOP of Jack Kemp and Bob Dole droning on about tax reform was subsumed into the wild-eyed conspiratorial worldview once walled off in fringe establishments like the John Birch Society. There is a long history of conspiracy theories fueling the

---

* In time, well-funded organizations like FreedomWorks, aided by conservative media carrying the correct talking points, would graft a specific issue agenda onto the formless antigovernment anger of Tea Partiers.

† You remember the line from *Cabaret*, right? "The Nazis are just a gang of stupid hooligans, but they do serve a purpose. Let them get rid of the Communists. Later, we'll be able to control them." Cut to Madison Cawthorn in lederhosen belting out "Tomorrow Belongs to Me."

nativist right in American politics,[6] including Know-Nothingism[7] or the anticommunist hysterias of the post–World War II era. But even McCarthyism looks tame compared to, say, Pizzagate and QAnon. And the progression of nuttiness has not abated yet; by 2021, Obama-era examinations of the "craziness" of the Tea Party seemed amusing in hindsight. We've moved on to much, much worse things.[8]

Immediately, though, keen Republicans including McConnell saw how the trend toward nativism and fake populism could be used in service of the important goals: tax cuts, judges, deregulation, power and money siphoned ever upward. The mislabeling of the Tea Party as "populist" ignores how perfectly it overlapped with, and was manipulated by, the existing right-wing power structure of the time. Within *days* of the televised rant by a D-list cable news personality that launched Tea Party fervor, heavyweight groups like FreedomWorks and Americans for Prosperity were bombarding friendly media and online groups with messaging and organizational "advice."[9] Longtime House GOP power broker Dick Armey—who rapidly churned out a "Tea Party manifesto" book—was a principal at FreedomWorks. Armey, the consummate Beltway insider, used the opportunity to resurrect his crackpot scheme from the 1990s to eliminate income tax in favor of a national sales tax. If former House majority leader Dick Armey is directing traffic, your movement isn't exactly an organic groundswell of populist sentiment.

Barack Obama's task was to build on his 2008 success to redefine a progressive populist worldview as a compelling alternative. Instead, his presidency, his natural caution, and his avowed preference for New Democrat–style solutions left a vacuum modern liberalism was ill equipped to fill. As with Clinton and the presidential also-rans of the intervening years, Obama's message that the establishment is made up of the smartest people and those people deserve to be in charge because they're so smart was not terribly appealing to the working class. Obviously, nothing the GOP did spoke to their economic needs either. If anything, as Donald Trump and Mitch McConnell have proven repeatedly, the GOP is more committed than ever to forcing American workers to endure increasingly precarious economic conditions. But the Obama era saw white grievance politics centered in ways that hadn't been seen since the battles over segregation and civil rights. In many ways, the former was simply a continuation of the latter.

Over the eight years Obama was in office, conservatives succeeded in generating or refining record-high levels of distrust toward government. Gallup poll data shows that trust in all institutions, including a Congress led by Republicans toward the end of Obama's presidency, sank to abysmal levels.[10] This is, of course, perfectly fine with the right. Right-wing politics and governance since Reagan have adhered to the "wrecking crew" model: they insist government is incompetent then get elected and govern incompetently to prove it. Vitriol toward Obama and his otherness helped, but the lingering effects of economic changes that began long before Obama and were continued unabated during his time in office were important as well. The "economic anxiety" narrative became a punchline after 2016, but there is little doubt that the appeal of this brand of nativist conservatism flourished in areas that have been in an economic downward spiral for half a century.*

Like Trump's 2016 election, the delegitimization of Obama and of government broadly speaking during his presidency was a phenomenon of better-off conservatives misrepresented by obsessive media coverage as average Americans who are fed up. The image of the Tea Partier or the Trump rally attendee defaults to white working class, something like an idled construction worker. But the movement has been wildly successful at turning suburban small-government conservatism into something darker. If Reaganism was the gateway drug, the Tea Party introduced that generation to the hard stuff: Dixiecrat racism, hardcore conspiracy theories, economic elitism, and cultural resentments too numerous to list. Conservatism in America has long included these strands, and it certainly occurred to Republicans to be racist before Barack Obama was elected.[†] What happened during those years, though, with a substantial assist from the conservative media, was a stunningly effective repackaging and

---

* The extent of Democratic losses in the factory towns of the Midwest and Northeast in the twenty-first century is detailed in Martin, J., "Democrats Lost the Most in Midwestern 'Factory Towns,' Report Says," *New York Times*, October 5, 2021.

† Ronald Reagan kicked off his winning general election campaign with a speech on August 3, 1980, lauding states' rights at the Neshoba County Fair, a stone's throw away from Philadelphia, Mississippi. Super subtle.

rebranding of what was once the extreme right into commonsense, main-stream conservatism. What is actually a narrow worldview that serves the rich and powerful was successfully rebranded as a popular, even universal set of demands for "real" Americans.[11]

UNDER THE BUS

The way Democrats chose to respond to the cheapest, worst-faith smear attacks by the emboldened Tea Party–adjacent right simply invited more attacks. Nothing better illustrates this than the way the Democratic establishment opted to throw one of its most reliable and effective voter registration organizations under the bus when the dumbest iteration of tabloid conservatism attacked it.

The Association of Community Organizations for Reform Now (ACORN) was founded in 1970 with the goal of uniting at the local level the working poor and the unemployed around basic, tangible issues like the provision of school lunches, housing, and medical care.[12] In time, it became an umbrella organization connecting street-level community groups nationwide, precisely the kind of effective conduit for activism and policy diffusion Democrats needed to supplement their growing appeal to the better-off and to help offset the waning strength of organized labor. ACORN did things unions did not, like reach the truly poor, the urban underclass, and Black voters to whom some unions were indifferent at best, openly hostile at worst.

In 2009, right-wing ass clown James O'Keefe dressed as a *Shaft*-style pimp to secretly record (and misleadingly edit) videos of low-level ACORN employees appearing to encourage illegal behavior. Conservative media mogul Andrew Breitbart used his online puke centrifuge to fling the story far and wide along with supposedly damning examples of ACORN submitting fake voter registration applications.* As elite liberals and the Democratic establishment had done in racing to criticize the activist group MoveOn in 2007 when the right erupted in paroxysms of

---

* Federal law requires the submission of every voter registration form, even if filled out incompletely or with obvious nonsense like "Mickey Mouse, 123 Ligma Street."

faux indignation over an ad tamely critical of Gen. David Petraeus,* in 2009 they briefly huddled and decided that ACORN was not worth defending. Democratic representative Gerry Connolly later put it: "The calculus for some of my colleagues was, 'How much political capital do I want to expend on this?'"[13] Liberal media outlets also ran with the story uncritically to show their both-sides objectivity, with the all-important Jon Stewart lambasting ACORN's dastardly corruption in a September 15, 2009, *Daily Show* segment hilariously called "The Audacity of Hos."†

In mere days, congressional Democrats decided that the best way to deflect the heat was to vote to defund—and thereby effectively destroy—the group that had been an important ally doing real, meaningful work for *four decades*. The accusations against ACORN were idiotic, transparently ridiculous, the kind of nonsense that collapses under the slightest scrutiny. One study later offered stark evidence that "opinion entrepreneurs" on the right had leveled baseless accusations of fraud at ACORN, and national (but not local) media had repeated these uncritically.[14] It was a hit job and a dumb one. A proper Democratic response would have been "piss off," or words to that effect. Instead, seeking a pat on the head from their Republican opponents, on September 17, 2009, 172 House Democrats joined 173 Republicans in voting to defund the group. ACORN's primary activity at the time was helping the poor avoid foreclosures and evictions.

In hindsight it is obvious that the Democrats made their usual bargain: they helped Republicans destroy something valuable in exchange for absolutely nothing. All the ACORN scandal did was, in the words of one Breitbart scribe, give the right a blueprint for how to win.‡ Democrats failed to, and still fail to, grasp that accepting the legitimacy of a clearly

---

* The ad, a full page in the *New York Times*, called him "General Betray Us." Real Alexander Pope stuff.

† O'Keefe and his collaborator Hannah Giles dressed as "pimp" and "prostitute" in some of the footage. Get it? Very droll.

‡ "I feel like this issue was a prelude to how conservatives would weaponize issues going forward in the tea party era that would follow," according to Kurt Bardella, quoted in Carter, Z. D., and A. Delaney, "How the ACORN Scandal Seeded Today's Nightmare Politics," *Huffington Post*, May 5, 2018.

dishonest smear (with poorly feigned moral indignation from Republicans) only gives credence to the attacks. It also makes them look weak and naïve, not to mention reminds political allies that Democrats will turn on them in a heartbeat. Hank Johnson (D-GA) regretted his vote to defund ACORN and said in 2018, "Having been there and done it, I think there's some wisdom now that would take hold that would perhaps prevent this from happening again." That Congress votes annually to ban funding from ACORN "or its successors" explicitly suggests they have not learned much. ACORN's organizing in marginalized communities certainly was missed in 2016.

The scandal barely registers now, but it is important as an example of how poorly Democrats of the era misread Republicans and their own electoral incentives. The liberal worldview held that partisanship was a tacky relic superseded by a neutral fairness that demanded, in this instance, siding with Republicans to destroy one's own allies. Accepting Republican accusations at face value has never yielded an ounce of benefit for Democrats. Republican attacks continue or even intensify, and the electorate shows little interest in rewarding Democrats for being nice, playing by the rules, and agreeing with bad-faith GOP attacks against them. The ACORN incident is the kind of thing Democrats think makes them look reasonable, dignified, and honest. What if it actually makes them look weak, appeasement oriented, and unreliable?

THE CBO SAYS NO

When Congress passed the ACA, you may recall that it did not go into effect immediately. Four whole years passed before it "began" from the perspective of ordinary Americans. Part of the delay was the necessity of preparing the groundwork for the enormously complex law.* But the most compelling reason was that by delaying implementation for four years, the Obama administration lowered something called the Congressional Budget Office (CBO) 10-Year Budget Projections. Ever heard of it?

---

* This delayed start did not, somehow, give the White House enough time to launch the ACA exchanges with a website that actually worked. See Anthopoulos, L., et al., "Why E-Government Projects Fail? An Analysis of the Healthcare.gov Website," *Government Information Quarterly* 33, no. 1 (2016): 161–173.

The CBO is a small, nonpartisan agency that estimates the economic impact of legislation under consideration in Congress. The assignment of a CBO score is an important step for a bill, at least among insiders like journalists, interest groups, and Capitol Hill staffers. To many Democrats, the CBO score is the closest thing to a "politics judge," an objective, nonpartisan arbiter who assigns a hard number to a bill. Liberals (and at moments when it is convenient to do so, other political factions) treat the pronouncements of the CBO as something approaching holy writ.[15]

Objective analysis seems like it would help a great deal in lawmaking, but in practice the CBO is wrong a lot.* In its defense, estimating anything on the scale of the national economy is difficult. With CBO scores treated as matters of grave importance by some insiders, however, the fact that their estimates are often wrong is a big problem. As Obama demonstrated with the ACA, there are also plenty of ways to juke the CBO score on a bill to one's liking. It is not *quite* as objective a process as it purports to be.

The four-year gap between passage and implementation of the ACA was used by Republicans to undermine the law in various ways, not to mention that it provided the public no benefits that it could see, experience, or use until 2014. Those are substantial political costs for manipulating some silly analysts' figure that nobody outside political elite circles cares about. Most voters couldn't tell you what CBO stands for (or does) to save their souls. A complete list of people who care about CBO 10-Year Budget Projections could fit on a matchbook. Yet within official Washington, it exercises what seems like tyranny over legislative outcomes and inconsistently to boot.

The worst and least appreciated part of the CBO's role in Congress is its inherent status quo bias.[16] Proposing something new—health-care reform, for example—will always produce a big scary number that aids opponents' attempts to frame it as big government and too expensive. The CBO score almost inevitably ends up being used as an argument not to do something. Not only do Republicans pretend to care about it when

---

* The CBO's analysis of its own accuracy in the 2019 paper "An Evaluation of CBO's Past Deficit and Debt Projections" admitted numerous mistakes in assumptions and predicted outcomes.

Democrats are in power,* but the Democrats have a long habit (the ACA example above notwithstanding) of letting the CBO dictate the scope of their ambitions.

The Clinton administration blamed (inaccurately, as we have already seen) the CBO for the failure of the Hillary Clinton–led health-care reform effort in 1993. In 2005 the Grad PLUS student lending reform saw Democrats "sacrifice a generation of students to the deficit god, in exchange for meaningless numbers in a report, because CBO scores are more real to senators than flesh-and-blood people."[17] In 2020, Speaker Pelosi exasperated even moderates in her own caucus by removing from the first COVID-19 stimulus package key provisions to automatically re-new parts of the stimulus if economic conditions failed to improve, citing the terrifying CBO score. Eric Levitz of *New York Magazine* summed that one up as, "Dems Nix Anti-Recession Policy After Learning It Would Help Too Many People."[18]

With her own party in favor and Republicans almost certain to use their Senate majority to refuse anyway, Pelosi kind of gave away the game in that example. For Democrats, the CBO score is a reason not to do things they do not want to do, the "I have a headache" of liberal pol-itics. The Democratic House majority knew that its bill was an exercise in symbolism—signaling to voters what Democrats want—yet the lead-ership would not even send the most ambitious possible version of the bill to the Senate for Mitch McConnell to reject. As the GOP regularly shows, and as Obama showed occasionally, the CBO score is malleable. If you really want to do something, you can make the CBO score look good enough to justify it to the tiny cult of people who care. But when you don't want to do something, the score is a full-stop argument against it. That's how progressive priorities die, not to mention why everybody hates the CBO except centrists with weird obsessions about obeying rules that aren't even rules because they're so easy to circumvent.

As with so many pathologies, the Democratic CBO obsession put down roots under Bill Clinton. Political journalist Elizabeth Drew re-counts a tragicomic scene inside a funereal Oval Office in 1993 when the

---

* In power, the Republicans not only ignore the CBO but openly deride it, as recounted in Prokop, A., "The Congressional Budget Office, Explained," Vox, June 26, 2017.

president and his inner circle learned that the CBO estimates of their budget revealed a shortfall that would require cutting at least 25 percent from all discretionary programs. The CBO, following procedures established under the earlier reign of Reagan appointee David Stockman, used an outdated, higher interest rate to inflate the White House cost estimates rather than using the lower interest rate prevailing at the time of the estimate. Without deep cuts, the budget would reduce the deficit by less than Clinton had committed to doing. At the beginning of his presidency Clinton promised—bafflingly—to use only the official CBO figures for all budgeting.* The moment he set foot in the White House, Clinton gave veto power over his economic policy to a supposedly nonpartisan agency staffed by unelected bureaucrats with a history of poorly estimating the impact of things like investments in education, infrastructure, and training—the focus areas of Clinton's proposals.

Consider the scene, then. Faced with a self-imposed choice between its own initiatives intended to improve the lives of ordinary Americans and two utterly arbitrary figures (the CBO estimates and the administration's own mysterious but sacrosanct $140 billion target for deficit reduction), it chose the latter. After a round of moaning about how unfortunate it all was, how depressing it was to take the axe to everything they wanted to do other than reduce the deficit, Clinton issued a soothing verdict: "We shouldn't push investments so hard that we lose our deficit-cutting message."[19] Only George Stephanopoulos, in Drew's retelling, broached the obvious: "Why should we accept the OMB number?" In time, he would learn that helping people, even in the indirect, technocratic New Democrat way, would always take a back seat to important matters like arbitrary deficit reduction goals based on dubious estimates.

THE DEMOCRATS FIGHT BACK

Just kidding. The Obama administration was an eight-year unlearned lesson that the GOP was lurching toward authoritarianism, a core white nationalist appeal, and mindless obstructionism. Until the end of his

---

* Republicans made a similar promise in the 1994 "Contract with America" but simply reneged once in power, correctly betting that nobody outside the Beltway would know or care.

second term—and possibly not even then—Obama failed to internalize that the GOP had zero interest in governing except to wrest power from the Democrats. Mitch McConnell had to tell Joe Biden to his face, as Biden recounted the merits of some policy or other, "You must be under the mistaken impression that I care" about governing. Even that wasn't enough to elicit more than a light scolding; in response to this nugget, Obama's memoir decries McConnell's "shamelessness" and "dispassionate pursuit of power."

Maybe the "dispassionate pursuit of power" is a definition of politics, and there is no referee to award one team points for taking the high road. Maybe politics isn't a game where the goal is for everyone to behave decorously but a struggle for power and resources that is literally life and death for some people.

SETTING THE TABLE

The Obama years ended with the Democrats unaware that they were walking into a disaster. That the GOP had changed into something viler and more dangerous should have been obvious, and certainly most liberals seemed to understand that was the case. The growing ugliness and authoritarian flavor of right-wing rhetoric was a frequent focus of liberal media, and coarseness of the kind of support whipped up by the Tea Party and anti-Obama right came to dominate liberal politics. The right was growing so ridiculous and scary compared to the cool, smart, credentialed competence of Obama and his people that liberals had a hard time assessing the Republican threat seriously. They assumed, wrongly, that the more extreme Republicans became the easier it would be for Democrats to occupy that valuable real estate in the political center.

It should have been apparent that Democrats entered 2016 having suffered tremendously since 2008 at the state level as well as in losing control of Congress. Republicans elected to state legislatures in 2010 also seized the Tea Party–McConnell ethos of using the redistricting process to pass restrictive voting laws to full partisan effect. There was no compunction from Republicans at any level to use the power they saw as hard-won to crush Democrats, by the rules or otherwise. While Democratic elites saw the Obama presidency as nothing short of an eight-year-long success story, the ground underneath the Democratic establishment had shifted.

In hindsight, very few people outside the Republican Party (and even within it) took the rise of reactionary right politics or the Tea Party, which seemed crafted specifically to be laughed at, seriously enough. But the Democratic Party continued to underestimate the right even as it started to lose ground. Who cared if right-wingers took over the capitol in Augusta, Maine? That's bush league. So long as Democrats controlled the White House and, importantly, the Supreme Court, liberals held effective power. And certainly that wasn't going to change in 2016!

CHAPTER 12

IF YOU'RE WAITING FOR A SIGN, THIS IS IT

Donald Trump's election is like the French Revolution: its causes and consequences will be debated well beyond our lifetimes. The moment the shock abated from the unexpected defeat of Hillary Clinton in 2016, a cottage industry of explanations, analyses, and hot takes stirred to life. Clinton was and in many ways remains the ur-mainstream Democrat, the apotheosis of everything modern American liberals value and believe about how the world should work. To see her rejected in favor of such a vacuous con man was, for many Democrats, a brain-breaking experience. Losses happen in politics, but 2016 was the kind of defeat that should prompt a complete reconsideration of every aspect of the approach, strategy, ideology, attitude, and worldview contributing to it. If losing to this guy doesn't shake things to the core, what will? Like a coronary patient who ignores all implorations to quit smoking four packs a day, though, liberalism for the most part succeeded in ignoring the potential lessons and came once again to their preferred conclusions: move to the right to appease moderates and bemoan the myriad ways Democrats were wronged by others.

Both popular and academic analyses of 2016 focused on the most appealing explanations from the Democrats' perspective, with an eye toward affixing responsibility to outside actors rather than to the party and the Clinton campaign. Voters are stupid. Voters are racist. Voters are misogynists.[1] Voters were lied to by the media. The Russians rigged the election. James Comey rat-fucked Clinton at the last minute. Trump was a solar flare of the American id, and nobody as dignified, brilliant, and accomplished as Clinton could compete with his appeal to the base instincts of the ignorant rabble. *Newsweek* catalogued *seventeen* distinct explanations (or, uncharitably, excuses) cited by Clinton herself in circulation as the Trump era began.

The appeal of these explanations is that all of them are at least plausible. Many Americans express racist and sexist attitudes, especially in politics. The information environment for voters is a cacophony filled with disinformation, exacerbated by social media platforms. The media, terrified as usual of accusations of liberal bias due to its relentless, well-deserved criticism of Trump, felt compelled to show "balance" by inflating the importance of Clinton scandals.* But all of this ignores a fundamental question, one we raised earlier in our look at the 2000 and 2004 elections (the latter of which 2016 shares much in common with): Why was an election against such a monumentally, even historically awful opponent close enough for these factors to tip the balance in the first place?

That is the part Democrats can control and change. In all the takes, reactions, explanations, and analyses, only on the left is the obvious question ever asked: Is there something fundamentally unpopular about the worldview of the modern Democratic Party? Those seventeen excuses

---

* Clinton has admitted that the use of a private email server was her responsibility and "dumb" but is correct to suggest the gravity of the problem was overstated in media coverage. It also is unclear if the Comey "revelations" mattered; subjectively, it is easy to assume that they must have, but actual evidence that votes changed on account of "her emails" is lacking. Poll data showing relatively high percentages of voters calling Clinton untrustworthy date to early 2015, far before the October surprise of 2016. For the media's role in boosting Trump and pushing Clinton scandals, see Searles, K., and K. Banda, "But Her Emails! How Journalistic Preferences Shaped Election Coverage in 2016," *Journalism* 20, no. 8 (2019).

cited by *Newsweek*, crucially, make no reference to either Clinton's issue positions or Democratic ideas overall. Let that sink in. At no point did the candidate or party establishment consider that "people might dislike us and what we stand for" as an explanation for a crushing loss. That's some real soul searching!

The election posed an insoluble problem for Clinton, who, as part of the Obama administration and of the Democratic establishment, could hardly tell voters: "This system is screwing you and I intend to fix it." Not only would her claim to fix it lack credibility, but it would imply that Obama, the Democratic leadership in Congress, Bill Clinton, and other power players of recent decades (including herself, as secretary of state and a senator) had screwed everything up. Thus, the Clinton campaign ran on the idea of unity, on "America is already great," which went over like a lead balloon with millions of Americans whose lives very demonstrably were not great and in fact had been worsening for decades. Even moderates like 2020 presidential contender Pete Buttigieg saw the weakness of that message; in 2019 he told an audience: "Donald Trump got elected because, in his twisted way, he pointed out the huge troubles in our economy and our democracy. At least he didn't go around saying that America was already great, like Hillary did." As timid as Democrats are about criticizing pedestaled figures like Obama or the Clintons, that practically counts as an assassination attempt.*

The disconnect between the campaign's rhetoric and reality was clearest in the Rust Belt. I am more familiar with this landscape than I prefer, having spent decades in Illinois, Indiana, and Wisconsin. Seeing firsthand, for example, Joliet, Illinois, in 1988 (when the only occupied buildings downtown were the courthouse and a newsstand, which, I discovered later in adulthood, had remained solvent by selling pornography under the counter) or Peoria, Illinois, in the twenty-first century (that avatar of the average American town) taught me much about the decades of accumulated mistrust, anger, misery, and memories of broken promises that make such places ripe for the kind of right-wing

---

* Buttigieg was immediately forced to reiterate his "enormous respect" for Clinton; see Frazin, R., "Clinton Aide Responds to Buttigieg Criticism of How She Ran Her Campaign," *Hill*, March 30, 2019.

demagoguery Trump sold. These are the places where factories have closed, and everything has gotten just a little bit worse every day since—for decades. These are the places where the Bill Clinton simulacrum from *Primary Colors* told blue-collar Americans that globalization was inevitable, that experts determined that their jobs had to go, and it was up to workers to "retrain."

Only the factory closures and economic desolation part of the prophecies materialized. The part where Decatur, Illinois,* and Kokomo, Indiana, and Saginaw, Michigan, replaced manufacturing jobs with something better did not. And by 2016 a large portion of the country was sick of hearing that the economic status quo was somehow going to work out for them, that the next scheme or public-private partnership was the one that would do the trick. Like John Kerry in 2004, Al Gore in 2000, and Walter Mondale in 1984, Hillary Clinton in 2016 represented that status quo. She had to; her candidacy made no sense in any other context.

Clearly, Donald Trump offered these voters no economic salvation either. His "populism" was *at best* a thin veneer over his demagoguery and sincere hatred of his fellow elites.[2†] But Trump offered them something the Clinton campaign could not offer: a dyspeptic volcano to rally around, constant reminders that they're being screwed, and a sense that the *we* of white, struggling America is special and important and deserves to rule the country—in their view, *their* country. Trump's sole moment of actual wisdom during the campaign was to pound on globalization and free trade—two issues Donald Trump would do nothing whatsoever to fix, of course—as the source of tremendous anger among the working class. "These trade deals are all bad!" hit a nerve because—stay with me—for so much of America those deals have been very bad. Democrats and Republicans joined hands in 1992 and declared free trade both inevitable and good, while on the ground, it has been an unmitigated disaster for many people and places. How could Hillary Clinton possibly fight back?

---

* This place manages the almost unbelievable feat of making Peoria look like the Left Bank in comparison.

† Trump's brand of anti-elitism was of the New York "Page Six" variety, where he held deeply felt grievances against other elites who rejected him from high society as crass and tacky. So even though Trump himself is obviously a wealthy elite, his hatred of other elites based on personal slights and his own ego allowed him to come across as sincere.

She could either alienate voters by arguing "free trade is good, don't you people understand?" or she could admit that her predecessors, including free trade champion Bill Clinton, had screwed up catastrophically.

Absent the desire or ability to craft an appealing economic message rooted in populism, the Clinton campaign competed on competence (like Michael Dukakis did in 1988 and Jimmy Carter before him), on the ability to manage a system that it viewed as working pretty well. The emphasis was on personal virtue and contrasts. Hillary is qualified; Donald is not. Hillary is a good person; Trump, a bad one. Hillary knows how to run things; Donnie will make a mess of it. All of these statements were plausible. None were persuasive to voters desperate for someone to be on their side or, in Trump's case, to pretend to be. Never did it occur to Democratic big brains that everything that made Hillary Clinton a slam-dunk choice among the liberal base made her unappealing to voters outside it. The dominant strategy for selling Clinton to anyone other than MSNBC addicts and Democratic consultants boiled down to pointing at her curriculum vitae and reminding everyone that Trump could be thrown further than he could be trusted or believed.

Mistakes of arrogance, cynicism, and the misguided belief that voters thought the America of 2016 was a pretty great place abounded for the Clinton camp. We were told to take the high road, while the GOP went low (and got everything they wanted). We heard that we should be grateful for the opportunity to vote for such a great candidate—the most qualified ever! We saw a campaign confident that it would win where it eventually lost, and a candidate who deferred on making an emotional appeal to struggling Americans and assumed the support of more successful ones was in the bag.

Critics of modern liberalism right and left saw—without straining—a Hillary Clinton candidacy that crystallized everything smug and unlikeable about the whole ideology. Her most genuine moment of passion in the campaign was a spontaneous onstage pledge to never, ever support single-payer health care. During the primaries she asked an audience: "Not everything is about an economic theory, right? If we broke up the big banks tomorrow—and I will, if they deserve it, if they pose a systemic risk, I will—would that end racism?"

That quote is worth lingering on. It is commonly cited without the middle clause ("and I will . . ."), although nobody sentient during 2009 and 2010 believed the threat anyway—if not during the Great Recession, then when? But not only is the quote a cynical straw man (why would that be an either-or?), it is demonstrably flawed logic. Much of systemic racism in the United States is in fact rooted in discrimination in the financial industry. This is uncontroversial. Not only is it bizarre to argue that a presidential candidate can fix racism more easily than she can regulate the financial industry—the powers of government are in fact designed to do the latter but not the former—but it also badly misrepresents the role of that industry in instituting and perpetuating racial inequality. It suggested that the Democratic Party would seek any reason, give any excuse, to avoid confronting an economic system that so many people felt, with justification, was rigged against them and in favor of elites.

Well-off liberals hear this stuff—take the high road, everything's fine, voters are the problem—and nod. This speaks to them. To anyone else it sounds like a tin-eared alien reading conservative talking points reworked to appeal to nonconservatives. Expecting the president to create a more active regulatory state (for example, by using the Justice Department to pursue antimonopoly action and crack down on financial crime) is Green Lantern magical thinking, and yet making economic reform and rebuilding the regulatory capacity of the state conditional on (somehow) ending racism is a more realistic alternative. In the end, it drove too many key voting blocs away. The story of 2016 was not the triumph of conservatism but the monumental fiasco of liberalism. Black and Hispanic voters—who, contrary to white Bernie Bro stereotypes, constituted some of Clinton's most vocal critics throughout 2016[3]— turned out in lower numbers and were less supportive compared to Obama's performance in 2012. Clinton underperformed Obama 2012 among voters under thirty, too.[4]

That is the lesson worth learning from 2016: that the centrist, neoliberal economic worldview that favors a winners-and-losers economy is unpopular outside successful, highly educated, professional liberals. It is at its least likeable when liberals couch their defenses of the economic status quo in *insincere* social justice language,* what Daniel Denvir called "peak neoliberalism, where a distorted version of identity politics is used to defend an oligarchy and a national security state, celebrating diversity in the management of exploitation and warfare."[5] It's not as if the 2016 version of the Democratic Party was doing a lot to address structural inequality based on race. Had that been undertaken more aggressively from 2009 to 2017, Clinton's base of support may have been stronger and her narrow loss instead a narrow win.

Some voters do hold racist beliefs, yet Barack Obama won twice with the same electorate. Sexism? Obviously pervasive and widespread.[6] Yet replacing Hillary Clinton with Joe Biden yielded only a small improvement—thankfully, enough to give Trump the boot—in 2020 despite the huge benefit accruing to Biden from an electorate exhausted by four grueling years of Trump's daily horror show. Whatever allowed Biden to improve incrementally upon the Clinton '16 performance to win—his gender, prevailing anti-Trump sentiment, his successful imaging as a safe moderate—it left untouched the underlying problem that the ideology for which Clinton carried the torch simply isn't very popular. Robert Reich, a cabinet secretary under Bill Clinton and once a firm believer in the New Democrat way, was among the first prominent party members to see through the haze: "The Democratic Party as it is now constituted has become a giant fundraising machine, too often reflecting the goals and values of the moneyed interests. This must change. The election of 2016 has repudiated it."[7]

Much has also been made of the bizarrely inept Clinton campaign strategy devised by the best professionals money could buy, but the campaign's mistakes can be overstated. For example, "Why didn't Hillary campaign in Wisconsin?" has become a trope, but everything we know about campaign effects suggests it is unlikely that more (or any!) visits

---

* This is not an argument against identity politics social justice warriors, both of which have become meaningless, all-purpose pejoratives in common use. It is a specific criticism of *insincere* co-opting of the language and gestures of those principles to defend institutions and actors that are responsible for the harm. Renaming a street Black Lives Matter Avenue while reinforcing the power of police is an example, as is offering the diversity of leadership in an exploitative or cruel system as a defense of its virtue. I trust the reader to understand the distinction.

to Wisconsin or Michigan would have impacted the outcome.[8] Huge resources devoted to Pennsylvania, for example, included regular visits that did Clinton little good there. The problem reflected in the lack of visits was that the campaign simply assumed it would win such midwestern states even when its own internal data said otherwise. It devoted resources on the ground in those places almost exclusively to targeting Republicans it planned to peel away from Trump. "Only in the last two weeks," a labor organizer in Ohio reported, "did the Democratic Party outreach effort really switch back to traditional Democratic voters."[9] Oops. The campaign bought whole hog into the "demographics are destiny" theory (more on that shortly) and assumed, crucially, not only that it would win the Hispanic and Black vote (true!) but that turnout among those voters would be robust (false!). Again, the signs were there well before Election Day.[10] By mid-October 2016, with Trump persistently, worryingly close in many state-level polls, prominent Black Democrats, including House Whip Jim Clyburn and G. K. Butterfield of the Congressional Black Caucus, were openly expressing worry that the Clinton campaign's strategy to turn out Black voters was a disaster.[11]

It was no surprise, then, when Black turnout fell and hurt Clinton. Who was responsible for ensuring that this essential Democratic voting bloc was primed and ready to vote in November? How did they fail? Rather than asking those questions, Democrats prefer to hand-wave this away to voter suppression. Republican voter suppression efforts are very real, but clearly they alone cannot explain 2016. Outcomes in 2018, 2020, and especially the 2020 Senate races in the GOP voter suppression mecca of Georgia undermine the idea that in 2016 the obstacles represented by voter suppression were insuperable.[12] More plausibly, either the Clinton campaign failed to offer Black voters something that secured their support or did so but failed to effectively communicate it. Alternatively, some Black voters may have become discouraged after the Obama administration fell short of expectations. Finally, it could be the case that the campaign team responsible for ensuring the Democratic base turned out did not do its job.

Two things can be true. One is that racism and sexism were clearly used by the Trump campaign and were, for the people who voted for

Trump, part of his appeal.* Another is that Trump won the election narrowly in a handful of states that "share certain characteristics in common, including specialization in manufacturing, slow population growth, a common pattern with regards to Hispanic population change, and higher-than-average percentages of non-college-educated whites."[13] And in all those places, a disproportionate number of people *who voted twice for Barack Obama* voted for Donald Trump. Clearly, there are social and economic factors, such as the statistically aberrant appeal of Trump in so-called landscapes of despair wracked by unemployment, drug addiction, poor health, and poverty, that broad-brush conclusions about racist and sexist voters obliterate.[14] We must digest the possibility that Trump's very narrow win is better explained by a small group of voters in key places, electorally, who were furious with the establishment—which included Hillary Clinton, in their view—and despairing or mad enough to vote for a vulgar cretin who seemed to hate the powers that be as much as they did.

"Republicans are awful" and "Look at how bad Trump is" were not enough in 2016, were barely enough in 2020, and will not be enough for long. Competing with the right to appeal to latent nativist, xenophobic, misogynist, or racist proclivities in the electorate is wrong, intellectually, ethically, and politically—a complete nonstarter. That leaves two options: be a permanent minority party or come up with a political and economic worldview that appeals to a wide enough coalition of working-class voters and professional-class liberals to prevent a repeat of 2016 and return to the days when Democrats could claim with legitimacy to be "the party of the people," fighting power rather than aligning with it and singing its praises.

If 2016 did not make that clear, I don't want to live through whatever will.

---

* The Internet abounds with compilations such as "25 Things Donald Trump Has Actually Said About Women" (*Cosmopolitan*, November 2, 2020) and "Donald Trump's Long History of Racism, from the 1970s to 2020" (Vox, August 13, 2020) if you require a refresher.

THE CHECKLIST

While researching this book, I read (or re-read) most of the published academic papers in political science specifically about the 2016 presidential election. As researchers are wont to do for practical reasons, they focus on what is measurable and quantifiable, using tools like surveys and demographic data. It was quickly apparent that the story liberals were coalescing around after the shocking loss—that voters were the problem—seemed to have some evidence to support it. Voters who express racist and sexist beliefs preferred Trump. A paper by a major scholar grabbed headlines by concluding that status threat—fear of someone taking one's place in the social pecking order—drove Trump voters, while economic concerns (endlessly parodied since 2016 as economic anxiety) did not.[15] Did that fit the Democratic zeitgeist of early 2017 or what? Republican culture wars and white nationalist revanchism explained everything.

A meta-analysis that replicated my own unscientific review of published work on 2016 found that the studies focused almost exclusively on vote choice and survey data.[16] In short, the research correlated individuals' responses to various questions with their stated vote choices. This is an effective way to match beliefs and votes—x percent of z voters who prefer y chose Clinton. This is useful and it tells us something. What it does not do is account for the changing electorate.[17] In fact, when lower turnout in 2016 and decreasing racial hostility among white survey takers is factored in,[18] Donald Trump received fewer votes from whites with high levels of racial resentment than Mitt Romney did in 2012. Racists and sexists voted for Trump on balance,[19] but such voters *always vote for Republicans on balance.* They did in 2012 and once again in 2020. They will in 2024. That sexists and racists prefer the Neanderthal* conservative worldview is not breaking news.

That "status threat, not economic hardship" paper? A subsequent analysis found considerable evidence to undermine the interpretation of the data.† The much-ridiculed economic anxiety was no less a motivator of

---

* Neanderthals were named after the Neander Valley of Germany where they were discovered; *neander* means "new man." Is life great sometimes or what?

† Using the same data as the original paper, "the relative importance of economic interests and status threat cannot be estimated effectively with the cross-sectional data,

vote choice than status threat.[20] This is not uncommon in academia, where the first paper on a topic is rarely definitive. No malice or deception was intended by the authors of the first study. They simply produced results that happened to align closely with what political elites wanted to hear: Clinton was good, but voters are dumb and racist and hate women and so they flocked to Trump. The question is why that should be explanatory in 2016, when those statements are not only true but *less true* than they were in past elections won by Democrats (especially Barack Obama, who really experienced the animal side of American racism). And the answer is typically avoided or explained away with activation theories positing that Trump made identity (race and gender, primarily) the determinative issue in the election.[21]

If so, why didn't Hillary Clinton's campaign successfully redefine the election to be about something more favorable to Clinton? They tried! It just didn't work because "qualified" and "experienced" were of very little interest to the voters (and nonvoters) who determined the outcome in 2016. The attitude that Americans more or less owed Clinton the presidency certainly didn't help.* (At one point the campaign seriously considered "Because It's Her Turn" as a slogan.†) If only there were something else Democrats could offer voters who have been ground into paste by the gears of the globalized economy, something more relevant to struggling people than "but our candidate is very, very qualified." Ah, nevertheless.

RED FLAGS, RED SENATORS

That there was competition in the 2016 Democratic primaries was not unusual. In fact, the winnowing of the field down to only two candidates

---

and the panel data are consistent with the claim that economic interests are at least as important as status threat."

* A celebrity Clinton endorser, campaign member, and surrogate stated after the defeat: "It was supposed to be her job. She worked her whole life for the job. It's her job." See Dunham, L., "Don't Agonize, Organize," *Lenny's Newsletter*, November 10, 2016, www .yahoo.com/lifestyle/dont-agonize-organize-164149299.html.

† The wordplay meant to suggest "America is ready for a woman president," but when read literally the statement suggested the candidate felt entitled to the job. They chose the deeply unmemorable slogan "Stronger Together" instead.

by February 2 meant the field was unusually uncompetitive for an open nomination.* Given Clinton's enormous advantage in support among the Democratic establishment, her win was not unusual either. You will find no endorsement of "the DNC stole the nomination from Bernie" conspiracy theories here; parties are not obligated to be impartial observers in their own nomination processes, and historically they have not been. Thus, the obvious preference among establishment Democrats and the major liberal media outlets for Clinton—even in light of the extraordinary, not to say questionable, commingling of the Clinton campaign and the DNC's finances and personnel†—is not proof of a conspiracy.‡ It is evidence that the New Democrat revolution that rose to prominence after 1988 is firmly institutionalized in a party establishment that prefers reliable, predictable, centrist candidates with money and name recognition who promise not to rock the boat too much.

Clinton's nomination was considered a lock from the moment Obama secured his second term in 2012. A key complaint among left or progressive liberal voters who were Clinton-skeptic was the oppressive sense of inevitability, that Clinton 2016 was "a feature of our reality that seemed intractable," with "no room for participation beyond absolute fealty."[22] It was simply going to happen, and the voter's job was to act thankful for the opportunity to support it.

That's unkind, admittedly. Yet the strong primary performance by Bernie Sanders should have caused more worry than anger among establishment Democrats, heeded as a warning that the Clinton juggernaut was vincible. Sanders, often tarred as a socialist, is in practice simply a New

---

* "Open" meaning without an incumbent president or vice president running.

† For that tawdry tale of insider back-scratching, see Gaughan, A., "Was the Democratic Nomination Rigged? A Reexamination of the Clinton-Sanders Presidential Race," *University of Florida Journal of Law and Public Policy* 29 (2018); and Holland, J., "What the Leaked E-mails Do and Don't Tell Us About the DNC and Bernie Sanders," *Nation*, July 29, 2016. I endorse the conclusion of both authors that while the DNC openly detested Sanders and wished to see his campaign defeated, evidence of rigging the process is lacking.

‡ This narrative is consistent with the robust finding that perception of fairness in elections is influenced by winning or losing; see Sinclair, B., S. Smith, and P. Tucker, "'It's Largely a Rigged System': Voter Confidence and the Winner Effect in 2016," *Political Research Quarterly* 71, no. 4 (2018).

Deal Democrat.* He was born in the wrong century. Slap an 1890 birth date on him, and his position that the government should robustly fund the social welfare state and focus on ensuring a minimum decent standard of living for every American would have been in perfect alignment with the rise of FDR. Crucially—and of the millions of words spilled on Bernieism since 2015 I think this best summarizes his appeal—he tells voters struggling to make ends meet despite working hard that their poverty, their needs, their failure to enjoy the American Dream is not evidence of their own moral deficiency. Lack of material success is not a personal failing. The economy needs cheap, insecure, compliant labor to function, and it has been designed to produce it.

That's it. That's the appeal of Bernie Sanders. He talks to people who have been shit on by a system rigged against them, a system everyone recognizes they cannot overcome by any "rise and grind" bromide, and tells them they are not morally, personally, or intellectually flawed for struggling within it. While the Democrats writ large have pivoted to the neoliberal mantra that it's your own damn fault if the economy leaves you behind, Sanders is among the last prominent people delivering the old message of economic equality and the need for government to protect the individual from powerful economic actors.

The whole party used to stand for this, but in 2016, it sounded refreshing to some frustrated voters and may have been brand new to younger voters for whom the New Deal might as well have been the Middle Ages. The Sanders campaign earned what success it had. It outorganized a complacent Clinton team, and its aging candidate seemed tireless and energetic about offering voters an alternative. Yet the hindsight afforded by 2020—when Sanders again contested the nomination and, in a crowded field, earned much less of the vote—suggests that there was more going on in 2016 than good campaigning by Team Bernie. Some portion of Sanders's strong showing in 2016 reflected antiestablishment and "anyone but Hillary" sentiments. Sanders, whom Democrats often note is not a Democrat, could credibly position himself as an outsider and appeal to

---

* Even Sanders critic Paul Krugman makes this point, for example, "Bernie Sanders Isn't a Socialist—but He Plays One on TV. That's a Problem," *New York Times*, February 13, 2020.

Democratic primary voters who had liberal or left sympathies but little faith in the Democratic establishment Clinton represented. But clearly there were also voters who saw what most liberals and Democrats could not: that her victory in the general election was anything but assured, even against a man with the personal appeal of a clogged septic tank.*

By 2016, Hillary Clinton had been a fixture in national politics for twenty-five years—as First Lady, as the architect of the Health Care Reform Initiative (1993), as the runner-up candidate in 2008, as a senator, and as secretary of state. Perhaps no active figure in American politics was more of a known quantity in 2016. Opinions about Hillary Clinton were well formed already. She had the risky combination of high favorable and high unfavorable ratings, meaning few people were uncertain or ambivalent about her irrespective of the Republican opponent. While her policy positions could pass for generic Democrat, Hillary Clinton herself certainly could not. Confidence that voters who weren't thrilled with Clinton would come around if the campaign pounded home the manifest unsuitability of Donald Trump proved to be misplaced.

A second red flag was Clinton's failed presidential campaign in 2008. Time and historiography have left her loss to Barack Obama a hazy memory, but that Mark Penn–led campaign was so spectacularly bad that it undermined the official narrative in 2016 of Clinton as hypercompetent and a masterful campaigner. Not only did her previous campaign get outworked and outsmarted by a relative political unknown, but the more Clinton '08 struggled, the worse the campaign got. By May of 2008, she was openly race baiting, suggesting she shouldn't drop out because someone might murder Obama and that "hard-working Americans" wouldn't vote for him (*wink*), and it ended with a two-month temper tantrum, with both Bill and Hillary bitterly complaining about disloyal superdelegates who owed them so much. It was not pretty, a bad campaign ending in the least graceful way imaginable.

Both the 2016 primaries and her previous campaign for president suggested that Clinton was more inevitable than unbeatable. She struggled to

---

* I was among the "most" who, despite not being enthusiastic about Clinton, felt that she was likely to win. The available data suggested she was ahead; I based my expectations on that data, and the rest is history.

connect with voters viscerally in 2016, with her own postcampaign reflections reinforcing that the technocratic approach is in her bones. It simply is who she is.* In the primaries, as Clinton staffer Jake Sullivan noted in hindsight, her rejoinder to Sanders's big, idealist visions was:† "Instead of aspiration, we gave people arithmetic: [Bernie's] numbers didn't add up!"[23] For liberal elites, that's catnip. For the kind of voters Democrats need to convince, it's minutiae. When Clinton did talk in terms of vision it was positive platitudes—strength, unity, togetherness—that gained little traction with the modal working-class voter who could give a shit if Democrats and Republicans get along if achieving basic economic security and a decent standard of living remains an elusive dream.

Despite every warning sign and flaw, it remained likely that Clinton would win. Any number of mistakes, it seemed, could be balanced against the sheer lunacy of putting someone like Trump in the White House. And when it happened, despite all the postelection promises that it wouldn't be so bad—"Trump will grow into the office and drop the heel act once in the White House" was a popular narrative—it was, in fact, so bad. Liberals committed to asking repeatedly, "Is this what you wanted, America?" instead of focusing on how a party that has the slightest idea what it's doing could have lost to a candidate so stupid that he began his presidency without the remotest idea of what the president's job entails. They lost an election to Peter Sellers's character in *Being There* and followed up that lamentable feat by insisting that it wasn't really their fault.

---

* In a 2017 retrospective, Elaine Kamarck (the DLC-affiliated scholar who coauthored the seminal "Politics of Evasion" essay) details Clinton's policy reflex: "Even in a book about the election she can't stop writing about policy—an entire chapter is devoted to gun control. She frequently digresses. [While] explaining a major gaffe she has to remind us that 'I got to work developing the detailed plan to invest $30 billion in revitalizing coal communities.' Even though she knows her obsession with policy is not widely shared, she simply can't help herself." See Kamarck, E., "Why Hillary Clinton Lost," Brookings Institution, September 20, 2017.
† Tellingly, Clinton expressed anger in her postelection memoir toward Sanders, noting that his big proposals "left [her] to play the unenviable role of spoilsport schoolmarm" (quoted in Kamarck). Who forced her to respond in that way? Was no other framing or rhetoric possible? As Kamarck notes, this specific response is entirely in line with Clinton's own preferences, style, and messaging.

BUT WAIT! IT GETS WORSE!

For all the energy Democrats have sunk into explaining Trump's improbable win, none have grappled with the fact that the rest of the 2016 election was a resounding *meh* as well. Democrats gained six House seats while losing the national House popular vote, meaning Clinton *outperformed* Democratic House candidates in defeat. Democrats also won back two Senate seats, but the majority remained in Mitch McConnell's weird, clammy hands.

At the state level, the string of disasters continued. Republicans added two governorships and won the gubernatorial popular vote while making minor gains to their significant nationwide advantage in state legislative seats. As Trump entered the White House, Republicans held 4,152 seats to the Democrats' 3,125—a lopsided GOP advantage not seen in decades—and the Democratic down-ballot problems continued from there.

You don't lose to a goo-brained reality TV star without something being seriously wrong; processing what happened in 2016 required reexamination of every fundamental assumption about electoral politics that were mainstream Democratic orthodoxy. Few took the opportunity.* Instead, Democrats largely determined Trump was an aberration, a one-time lashing out of Americans' worst impulses. Much effort was devoted to determining what was wrong with Trump voters (bad people, racists, sexists, pieces of shit—please vote for us next time, though!), focusing only on examples that validated the hypothesis.

Crucially, sober postelection analysis undercut every pillar of the theory that toothless, unreachable racist hillbillies pushed Trump to victory. His strongest supporters and his narrow victory margins came from suburban professionals[24]—the kind of educated, successful voter at whom Democrats had been tailoring their electoral appeal for decades. These were the people Chuck Schumer infamously claimed would swarm to the Democratic camp even as Democrats lost ground in rural areas. The uncomfortable question arose that if slick, centrist, professional Democratic

---

* Rick Perlstein, for example, thoughtfully examined how he misunderstood American conservatism; see "I Thought I Understood the American Right. Trump Proved Me Wrong," *New York Times Magazine*, April 11, 2017.

friends of Wall Street can't win in the suburbs, who exactly can they win with? What is the point of Hillary Clinton if she couldn't win over the highly educated professional class for which she was a standard-bearer?

Instead of an answer to that question, we got a billion interviews with trucker-hatted Trump voters and daily, even hourly reminders of just how appalling Trump and his administration turned out to be. As a short-term strategy, "Trump is awful" produced some dividends in 2018 and 2020. Whether any of the underlying problems that made 2016 possible have been solved is less certain.

CHAPTER 13

LESSONS LEARNED

In *Learning from Loss* (2020), political scientist Seth Masket takes a systematic look at how Democratic Party insiders came to understand what happened to Hillary Clinton in 2016. His sifting identified a small number of common narratives.* One was Clinton's inability to connect with white working-class voters due to her handling of identity politics, as the insiders understood it. Another posited that Clinton and her campaign made many poor strategic choices. Finally, questions of electability posited that Democratic insiders had misidentified Clinton as a strong candidate when her gender (and the way voters perceive certain messages differently from women candidates) made her a poor matchup against Trump.

Though competing explanations abounded and remain today, Masket concludes that "the preponderance of narratives suggested a similar remedy: scaling back on some of the party's commitments and picking the 'safe' nominee who could best guarantee a win."[1] In other words, what the Democratic Party learned from 2016 was to maximize the odds of beating Trump (the top priority, obviously) by minimizing risks. The safest,

---

* See Hershey, M. R., "The Constructed Explanation: Interpreting Election Results in the 1984 Presidential Race," *Journal of Politics* 54, no. 4 (1992): 943–976, where postelection periods feature many competing explanations for outcomes before settling over time on a (general) consensus.

least objectionable, most experienced, most politically mainstream white man available would give voters the fewest excuses to reject the Democratic nominee due to some factor beyond the party's control (in the way, for example, voters' racism or sexism could repel them from a candidate they'd otherwise support).

Hence, Joe Biden. Implicit in this electability narrative is the continued Democratic hyperfocus on moderate, independent, and disaffected Republican voters—especially the white ones Trump won so handily—as the key to victory. Biden, Masket explains, was the choice among Democratic Party elites well before the Iowa caucus in 2020. While the pro-Sanders and left factions cried foul, Democratic power players, including Barack Obama and DNC chair Tom Perez, did in fact act in a coordinated fashion to rally the party around Biden once the primary season began, persuading competitors like Pete Buttigieg and Amy Klobuchar to withdraw prior to Super Tuesday.*

Were the Democrats wrong to conclude from 2016 that replacing a moderate white woman with a moderate white man would work? It depends on where the goalposts are. If the focus is exclusively short term, no. Biden defeated Trump, and defeating Trump was the dominant, perhaps sole, focus of Democratic politics after 2016. Masket quotes numerous activists and insiders who expressed a willingness to punt on policy if doing so helped defeat Trump. But that short-term view merely exacerbates the long-term problem Democrats will not, maybe cannot, confront. The 2020 strategy, in the context of the last four decades, looks less like something the Democrats learned from 2016 and more like a case of the Democratic Party doubling down on the only trick it, as currently constituted, knows: move toward the center. Appeal to moderates in the GOP along with undecided centrist voters, tout bipartisanship rather than transformative policy, reject extreme ideas both right and left, mollify the status quo, and offer oneself to the electorate as the adults in the room to the GOP's posse of insane clowns.† If Masket's analysis is right—and there is every reason to believe it is—then learning is the wrong frame.

---

* It was assumed correctly that a race coming down to Biden and Sanders would favor Biden.

† No relation to any artist or artists.

The strategy insiders chose for 2020 is almost indistinguishable from the strategy that has dominated the Democratic response to every electoral or political setback since the Reagan years, difficult to distinguish from the arguments for the Bill Clinton, Al Gore, and John Kerry campaigns, not to mention countless statewide and congressional candidacies. While the campaign did try to shore up support on its left flank by touting Biden's personal platform (detailed on the candidate's website, not necessarily featured in the campaign) as the most progressive positions ever taken by a Democratic candidate, the dominant focus throughout was to present Biden as a safe, predictable alternative to the manic Trump presidency.

The euphoria of beating Trump in 2020 may, then, be short-lived if he or something worse than him returns to the White House in 2024 while Democratic wheel spinning down ballot continues in 2022. The evidence that all is not right in Liberalville now that the bad orange man is gone is right in front of us: the 2018 and 2020 elections delivered more of a blue trickle than the promised or hoped-for blue wave, and the short time in which Democrats have had power strongly suggests they didn't learn enough. Falling back on the post–New Deal Democratic Party repertoire—campaign to the center, attack extremes on both sides, promise good stewardship instead of big changes—has always been the plan. What is different this time is that with the GOP already openly playing footsie with undemocratic minority rule, Democrats' failure to address that threat directly could lead not merely to defeat but to the minority with no clear path back to the majority.

MIDTERM RALLY

Like the 2006 election, Democrats regained control of the House in 2018 with two things in their favor. One was an unpopular Republican president who fired up liberal activists and motivated some ordinarily apathetic voters. The other was the imbalance created by several consecutive poor Democratic showings in congressional elections. Some seats Republicans had no business winning in the first place in 2014 and 2016 were ripe for Democrats to reclaim.

Democratic activists tried to credit a focus on a tangible issue—health care—with their good showing in House races in 2018.[2] Polling data did show that health care was the most commonly cited voter concern, and many Democrats' campaign ads were devoted to the topic.[3] But as with 2006, when Democrats took Congress as George W. Bush's popularity was plummeting, the 800-pound gorilla of a flailing autocratic Republican in the White House loomed larger than any substantive issue. There is strong evidence to suggest that the election was a powerful referendum on Trump by an electorate forced to witness his grotesque act for two years.[*] If voters cited health care as the top issue in polls, it is likely because "I can't stand Trump" was not an available alternative.

In another parallel to 2006, when the Democrats identified Iraq as the top issue in their midterm win and then did next to nothing about it, it was not clear to House Democrats what to do about the putatively crucial health-care issue with McConnell's Senate and the Trump White House in their way.[4] By 2020, the issue was all but forgotten as COVID-19 flared and Trump's behavior grew increasingly deranged.

In a preview of 2020, 2018 was a victorious letdown for Democrats. Taking the House was important, yet Democrats simultaneously lost two seats in the Senate. This was in part due to an unusual (and unlucky) number of Democrat-held seats up that year and partly due to the continued belief of the Democratic Senatorial Campaign Committee (DSCC) that lavishly funding supposedly electable moderates is the only winning play. One shred of good news aside from the House, though, came from gubernatorial elections, where Democrats picked up seven seats after a brutal stretch of losses in state capitols beginning in 2008.[†]

Biden's win, which was disappointingly narrow and fraught with suspense until days after the election, dulled the euphoria many expected to feel when Trump was defeated. A heroic effort in run-off elections for two Senate seats in Georgia produced a miniscule Democratic majority from a tied Senate. Georgia was an all-out blitz by both parties, with a Democratic ground game organized by one of the few modern

---

[*] The dean of political science postelection analysis argues convincingly that the long-held view of midterms as referendums on the incumbent held for 2018; see Jacobson, G., "Extreme Referendum: Donald Trump and the 2018 Midterm Elections," *Political Science Quarterly* 134, no. 1 (2019).

[†] This too proved short-lived, with the off-year 2021 gubernatorial races producing a Democratic loss in Virginia and an unusually narrow Democratic win in New Jersey.

high-profile Democrats with a strong grasp of the tedious basics of electoral politics, Stacey Abrams. In line with liberals' tendency to attribute outcomes to individual actors (a theory of politics akin to the "great man" theory of history, and with the same integral flaws), Abrams was immediately deified. As three *Slate* writers tactfully put it, the reaction to Abrams among the predominantly white, very online liberal base was "icky."[5] Abrams deserves credit and praise, but lost in the shuffle is how her smart strategy relied on thousands of volunteers on the ground who did the dull, repetitive, hard work and how she rarely passed up an opportunity to point this out, reminding voters that Georgia was a team effort and not something she did on her own by sheer force of will. That did little to stop enthusiastic liberals from talking about her like the white parents in Jordan Peele's *Get Out*.

The Abrams-led Georgia miracle exposed exactly what Democratic candidates and state parties were failing to do elsewhere, a dereliction of some of the most basic aspects of campaigning. The COVID pandemic was cited as a reason to skip canvassing in 2020, for example, yet *before the pandemic even began* the abortive Pete Buttigieg primary campaign's virtual campaign for the Iowa caucus was being touted as a blueprint for the presidential race. Unsurprisingly, every election postmortem of 2020 ended up highlighting the absence of canvassing as a flaw. Even dedicated centrism apologists of the Third Way public policy think tank gingerly concluded that "many [insiders and professionals] included in this analysis said in hindsight Democrats could have been on doors safely in more places—and Democrats would have won several close races if they had gone back on the doors either sooner or in a more robust way than they did."[6] Sources across the ideological board from Alexandria Ocasio-Cortez to defeated Alabama Senate candidate Doug Jones to presidential also-ran Beto O'Rourke highlighted the failure of the virtual campaign idea.

Rather than mask up, carry plenty of hand sanitizer, ring doorbells, and take three big steps back to preserve social distance, liberals were satisfied to have an excuse not to canvass while Republicans blitzed voters in critical areas. One apparently serious take argued that "Biden may well [have] trimmed his prospects by taking the ethical path of campaigning safely, limiting his interaction with voters, in contrast to Trump's super-spreader events. He deserves praise for that."[7] Does he? Given the stakes and the consequences of losing what was touted (plausibly!) as an election of epochal importance, "praiseworthy" would have been doing everything humanly possible to win, even things of uncertain efficacy that might require extra COVID precautions to do safely. What prize do candidates get for being most ethical?*

Whatever the cause, poor down-ballot performance and narrow Biden wins in several states cast a pall over what Democrats were hoping would be a resounding anti-Trump and anti-Republican statement. They lost House seats, lost control of two more state legislative chambers, and saw two more states gain Republican trifectas (partisan control of the governorship and both legislative chambers), all with post-2020 redistricting looming. Democratic struggles in state politics, which showed signs of abating in 2018 and 2019, continued in 2020. This wasn't hugely surprising; the Biden-Harris campaign was a rare example of the Democratic establishment settling on a strategy and having it work out *exactly* as intended: Hillary Clinton's narrow losses in several key states were turned into narrow Biden wins. As it happened, that plan to minimize risk also limited the upside the Biden campaign could have offered Democrats down ballot. His safe, low-key campaign didn't hurt other Democrats, but it didn't give them much of a boost either.

The good folks at Third Way—a spiritual successor of the Democratic Leadership Council, found wherever the treacliest centrist pablum is sold—offered a postmortem on 2020 that avoided unimportant questions like: "Is that thing where we rebrand Reaganism as a liberal economic worldview unpopular?" Instead, they zeroed in on the real problem: activists saying "defund the police." Republicans repeatedly and successfully painted Democrats not only as antipolice (note: Democratic candidates' support for defunding police was virtually nil) but

---

* Of all elections, canvassing has the least impact in presidential general elections; see Kalla, J., and D. Broockman, "The Minimal Persuasive Effects of Campaign Contact in General Elections: Evidence from 49 Field Experiments," *American Political Science Review* 112, no. 1 (2018). So it is unlikely that Biden lost many votes by failing to canvass. It is likely, however, based on extensive research on canvassing in down-ballot races that nearly every other Democratic candidate who declined to canvass lost votes.

as socialists. Candidates were tarred with "Dem potpourri," a bunch of common attack points like pictures of Alexandria Ocasio-Cortez, references to activist demands Democrats had zero intention of fulfilling, and a pervasive, nonspecific specter of socialist revolution. The solution? Better marketing! "Make it exciting" to be a Democrat, and the avalanche of Republican attacks will surely lose its impact. That the report noted Democrats "lacked a core argument about the economy,"* in the words of the *New York Times*, and "leaned too heavily on 'anti-Trump' rhetoric" is mentioned almost in passing. First, scold the left.

The *New York Times* declared this report "the most thorough soul-searching" either party undertook after 2020—a curious claim about a document that contains at best a light rehashing of exhausted talking points.[8] The report, incidentally, was authored by principals of a consulting firm that did work in 2020 for the DCCC (Democratic Congressional Campaign Committee) and ludicrous "pro-Trump Democrat" Kentucky Senate candidate Amy McGrath.† Obviously, the best people to interpret an election were the ones who oversaw the *Starship Troopers* of Democratic Senate campaigns and yet another embarrassing bellyflop in the fight for control of the House.[9]

To an extent, Third Way analysts sound like they get it: they highlight the need for Democrats to combat Republican disinformation, to define themselves rather than letting Republicans define them, and to present a positive economic agenda. Valid points, all. Things fall apart quickly, though, when it becomes clear what they mean by each of those. Combatting disinformation means pointing out that Republicans are liars. (Wait 'til voters hear about that!) Defining themselves means branding, finding the right combination of marketing speak, buzzwords, and corporate HR jargon—the kind of stuff Americans who are not political consultants detest. And the positive economic agenda is the same tired mix of Bill Clinton–era solutions—public-private partnerships, means-tested social programs, tax incentives, fiscal austerity, opportunity and entrepreneur

---

* I bet you can guess what core message on the economy Third Way recommends.
† The problem of futile Senate campaigns wasting scads of money raised from gullible out-of-state donors includes but is not limited to McGrath; see Sokolove, B., "The Losing Democrats Who Gobbled Up Money," *New Republic*, February 14, 2022.

fetishism, getting cool CEOs and the market to fix problems—all solutions working-class voters didn't trust twenty years ago and now utterly despise. It's a prescription for more of the same thing that, judging by present circumstances, has not only failed but has American democracy on the verge of heading down a very dark path.

STORM CLOUDS

Third Way does highlight the worst news from 2020 for Democrats: the decline of support among Black and Hispanic voters. Trump actually *improved* his performance among voters of color after four years of waking daily and challenging himself to somehow be more racist than he was the day before. It is difficult to overstate how alarming is the prospect of Republicans making inroads with Black and Hispanic voters, however slight. For nearly three decades, "demographics is destiny" has been a cornerstone of liberal thought—that Republicans might dominate an aging white base, but a changing country and changing electorate will eventually, inexorably crush the GOP beneath a diversifying electorate where groups loyal to Democrats make up the majority.

The idea, popularized by John B. Judis and Ruy Teixeira in their 2002 bestseller *The Emerging Democratic Majority*, is enormously comforting to Democrats. The future is ours! But the theory has some holes. What if, as we see today and have seen since the push for voter ID laws during the George W. Bush years, Republican voter suppression efforts succeed at disenfranchising enough Black and Hispanic voters to counteract demographic changes? What if years—decades, really—of broken Democratic promises to Black and Hispanic communities leave voters disconnected from politics altogether? What if the treatment of the Black and Hispanic electorates as monoliths is foolish, and some of those voters are more receptive than liberals realize to right-wing messaging on culture war issues? What if authoritarian strongman posturing has as much appeal to some struggling, frustrated, fed-up Hispanic or Black Americans as it seems to have for some white people? What if the racism and xenophobia inherent in Trumpism has a core of appeal even to some voters of color who like the idea of keeping someone, even people with whom they share aspects of their identity, beneath them on the socioeconomic ladder?

The assumption that Democrats can win the Hispanic vote simply by virtue of the racism and xenophobia embedded in American conservatism has always been dubious. George W. Bush did well among Hispanic voters in 2004 with only the most minimal feints toward softening Republicans' hard-right immigration stance. Conservative ideas are also more popular among Black voters, especially older ones, than the Democratic voting habits of the Black electorate suggest.* It is highly unlikely Republicans will win majorities of Black or Hispanic voters anytime in the foreseeable future. But that's beside the point. Democrats can so little afford to lose support that any defections are critically important.

Third Way offers no good solutions to the dilemma, only the ominous warning that "voters of color are persuasion voters who need to be convinced." Imagine, if you can, a major political party that needs reminding that voters must be persuaded, that votes cannot simply be taken for granted as owed. Even those voters with "nowhere else to go" because the GOP is so much worse can, and do, give up on voting altogether if they feel that their party is not fighting for them. This is so obvious that merely typing it out is enough to drive one mad; it's like having to explain to one of the teams in the World Cup that they must kick the ball toward the goal in order to score.

Democratic efforts to reach the diverse electorate on which they depend (including younger voters) tend toward the symbolic, the superficial, and the downright patronizing. We'll break our promise to cancel student debt, but here's a campaign video featuring Billie Eilish! The kids these days like that, right? What if, while pursuing a policy of showering police with money and sheltering them from accountability, we cloak ourselves in the outward symbols of the Black Lives Matter movement? What if we promise to maintain 99 percent of Donald Trump's border policies but have better, smarter, more diverse leaders running the deportation machine?

---

* Ideology and partisanship are different; voters, individually or as groups, can be extremely loyal about casting Democratic ballots without being very liberal. This dynamic is especially important to understanding the Black electorate, where Democratic loyalty does not map neatly on a survey-based measure of ideology; see Jefferson, H., "The Curious Case of Black Conservatives: Construct Validity and the 7-Point Liberal-Conservative Scale," SSRN, July 6, 2020, https://ssrn.com/abstract=3602209.

The problem might not be merely that Democrats treat their base as monolithic groups but that they treat them like monolithic groups of idiots and ingrates who fail to show fealty to the party that does so much for them.

STUPID COUP

It would be repetitive to rehash the January 6, 2021, events at the US Capitol and the various inept attempts by the Trump campaign to overturn the results of the 2020 presidential election in detail. What is important is to recognize that the Trump "stop the steal" debacle was an effective dry run for Republicans to overturn future election results. What was absent in 2020 was the full backing of the conservative establishment; with it, in the future, even a putsch as transparently stupid as Trump's can work. Republican efforts at voter suppression continue to escalate, although 2020 did build Democratic confidence that hard electioneering work can overcome these barriers.* The weak points in the system, however, remain the constitutional power of state legislatures to choose electors independent of the popular vote, and the ability of appointed state election officials to invalidate votes or otherwise manipulate outcomes post hoc.

There is no insurmountable safeguard to prevent this from happening. The Constitution clearly states in Article II, Section 1: "Each State shall appoint, in such Manner as the Legislature thereof may direct, a Number of Electors." The manner chosen by the legislatures can be proscribed by state law, but Republican-led chambers are already revising those legal niceties. The federal courts as currently composed are overwhelmingly likely to stand aside with a strict, literal interpretation of the "in such manner" clause. They'll shrug and declare the matter up to the states, and then state legislatures full of QAnon-poisoned car dealers will have free

---

* Unable to convince even the fifty Senate Democrats to pursue voting rights legislation, let alone the Republican senators that Biden claimed during the election would have a post-Trump "epiphany" and work together with him, as of August 2021, Biden asserted that Democrats could outorganize the rising wave of GOP voter-suppression tactics. See Derysh, I., "Biden Team Calls for 'Out-Organizing' Voter Suppression—Activists Say That's Insulting," *Salon*, August 3, 2021.

rein to let their paranoia govern. Any faith that Republicans' decency, or institutions like the Supreme Court, will stop such a scheme is hard to justify under the current circumstances.

So if it can happen, why didn't it happen in 2020? One possibility is that Republican leaders like House Minority Leader Kevin McCarthy and Senate generalissimo Mitch McConnell felt that they had achieved enough of their big-picture goals under Trump to keep the election-overturning powder dry for the future. With the massive Trump tax cuts, considerable deregulation, and, just weeks before the election, the death of Ruth Bader Ginsburg (which allowed McConnell to confirm another Federalist Society–stamped Supreme Court justice and secure an un-breakable 6–3 right-wing majority), Trump just wasn't worth going to the mat for.

We are unlikely to be so lucky indefinitely. Democrats' ongoing strug-gles in state legislative elections give Republicans an effective veto power on the Electoral College at the state level in a close presidential election, should they choose to go down that path. Furthermore, extreme steps like a GOP-majority House refusing to certify election results are at least plausible now. Combined with voter suppression efforts now ratcheting up the war against mail-in ballots and people of color, the postelection period in 2020 was not the last pratfall of a confederation of dunces try-ing to do the impossible. It was an effective demonstration for the future of exactly where the weaknesses in the system are and how a united GOP might exploit them.

The Democratic response has been, well, mixed and uninspiring. Con-gressional Democrats remain torn between the conflicting messaging of the Republicans as an existential threat to democracy and as partners in governing. Are they power-mad autocrats or good sensible folks to sit down with and hash out a bipartisan infrastructure bill? Overall, both Biden and the congressional leadership show no sense of urgency. If this is a crisis, you wouldn't know it from the response. Democrats have been unable to even keep their own coalition united behind basic voting rights reforms, let alone to take any of the big, structural changes necessary to begin rolling back the Republicans' power grabs: expanding the Supreme

Court, abolishing the Senate filibuster rule, making statehood for DC and Puerto Rico* a priority to ameliorate the disproportionate power of small states in the Senate, or doing much of anything beyond embarrassing wheedles for a better, nicer Republican Party to play by the rules.

If Democrats are so concerned about the current iteration of the GOP, the way to reform it is to crush it electorally so thoroughly that it will have no option but to change. Shaming, finger wagging, hectoring, and begging won't work. Devoting an entire prime-time night at the Democratic Convention to Republican apostates (as Biden did in 2020) won't either. At every step over the past four decades, Democrats have insisted on downplaying or refusing to see what the American right was becoming. Now there is legitimate reason to worry that they can't or won't see what is happening until it's far too late. Post-2020 Democratic governance has bet heavily that a return to something resembling normal Washington politics will appeal to voters after the daily adventures of the Trump presidency. It's a long shot, the kind of strategy you convince yourself is brilliant because the better ideas have all been ruled out. Why, instead, didn't Biden and his thin congressional majorities approach the two years following 2020 as the Democrats' last, big chance to show voters just how much they can do when entrusted with power? History and the midterm loss phenomenon strongly suggest that the GOP will return to the majority in one or both chambers of Congress in 2022. Yet Democrats still lack a strategy beyond telling voters to vote blue even harder to empower them to get things done. Too little weight is given to the more obvious explanation that getting things done would encourage more voters to vote blue without needing to be cajoled, begged, scolded, or threatened. The choice between "vote for us and we might do what you want" and "we did what you wanted, now it's your turn to do your part" seems, but apparently is not, clear.

THE TWO-BODY PROBLEM

The Biden presidency started promisingly when both the White House and congressional Democrats refused to wait around seeking Republican

---

* Contingent, of course, on the residents of each indicating a desire to pursue statehood.

support for the planned COVID relief legislation. When it was clear none was forthcoming, the bill was passed through the Senate reconciliation process, which circumvents the filibuster and enables passage with a bare majority of votes. Hosannas were sounded. Bells were rung. Paeans were written. The Democrats, it seemed, finally got it. Republicans only want to obstruct, defeat, and destroy. Democrats should stop trying to entice them to the bargaining table and instead use whatever powers are at hand—executive orders, parliamentary maneuvers, threatening Senate recalcitrants with dismemberment on the National Mall—to do good things Americans will like. Nobody knows or cares what reconciliation is or whether a bill is bipartisan; people know only whether the government is doing something to help them.

Some of the celebration bordered on manic. "Welcome to the New Progressive Era" blared the usually reserved Anand Giridharadas in the *Atlantic*.[10] Paul Krugman took to the *New York Times* three weeks into the Biden presidency to explain "How Democrats Learned to Seize the Day."[11] *New York Magazine* asserted that Democrats' "approach to legislative strategy has fundamentally changed."[12] MSNBC assured viewers that Democratic leaders were committed to learning from 2009 and even offered an uncharacteristically hard assessment of the Obama White House: "The mistake was Democratic efforts to pass key legislation with Republican support, and it happened over and over again."[13] Even the left-leaning *New Republic* (with some prescient skepticism*) allowed that the COVID relief bill and strategy were winners.[14]

There was reason to question this narrative, but Democrats can only exist at the poles of dejected hopelessness or smug triumphalism. Despite Biden campaign promises to enact a fifteen-dollar minimum wage and student debt relief (which does not require Congress but can be done through executive action), both populist priorities were casually jettisoned. The minimum wage hike was considered for inclusion in the COVID relief bill—reconciliation broadly interpreted can encompass any budgetary matter—but was excluded on the cartoonish excuse that the unelected, advisory-only Senate parliamentarian said no. A vote on the

---

* "Party leaders like Joe Biden and Chuck Schumer say they won't repeat the missteps of Barack Obama's first term. They haven't proved it quite yet."

Bernie Sanders–chaired Budget Committee's attempt to waive the rules and allow the minimum wage increase to go through quickly revealed the real reason: at least eight Senate Democrats opposed it.*

The COVID bill, it seemed, was both the beginning and the end of the lessons-learned phase. After the victory lap, Senate Democrats fell hard back into old habits, with caucus "moderates" Joe Manchin and Kyrsten Sinema taking the most visible positions opposing the institutional changes the political moment required. Both defended the filibuster with categorically ridiculous, reality-free arguments about the need to compromise. A District of Columbia statehood bill was introduced, as usual, and went nowhere, as usual. Even the cornerstone of the Democrats' acknowledgment of the reality of Republican voter suppression, the John Lewis Voting Rights Enhancement Act, stalled. A massive White House–led infrastructure proposal, with numbers as large as $5 trillion over a decade initially proposed, became a bipartisan bill obsessed with "pay-fors" and subjected to one round of cuts after another.

Build Back Better (BBB), which encompassed a range of items from the Biden-Harris campaign agenda touted as the most progressive in history,[15] turned into a public showcase of congressional Democrats relapsing into their worst habits. With Manchin, Sinema, and others (behind closed doors, of course) grousing about the cost of even minimal, insufficient measures to address climate change and a variety of social welfare needs, BBB was eventually split into three bills: the aforementioned COVID-19 relief package passed early in the Biden presidency, an infrastructure spending package (enacted as the Infrastructure Investment and Jobs Act on November 15, 2021), and the American Families Plan (AFP). House progressives initially insisted that infrastructure and the social-spending-heavy AFP pass as a single bill, knowing full well that separating it from infrastructure was a ploy to let AFP wither on its own. Eventually, House progressives yielded in exchange for a verbal promise from President Biden that he would secure Senate passage of AFP after the bills were separated.[16] You won't believe what happened next.

---

* Including Democratic-caucusing Angus King (I-ME).

This is not to argue that nothing good has happened since Trump was sent packing. But the narrative early in 2021 that Democrats have turned things around and renounced their errant ways was premature. Biden and his fellow aging Democratic leaders have failed to show that they understand the gravity of the current crisis and can respond accordingly—as robustly and aggressively as possible, not with as little as they think they can get away with while still claiming "we fixed it." The filibuster remains in place as an excuse not to make more substantive changes, now joined by the darkly comic claim that they were thwarted by the unelected parliamentarian atop the list of excuses voters don't want to hear. Major voting rights legislation looks impossible with the filibuster in place, as does meaningful domestic legislation to follow up the COVID relief bill. Far from expanding the welfare state as one might expect from the New FDR, the Biden-led interventions into the social safety net are temporary and depend upon future political capital and willpower to expand or renew.

In short, Democrats plan to stand before the electorate in '22 with the kind of message they've been relying on for thirty-plus years:

- We did some things. If you are mad about the things we could have done but chose not to, you're a whiner with unrealistic expectations. We can't scare away moderates!
- The Republicans are bad. Very, very bad.
- We did all we could. Nothing better was possible. Here are all the excuses for why we couldn't do more. Stop laughing at the part about the parliamentarian.

The reader has an advantage here, as the outcome of the midterm elections may be known by the time your eyes reach this page. From this perch, however, it looks like the Democratic Party, facing what may be its last chance for the foreseeable future to govern, is reacting by declining to govern in a misguided effort to keep itself in power longer. The point of political power is to wield it before losing it again—especially when, as is clearly the case with the Republican Party of today, the opposing party is gearing up to ensure that its grip on power is decoupled from election outcomes. Instead, we see evidence that Democratic leaders believe voters will give them another shot, ideally with bigger majorities, in 2022 or 2024. There is a fine line between optimism and wishful thinking.

THE PRESCRIPTION

As the Democratic establishment sees it, the inability to pass a more ambitious agenda in Congress is not an indictment of the party; the solution is—and stop me if you've heard this before—down to the voters. With only the barest Senate majority, two dastardly villains, Manchin and Sinema, have waylaid the noble goals of an otherwise enthusiastic coalition. As always, the party and its geriatric leadership have done no wrong. The problem comes down to two people. Vote blue a little harder and the problem is solved.

This annoyingly familiar narrative is both an article of faith among the liberal base and holier than a colander. Voters have no reason to believe based on past experience that fifty-two Democrats will pass anything fifty will not. It is as likely that the two intransigents would be joined by additional "moderates" with many concerns about whatever changes are on the table. Obama's experience in 2009, for example, showed that even with fifty-eight or fifty-nine in the Senate, there were too many concerned moderates to engage the most progressive ideas he floated during the campaign. Only voters with memories that wipe clean with every election think that "Manchin and Sinema" isn't likely to turn into "Manchin and Sinema and (just for example) Chris Coons" were the majority increased. As usual, Democrats' strategy boils down to "trust us," while their track record argues powerfully against doing so.

More importantly, the process of attaining power and then being unable to enact the party's supposed agenda because not even all the Democrats are on board with it (Republican opposition is a given) has the exact opposite impact of convincing voters to vote blue even harder. Voters who put time and effort into getting Democrats into power might reasonably ask why they hear excuses and see fingers pointed at them. Even worse, they may question the point of supporting a party that sells itself as the smart people who "know how to get things done" but once in power is forever explaining what it cannot do and why.

This is a crucial disconnect between how Democratic elites and loyalists see politics and how the voters who so disappoint them seem to see it. The party has long argued that it needs people like Joe Manchin to attain majorities. Building a winning coalition requires, they assert, electing a few conservatives like Manchin in states Democrats could not otherwise win. The appeal of that argument is immense and obvious: find candidates who can win and hash out the policy differences later.

What if, contrarily, putting together a coalition that includes members who explicitly reject most of their party's agenda and who are willing, even eager, to obstruct it *is the problem* rather than a solution to the problem? The cycle of taking power, delivering only a fraction of what was promised (or what is required to address the problems voters face), and then moaning about how voters didn't show up for you in the subsequent election is a predictable one. Instead of insisting that attaining the majority is the most important thing, even if it takes a few Manchins to get there, what if instead candidate recruitment focused resources on House and Senate candidates who will vote with their party when a rare chance to govern arises?

Obviously, it's preferable to have the majority; that much Democrats certainly understand. But if the majority is attained with a coalition that can't agree on some basic, core agenda items and includes members whose purpose in life is to make everything worse, then the party's tenure in power is almost certain to be very brief. No majority that depends on Joe Lieberman or Joe Manchin can or will last long. It merely reinforces the perception that Republicans use power to enact bad policy with little public support, and Democrats respond by failing to use power to enact good policies people like.

The problem isn't Manchin or Sinema; the problem is that there is always a Manchin or Sinema to block, ruin, pare back, or water down whatever a Democratic majority purports to pass. Unfortunately for the party as a whole, voters' regular and predictable disaffection after delivering a Democratic majority suggests that everyone except the

Democratic establishment has figured this out. You have to deliver. It's that simple.

CODA

A final, illuminating anecdote.

In 2020 the House Democrats' campaign arm, the DCCC, instituted a blacklist policy for campaign professionals who worked for Democratic primary challengers. The policy was intended to protect incumbents from expensive primary campaigns, theoretically allowing them to devote their full attention to beating Republicans. The same Democratic leaders who regularly feign impotence when asked to apply pressure to recalcitrant moderates knew exactly how to play hardball when threatened by left-of-center primary challengers.

The policy was withdrawn in 2021 among general furor from Democratic progressives but not before a curious thing happened. As then DCCC chair Cheri Bustos (D-IL) was trying to enforce party discipline against primary challengers in 2020, Nancy Pelosi, Steny Hoyer, Hakeem Jeffries, John Lewis, and dozens of other prominent House Democrats endorsed Rep. Joe Kennedy III in his primary challenge against Massachusetts incumbent Sen. Ed Markey. Even Mark Pocan, chair of the Congressional Progressive Caucus at the time, gave his imprimatur to the scion of the Kennedy clan.

Nobody could explain convincingly why Markey—a wholly reliable team player since entering Congress in 1977—needed to be replaced. True, he was in his seventies, but the senescent House Democratic leadership could hardly hold age against him. Pelosi, whose support for Kennedy was especially emphatic, explained through an aide that she endorsed him because she "was concerned by attacks by the Markey campaign on Joe, his family, his supporters and the Kennedy family policy legacy."[17] It was not clear how high the Kennedy family legacy ranked among voters' most pressing concerns in 2020.

Kennedy seemed unable to explain why he was challenging Markey beyond the vague sense that he deserved to be in the Senate and he's a Kennedy. His hilariously inept campaign boiled down (predictably, inevitably) to ads featuring pictures of Robert F. Kennedy, very subtly reminding voters that he's not just some moist-mouthed, soulless cipher; he's a moist-mouthed, soulless *Kennedy*.

It was a spectacular waste of time and money. Markey defeated Kennedy by over 153,000 votes before demolishing his Republican challenger in November. Like the anecdote about former Kentucky governor Steve Beshear that began this book, ultimately the Kennedy primary challenge mattered little. Substantively, nothing changed. Yet it gives us useful insight into the party and its problems.

What are these people's priorities? What do they think politics is for? In the midst of an election of existential importance—Pelosi herself was emphatic and repetitive on the gravity of 2020—the most powerful Democrats in the House and quite a few big shots outside Congress thought that a good use of time and resources was to challenge a loyal Senate Democrat who caused no problems, toed the party line, and represented one of the few states blue enough for a senator to push a liberal agenda without provoking a constituent backlash.

And for what? Why? So Kennedy could have a bigger stage to haplessly point out the banality of neoliberalism with statements like "not a single patient should be forced to fight off medical bankruptcy in the midst of a global health pandemic without a lawyer by their side." Not that they shouldn't go medically bankrupt, not that a civilized, wealthy nation should go off to the woods and reflect on its moral failings for allowing "medical bankruptcy" to be a thing but to make sure everyone had a lawyer next to them when the bankruptcy judge summarily pronounced them destitute. Dream big, JK III.

The rank hypocrisy of blacklisting primary challengers and their paid support staff while lining up behind a blue-blooded and well-connected primary challenger was both obvious and beside the point. What do Pelosi and the others who endorsed this scheme think is the point of politics? What is all this *for*? If the goal is to get elected and hopefully take the majority, Markey was doing his part. If the goal is to pass an agenda, Markey was an entirely loyal and reliable vote. But maybe that's not what a lot of people within the Democratic establishment really think is the point. Maybe they see the point of politics as making sure that the right people have access to the power they deserve.

What lingers from this ultimately irrelevant campaign is the peek into the mindset of the thing we call the party establishment at its highest levels. With a deadly pandemic raging and Donald Trump actively trying to get us killed as the nation drifted away from democracy, someone thought, "We have to make sure Joe Kennedy III gets to write 'United States senator' on his résumé. Please understand that Joe *really* wants to be a senator." Everything felt (and feels) on the verge of collapse, and yet this is something they thought was important to do. This is what they thought was a good use of time and resources and the finite attention activists and ordinary voters can devote to politics. More desperate than ever to recapture working-class votes, prominent Democratic leaders signaled that their priority is making sure a spectacularly unlikeable rich kid from the American aristocracy got the lollipop he wanted. It was like the captain of the *Titanic* spending the ship's final moments before going under the icy black waters arranging a cabin upgrade for Mr. and Mrs. Astor.

For a political faction utterly obsessed with messaging and appearances (the "optics"), it's impossible to believe that they don't understand what kind of message this sends. It's business as usual up at the top, among our social, economic, and political betters. Our crisis is not their crisis. Things are fine. They're doing a great job. Their only responsibility is to one another. They owe us nothing.

CHAPTER 14

THE LAST CHAPTER PROBLEM

Two of the left's sharpest minds, Adolph Reed Jr. and George Scialabba, had an important exchange in 2014. Reed's "Nothing Left: The Long, Slow Surrender of American Liberals" in *Harper's* (March 2014) is a modern classic, laying bare Obama-era liberalism's self-satisfied vacuousness. Scialabba's critical response in the *Baffler*, "Now What, Left Wing?" (February 21, 2014), received little notice.* Describing Reed's critique as "wholly persuasive," Scialabba nonetheless wonders, paraphrasing Lenin: "Well, what is to be done? Fifty-two hundred words into his 5,450-word essay, Reed suddenly turns to this question . . . precisely where Reed's essay ought to begin, it ends. Admit you have no power; now go and get some. Don't expect *me* to fill in the program." Explaining what is wrong is one thing; offering a solution is much harder.

That's a great distillation of the "last chapter problem"—a dilemma for nonfiction books thoughtfully examined by David Greenberg in the *New York Times*. Even the best books tend to conclude, Greenberg argues, with "an obligatory prescription that is utopian, banal, unhelpful or out of tune with the rest of the book."[1] The basic demands of storytelling and narrative structure mean that a book devoted to a problem must conclude

---

* *Harper's* March issue published in February, hence the odd sequence of dates.

with some idea of what to do about it. Even if there are no answers, answers must be given. So they are, and often the answers are unrealistic, unhelpful, or even silly.

This problem looms large for books about politics. American politics presents daunting barriers to change, and even the simplest solutions prove to be complex, difficult, and unlikely under scrutiny. Writers often resort to "solutions" with no basis in reality, like wholesale mental reprogramming of the electorate ("teach people to be more critical consumers of information" or "educate voters" are personal favorites) or structural reforms to the political process (proportional representation, abolishing the Senate or Electoral College, ranked-choice voting) that sound great but have no obvious path to implementation in the near future. Anything we can imagine is possible over time and with great effort, but answers that defer results beyond our lifetimes aren't terribly satisfying. What can we do now? How do we fix this before it's too late?

Rather than take the flippant, even dishonest approach of claiming that I have the answer, I prefer to address Scialabba's charge to Reed upfront. We are in a bad situation politically, and there is no easy way out. Nothing—no radical reorientation of Democratic ideology or alternative electoral mechanism or piece of legislation or savior president or devastating tweet—will turn things around rapidly. Even if the Democratic Party flips a switch and backs an economically populist agenda speaking directly to the material needs of every poor and working-class person, voters will not be convinced until they see results. Promises won't cut it, and results take time to deliver.

The most optimistic scenario involves things getting worse before they get better because the mistakes that led us here were made repeatedly for a long time and have compounded to increase the difficulty of undoing them. An excellent example is the Supreme Court: its current right-wing majority became entrenched not because of one costly error but because Democrats' approach to the federal courts has been lousy *for decades.*[*] That can't be fixed overnight except by a structural reform (court packing)

---

[*] Emma Green argued effectively in "How Democrats Lost the Courts" (*Atlantic*, July 2021) that "some Democrats are starting to suspect that the story is simpler: They've been chumps. They have clung to norms Republicans long ago abandoned. They have

Democrats show no interest in pursuing. Popular but difficult answers like "primary Democratic legislators and replace them with candidates who support court reform" would achieve change only slowly if it worked at all. And it very well might not, given the obstacles to reforming something that people in positions of power do not want to see reformed.

Not every problem we face can be solved; no problem can be solved until it is faced.* So let's start there. The Democratic Party continues to show little inclination to engage in honest self-criticism in favor of doing the one thing it knows how to do in its current iteration: backpedal from its stated agenda to appease moderates, then blame the left (and a rotating cast of voting blocs that failed to vote blue with sufficient fervor) when it doesn't work.

Declining to offer fully formed solutions, to conclude the book with The Answer, constitutes taking the easy way out on my part in one sense. I plead guilty. But even if I did believe that I had all the answers, the sheer complexity of the problems would preclude condensing them into one neat chapter. Consider the situation—an inane media, a broken legislative process, elections drowning in money, a Republican Party marching toward authoritarian managed democracy, institutions biased toward rural and predominantly white voters, an economic playing field sharply tilted against workers, and staggering economic inequality are just a handful—and ask yourself what kind of "answer" could be simple and succinct. Only a magic-wand answer untethered from reality would fit the bill. That, in my view, would be the real easy way out. "Start a third party and that will fix it" or "primary them all" are every bit the bullshit cop-out as "I don't have the answers." They leave the how-to and the heavy lifting to you.

So what *can* I tell you?

THE SOLUTIONS THAT AREN'T

Two frequently proposed fixes for what ails the Democrats, and American liberalism in general, deserve a moment of our time: third parties and

---

championed moderates to appeal to their enemies, only to watch those moderates twist in the wind." Indeed.

* Paraphrasing, with respect, James Baldwin.

structural reforms like ranked choice voting and term limits. These aren't the solutions they purport to be. Sorry.

The French polymath (and communist) Maurice Duverger is best known as the namesake of Duverger's law, which posits that certain kinds of rules about voting and elections reinforce a two-party system. The most important of these rules are first-past-the-post plurality elections (whoever gets the most votes wins, even if he or she fails to receive a majority of votes) and single-member districts (candidates who do not finish first win nothing). In some voting systems around the world with proportional representation, our Libertarian Party (just for example) would win a small handful of seats in Congress as a reward for finishing with a small percentage of the vote nationwide. Instead, in the American system the party gets nothing. A revealing example is the 1992 presidential election when winning nearly 20 percent of the popular vote nationwide gave Ross Perot a grand total of zero electoral votes. Because he failed to win a single state, his getting nearly one out of every five votes meant nothing. He won exactly as much by getting nineteen million votes as he would have by getting nineteen.

That's an example of how our rules make it difficult for third parties to succeed even if they receive a decent amount of support. But just as important is the psychological effect on voters who might prefer a third-party candidate but don't want to waste their vote on someone they know cannot finish first. Throughout American history, no third party has been able to overcome this problem except briefly. Bearing in mind that electoral rules are made by representatives of the major parties, it's difficult to see how or why a system dominated by Republicans and Democrats would change the laws in ways that would benefit third parties.

Third parties can serve an important purpose without winning elections. When they achieve some measure of success, the major parties theoretically respond by stealing whatever issues or positions have contributed to the third party's success. A socialist or left-wing third party that finishes third in an election could force the Democratic Party to move to its left to recapture those votes. But this logic runs up against the seeming willingness of Democrats to lose and assign blame instead of changing their approach and agenda to satisfy more voters. It's as likely as not that the outcome would simply be to maintain the status quo and scream at voters for daring to vote elsewhere. I've yet to see a convincing argument of how a third party, even a successful one, would change that. So I'm not going to tell you there's nothing to be gained by a well-organized, coherent third-party movement. I am telling you to have the right expectations about what a third party can accomplish. Racking up wins over Republican and Democratic candidates isn't likely, nor is it likely that the Democratic Party will quickly see the error of its ways and change.

Ranked-choice voting and statewide runoff elections are now used in a few states, with no discernible consequences for the two major parties. If these reforms were to fuel the rise of third parties or independent candidates, there is every reason to believe Republican and Democratic legislators would push back to protect the two-party system. Another popular panacea—term limits—sounds like a great idea as long as one ignores the evidence that term limits in state legislatures have largely benefited interest groups and lobbyists.[2] They also increase partisan polarization, reduce legislative output, and encourage legislators to spend their brief time in office auctioning their votes to the highest bidder.[3] All three of those things are already problems. Term limits exacerbate rather than solve them.

It is useful to devise ways to fix our clearly broken system. However, it's important to be honest about the consequences rather than simply insisting or believing that a given reform will be a solution. Neither third parties nor alternative voting methods are bad ideas in a vacuum. They just aren't the quick fixes they are often presented as. Even in the best scenario, assuming that the infamously fractious American left can co-ordinate rather than splinter, third parties are unlikely to win elections outright and might not motivate Democrats to do anything differently. Party building is hard and takes a long time. Don't expect miracles or instant gratification.

DO THEY NEED YOU MORE THAN YOU NEED THEM?

The question of how to fix the Democratic Party coexists and often over-laps with a separate question about how to advance progressive or left politics. They're distinct topics. The Democratic Party isn't the sole or even the best vehicle for achieving social and economic justice. Things can get better without them. Similarly, Democrats could start winning more elections and our social and economic problems as a country could easily stagnate or worsen. Consider, then, that "How do we fix the Democratic Party?" may be the wrong question. If they are not addressing the problems you want to see addressed, then the cold reality is that they need your vote more than you need them. All they can do for you is to be "not the Republicans." That is, as the previous pages have hopefully made clear, by design. Democrats' ideal constituent is a well-off person who demands nothing more than that, and they have found enough of them to justify continuing on their present course. If "not the Republicans" isn't enough for you, then your own view about voting and of how change can be achieved might need revising.

This explicitly is *not* a book about the wide range of nonelectoral means to achieve change: social movements, community organizing, union advocacy, debt collectives, mutual aid—you name it. The separation between activism and electoral politics is growing as activists disillusioned by unfulfilled promises and symbolism over substance are increasingly skeptical of promises. What once looked like Democratic outreach to activist groups now looks like attempts to co-opt movements and reorient leadership away from goals and toward managing expectations.[4] You may need to accept that we have reached the limits (forgive the burst of Marxist rhetoric) of what bourgeois electoralism can accomplish. Maybe the Democratic Party can't be fixed, or maybe fixing it isn't the solution you're looking for. It would be ideal and convenient if voting regularly and responding to some of the fifty daily email solicitations to donate money to Democratic candidates were enough to bring about the society we want to live in. But it should be clear that it isn't. We'll return to this dilemma shortly.

Obviously, power brokers in the Democratic Party are not waiting with bated breath to hear what Ed Burmila thinks they should do. The world is full of policy and strategy advice offered up unsolicited for Democrats' consumption. The problem is that they have concluded that they don't want to do any of those things. They're confident that their preferred course of action is the right one, and it's up to voters to accommodate them. As with the New Deal–era Republicans who were satisfied being in the minority, they'll continue to spin their wheels until they decide that the most important thing, the only acceptable outcome, is to win and enact their agenda. That's unlikely to happen unless and until they are forced to change by circumstances beyond their control. It may take a McGovern- or Mondale-type drubbing to rattle their cage sufficiently.

This problem is not one that gets resolved by nominating a savior candidate or improving the party platform. Having the best platform on Earth won't matter if Democrats can't win and can't (or won't try to) pass anything once in power. The problem is a mindset; the way they think voting, elections, governing, and politicking work is flawed. There is no easy way to fix that. Hell, there may be no *hard* way to fix that. Within the limits of electoralism, change will come only when voters demand it. Until then, the tension between core Democratic constituent groups that demand results and those that accept excuses in lieu of results will continue, producing occasional majorities that disappear quickly.

THE CENTER-RIGHT COUNTRY THAT ISN'T

Consider the following graph, which depicts an estimate of liberal policy mood based on responses to the large American National Election Studies survey. Note that these estimates are minimally influenced by Americans' increasingly liberal attitudes on so-called social issues involving race, equality, LGBTQ+ rights, abortion, and more. In other words, the survey overemphasizes Americans' preferences on core economic policies—taxes, funding the social safety net and welfare state, economic inequality, government spending, and more.

How can Americans favor liberal economic policy so strongly (even the low ebbs on the graph are above 50 percent) and yet the ostensibly liberal party struggles to win elections? Baffling, right?

There are two ways to interpret that disconnect. One is what I call the James Carville hypothesis: that Democratic economic policies are broadly popular while activist positioning on social issues is not;[5] see Carville warning in 2021 that "wokeness" was hurting Democrats who lost the plot with ordinary Americans by using academic-tinged

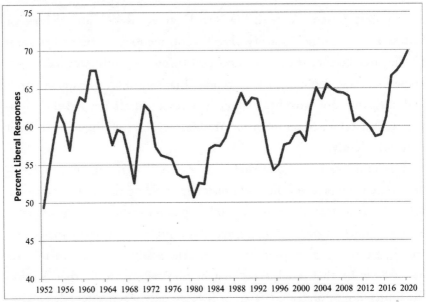

Estimated liberal policy mood of the American electorate, 1952–2020. Based on survey responses to the American National Election Studies analyzed by Prof. James Stimson. For detailed data and methodology, see James Stimson's site, https://stimson.web.unc .edu/.

language like BIPOC communities.* This "popularism" narrative remains a powerful force in Democratic political strategy, exemplified by the surge in popularity (pun welcome) of star strategist of the Biden-era David Shor. His version of popularism—that Democrats should talk about (and do) popular things while not talking about unpopular things—is the updated version of Carville's famous take on the economy. Democratic elites love to hear this (Shor, as of early 2022, has the ear of people in the White House) because it confirms their preexisting beliefs: that Democratic ideas are popular, but activists repel voters with demands like "defund the police." The solution, as ever, is to discipline activists and push nonthreatening, strong-polling technocratic

---

* Carville has the kernel of a point; elected officials and candidates *should* speak familiarly and without excessive jargon to audiences and BIPOC may not be vernacular yet. Nonetheless, he overestimates both the prominence and the impact of such choices. If "BIPOC communities" is alienating terminology in his view, it is hardly a crucial component of Democratic messaging. Even if he is correct, how big of a problem is this? Who is losing elections because they said BIPOC?

economic ideas paired with, if not explicit racist appeals, an implicit agreement not to talk about that race stuff.

There is scant evidence to support this idea, which is a problem given its powerful implications for Democratic strategy. Mountains of survey data over time suggest that Americans, especially self-identified liberals or Democrats, express greater tolerance on a range of social issues— from women in the workforce to divorce to single-parent households to LGBTQ+ equality to varying proposals for ameliorating the consequences of racism.[6] The story of the American polity since World War II has been one of more, not less, professed tolerance on many issues.[*] The Democratic Party has contributed positively to this, however unevenly. The whole hypothesis that it repels voters from Democratic candidates is based on two huge and questionable assumptions: that Democratic economic proposals are as popular as claimed and that their appeal is negated by the lack of appeal of Democrats' social liberalism.

An alternative interpretation is that the Democratic Party shuns, rather than champions, popular economic policy because its electoral strategy obsessively tries to appeal to people who oppose those policies. What the Democratic establishment now sees as its most important supporters includes a category of voters (our HEPs) and a range of industries (think Wall Street) that stridently oppose the kind of policy working-class voters used to like about Democrats. Convinced that the working class, the poor, and other former components of the Democratic coalition will not reliably turn out to deliver wins, the mainstream Democratic view endorses the Mark Penn theory of elections: focus only on the voters who are undecided and are almost certain to vote. Turnout is most likely among better-off, whiter, more suburban, older Americans. In other words, the people who would like economic populism are already voting Democratic or will not vote; the only way to win more votes is to reach for voters who actively dislike it.

Note the seeming incongruity baked into the Clintonian strategy of opportunistic centrism. Public opinion is used to justify the New Democrat

---

[*] This does *not* imply that racism, sexism, homophobia, and other issues have been solved or have necessarily improved. It means only that the attitudes Americans profess using the imperfect tool of survey research have gotten more liberal.

evolution everywhere *except* on economic issues. If voters say they want a more punitive criminal justice system, Democrats shrug, throw liberal principle over the cliff, and become tough on crime. If a similar majority of voters says it wants a higher minimum wage, suddenly the popularity of that policy is irrelevant. It is replaced by a stern warning that moving left on economic policy will alienate persuadable moderate voters. So sometimes it matters what voters say they want, and sometimes it doesn't. Generally, if a policy punishes the poor, marginalizes already marginalized people, or reinforces the economic and social status of the better-off, then public opinion means Democrats must support it. If the public supports universal social programs or things that directly help the poor or working class, then public opinion is bad and should be discounted.

One needn't be hugely cynical to conclude that the difference, the deciding factor in when polls reveal the correct policy and when they do not, is *what Democratic elected officials and elites do or do not want to do.* Embracing center-right economic ideology is what they do because they and the people whose opinions matter most to them are big fans of it. That most voters—especially Democratic voters—are not fans is no deal breaker. HEPs will rally around something that looks like economic populism but is "smart," which is to say it is complicated, heavily means tested to weed out the undeserving, and ultimately ineffective. Universal health care is bad; the ACA is good. Higher wages are bad; Rube Goldberg machines that funnel money to small business owners and major industries to "encourage investment in communities" are good. People who oppose economic populism get what they want; people in favor of it get lectures about how nothing can be done now. Democrats hear and see you and share your concerns, but they do not intend to do anything about them.*

The result is both where we stand now and the root of the problem that animates this book: a Democratic Party that is not merely responsive to

---

* Like an alarming number of contributions to the lingo of mainstream liberalism, this comes directly from the organizational management, human resources playbook—to diffuse anger and demands by giving employees an opportunity to vent and be heard by those in power. It remains questionable how many working-class voters want to vote for people who talk like the consultants their boss brings in to fire them.

but hyperactively defensive of the interests of one kind of voter to the exclusion of others. The party that still fancies itself the party of the people rejects all manner of liberalism that offends the sensibilities of well-off, mostly white, often-suburban, resplendently degreed professionals. These constituents happily embrace symbolic liberalism while rejecting the substantive kind. Their insistence that GOP Lite is the only acceptable ideology is the—not among the, but *the*—limiting factor on how successful the Democratic Party can be. With time, the voters who were promised rose gardens that turned out to be Superfund sites have seen clearly that the party is not responsive to their demands. The Clintonian solution of offering one group pleasing rhetoric or performative politics while the other gets policy is losing its impact with time.

Historians Lily Geismer and Matthew Lassiter put it well: "The relentless pursuit of moderate white suburbanites is at once a symptom and cause of the Democratic Party's unwillingness to fight for a working-class agenda that attacks economic inequality, systemic racism, and the global climate crisis by guaranteeing quality housing, health care, and employment; freedom from police brutality and the carceral system; and enacting a Green New Deal."[7] We are told those policies are too liberal, too extreme, and that Americans simply will not tolerate them. The best we can ever have are half measures, perhaps some streets renamed after victims of brutal police violence.

That leaves us with a system in which the Republicans set the terms of acceptable debate for Democrats, and the Democrats' role is to police and to define what is possible for the left and for progressives. You end up with a political party whose primary function is to manage the expectations of its own voters, or would-be voters, and then seems baffled when it cannot achieve more electoral success, and then insists that the only way it can do better is to be even more like its opponents. When diluted economic policies fail to win voters' hearts, Democratic strategists emerge like clockwork after every election to insist that the only way to make the party more appealing is, frankly, to knock off all that woke stuff and focus on underwhelming economic policies they insist and believe are far more appealing to voters than they really are. It is the definition of a vicious cycle.

THE POPULARITY PROBLEM

Moderates, undecideds, swing voters, floating voters to our friends in the UK—whatever term you prefer—they're a risky target. They have preferences that make no sense cumulatively, such as favoring expensive government programs while demanding tax cuts, and tend to be poorly informed overall.[8] They gravitate toward simplistic, ineffective "common-sense" solutions on issues like crime (lock 'em up!) and poverty (get a job!) and are eager to avoid addressing problems in the present if action can be deferred to the future.[9] The brain of a persuadable moderate voter is not the place to look for a coherent worldview.*

Consider the 2016 or 2020 presidential elections. Who were swing voters? The venerable Cook Political Report concluded that they were overwhelmingly people who pay little attention to politics.[10] But consider, nonetheless, a hypothetical well-informed, conscientious moderate deciding between Trump and either Hillary Clinton or Joe Biden. What goes on in that person's head? On the one hand, they seem to recognize that Trump is a dangerous authoritarian con man. On the other, they'll gladly vote for him if the Democratic candidates propose an economic agenda to the left of Mitt Romney. That's not moderation or ambivalence: "Lower my taxes or I'll vote for the fascist" is the ideology of *the worst human being on Earth.*

For how long and how effectively can a party pander to the basest, most ambivalent, least-informed people until it becomes substantially like them? Practically, how can a party tell its millions of loyal voters that they can't have things they want because it might upset the handful of mouth breathers who see authoritarianism as preferable to modest tax increases on the wealthiest Americans?

This is the inescapable risk of a strategy of opportunistic centrism. It requires telling your most loyal voters that they must accept policies they don't want in order to win over new voters. If the new voters cease to be won over, then the steep ideological compromises the base has been asked to accept no longer seem worth it.

---

* This also is true of many with partisan voting behavior.

This led Democratic elites to a lamentable conclusion: the easiest way to avoid this awkward situation is to build a base of loyal partisans for whom *failing to achieve liberal policy goals will not be a deal breaker*. And this, reader, is where all roads merge, where the HEPs become essential to the Democratic Party not only because they were identified in the 1960s and 1970s as a growing, important share of the electorate in a changing economy. They became important because, as a successful demographic made up of people who can meet their own material needs and do not, as a whole, suffer oppression and discrimination, they have remarkably little skin in the political game. Politics is important to them in the way their favorite TV shows are important; they care what happens to the characters because they're emotionally invested, but ultimately the outcome is irrelevant. Their preferences are just that: preferences, not demands. The distinction matters.

Health care and access to health care are interchangeable to people who already have health care and have never worried about not having it. A program named Home Affordable Modification Program is great, even if it does nothing to help foreclosed homeowners stay in their homes and instead is a cynically named handout to mortgage lenders. HEPs aren't generally the kind of people at risk of foreclosure; instead they are the kind of people who work in real estate, lending, and banking. Immigration policy may have changed little between Republican and Democratic administrations, but HEPs either have high-education skills that grease immigration processes or see the whole issue in the abstract. A social welfare program guaranteeing everyone a minimum standard of living is effectively the same as a means-tested program that excludes the undeserving by middle-class standards or is bureaucratically complex to the point of being impossible to access. The difference between a policy and *some version* of that policy, even if only symbolic or in name, is negligible.

But the HEP base is not only ambivalent about outcomes on the policies it claims to support; it also stridently opposes liberal policy in key areas. Journalist Ronald Brownstein distilled what he called the four core ideas of Clintonism, all of which attained scriptural status in the Democratic Party: opportunity and responsibility, economic globalism, fiscal discipline, and government as catalyst rather than problem-solver.

These are worth looking at briefly because each one is aimed squarely at the preferences of professional-class liberals. "Opportunity and responsibility" means Democrats are all in on Republican framing on the welfare state. People no longer deserve a minimum standard of living; they must earn it by meeting standards laid out according to contemporary middle-class mores. Being a professional and managerial class, HEPs grudgingly tolerate Democratic lip service toward unions, labor rights, and issues of inequality, but to your average middle-management liberal, labor is a pain in the ass. It needs to be disciplined and powerless, cheap and easily replaceable. Free trade means economic growth, however unequally distributed, and to people nearer the top than the bottom, a disproportionate share of economic growth is their just reward for having "earned it." "Fiscal discipline," similarly, becomes an unemotional data point on which to base opposition to the welfare state. Of course, I want to help the poor, but, but, but the deficit! Finally, a preference for deregulation and limited government activism requires liberals either give up goals like environmentalism, racial and gender equality, and fairness or embrace a worldview in which the market, employers, corporations, and individuals will resolve those things. Believing that the market will do it conveniently frees elected officials from the need to do anything difficult to advance those goals.

HOW TO BE A POLITICAL PARTY 101

The cycle described above can continue, at least until Republicans abandon any pretense of endorsing the basics of electoral democracy. Democrats can win one election for every two or three they lose and take a half step forward for every ten steps the GOP drags the country back to the right. The way to break this cycle requires more than people like me lecturing Democrats on how to make their policies better, more effective, and more appealing. Those things won't matter unless and until they fix a much more fundamental problem for a political party: they refuse to be partisan.

Isn't partisanship bad? Isn't polarization at the root of so many problems, as the last three decades of political science and popular analysis have reminded us endlessly? In a sense, yes. But the polarization and the increasingly vicious partisanship are being driven by the right, while

Democrats insist, in line with modern liberal values, that the solution is to pursue neutral, meritocratic, rule-abiding fairness. A great example is the parties' competing approaches to redistricting and gerrymandering. Republicans believe, as New Deal–era Democrats believed, that control of redistricting is a powerful opportunity to extract the maximum advantage for one's party. Democrats respond that the true goal of redistricting should reflect a high-minded good governance commitment to doing things the right way. The problem should be obvious. Republican state legislatures and governors draw maps that wring every last possible benefit for the GOP out of the political landscape, while Democrat-controlled states fail to respond in kind. Imagine you're driving a car, and the passenger reaches over and yanks the steering wheel hard to the right every few minutes. If you as the driver refuse on principle to yank the wheel to the left but instead insist that bringing the wheel only back to the center is the right thing to do, what direction will the car be headed after a few iterations of that cycle?

As the political theorist Nancy Rosenblum has argued convincingly, the solution cannot be bipartisanship or nonpartisanship but *better* partisanship.* Ceding the moral high ground to moderates, the center, independents—whatever term you prefer—is a change that occurred in the Democratic Party under Bill Clinton. It's a recent phenomenon, not some long, proud tradition that needs to be defended or revived. The results have been abysmal. The car continues to tack farther to the right, and no one even tries to correct the imbalance by steering it to the left. Over time, the conservative movement inevitably wins in that scenario. That is why exhortations to vote blue because putting the Republicans in charge will make things worse fall flat after three decades—because the Republicans are winning. Things are getting worse. Politics are inexorably drifting to the right. The Democratic political worldview that disdains the idea of a political party being partisan is a suicide pact; this strategy guarantees that the right will win, whether it happens quickly or gradually.

---

* Required reading on the value of parties and partisanship and the moral vacuity of the veneration of nonpartisanship or bipartisanship is Rosenblum's *On the Side of the Angels: An Appreciation of Parties and Partisanship* (Princeton, NJ: Princeton University Press, 2010).

That is why a useful understanding of the current political moment has to go far beyond "the Republicans are bad" because, as obviously true as that statement is, it fails to force the Democrats to reckon with the reality that they are utterly failing to stop their opponents and are refusing to consider how their own bad politics, bad ideology, and bad strategy are abetting the GOP.

Democrats complain with justification about the institutional factors that favor the GOP—the Senate, the filibuster, the conservative-packed judiciary, and so on. None of these obstacles can be overcome without embracing partisanship, which too many Senate Democrats in their razor-thin majority refuse to do. They worry, for example, that court packing would be seen as a partisan power grab. Here's the thing: it is, and that's OK. Partisan power grabs are an acceptable aspect of partisan political competition unless losing is an acceptable alternative. The solution to the problem of the Republicans' constant power grabs is not to scold them until the "good GOP" reasserts control over the party. Nor is it working to appeal to a nonexistent politics judge who will rule the Republicans' actions as bad and unfair and award the Democrats a victory for behaving like good boys and girls. The solution is to push back in the seemingly rare moments in which Democrats have the chance to do so. And, knowing that whatever Democrats do the GOP will later seek to undo, they must push back as hard as possible and then some.

There is no future for a political party that rejects the idea of being partisan. This is the most toxic legacy of New Democrat thinking, the belief in a postideological politics in which parties and labels aren't central to the process. In the wake of the Trump presidency, the ideal governing strategy for the first two years of the Biden administration would have been to attack every institutional disadvantage to Democrats with gusto and to use every tool at the president's and Congress's disposal to shower voters with tangible, direct benefits. Instead, they proceeded with their usual caution and self-negotiating, abandoning some explicit campaign promises and yielding to moderates, whose only purpose seemed to be to take every pending bit of legislation and make it worse.

Liberals forever scold the left about the harmful influence of purity tests: don't brood about what the candidates stand for, just vote for the blue team. The Biden presidency demonstrates with lamentable clarity the shortcomings of that approach. If a party attains the majority but does so with a handful of members who are not interested in supporting the broader agenda, then the whole point of holding power is undermined. All parties are coalitions with ideological range, but there must be some limit, some line in the sand on which one side is Democrat and the other is not. Having some purity tests on crucial issues like voting rights reform or abolishing the filibuster would, notwithstanding what "vote blue no matter who" advocates tell you, be of great benefit to the party as a whole. American politics offers few opportunities for a party to exercise unified control, and if those opportunities are not exploited to the utmost, then the party's position can only weaken over time. Simply put, Democratic wins when in power are not impressive enough. "Half a loaf" and "better than nothing" aren't the resounding arguments moderates seem to think, and failing to address the Republicans' continued tilting of the playing field in their favor makes something like permanent minority status inevitable for Democrats.

So, a basic first step is not to engage, as we so often do, in the endless cycle of proposing different policies until Democrats find the magic recipe that wins more voters more regularly. Instead, focus on the many things Democrats do that make it harder for them to win elections and render them ineffective (or less effective than they need to be) when in power. If the party is not willing to rediscover, relearn, and embrace self-interested partisanship, then all the great policy prescriptions in the world won't matter. If nothing else, fighting back in kind against Republicans' baldly partisan efforts to rewrite the rules of the game to their advantage would suggest to voters that Democrats have a basic self-preservation instinct. If party elites continue to insist that the recruitment, endorsement, and support of candidates can be free of any kind of ideological litmus testing, that any warm body with a D next to the name is good enough if they deem that person electable, then this cycle will never end. They will attain infrequent majorities that fail to accomplish much because they are majorities built on a coalition that lacks commitment to a basic, shared agenda. To be stymied and undermined by the opposing party is expected in politics; to regularly be stymied by elements of one's own party says that the party is incapable of governing effectively.

That's my magic-wand prescription for the party: be partisan and stop throwing the weight of the Democratic campaign apparatus at candidates who do not demonstrate a basic commitment to core matters of survival for the Democrats, like voting rights legislation, procedural reform in the Senate, and addressing the imbalance of partisan power in the federal courts. Any Democrat who can't commit to that will do more harm in the long term than any contribution they might make in the short term to a Democratic majority. When faced with questions like this, responsibility is palmed off on primary voters. Hey, the primary voters of Arizona wanted Kyrsten Sinema, don't look at us! This omits the crucial fact that when Schumer uses the DSCC to shower Sinema—whom he handpicked even though she was well established as one of the most conservative House Democrats—with money, party elites are placing a heavy thumb on the scale in primaries. You might be able to build an occasional majority out of candidates who exist only to undermine the rest of their party, but it won't be a majority capable of sustaining itself. In fact, by reinforcing public perceptions that Democrats cannot or will not deliver on their promises, it is likely to cause more long-term damage than any temporary wielding of power can offset.

WHO'S IN CHARGE HERE?

Another straightforward problem for Democrats at every level is leadership. Bluntly, people who are not very good at their jobs get into positions of power and hold what appear to be lifetime appointments. Are you picturing Steny Hoyer or Chuck Schumer? Either will do. At the state level, similar Democratic figures are entrenched around the country. This is the worst aspect of liberal politics as fan culture, latching onto individuals (Obama, Pelosi, RBG, Biden, Harris, etc.) as though their personal success and advancement are what matters. More baffling is why this extends even to uncharismatic blobs like Hoyer and Schumer. Ask yourself, what have these people done? What is their track record? What record of achievements suggests that they should continue in positions of power?

I humbly suggest that any and all leaders who led the party to the dire situation in which it finds itself right now should be, if not marooned on a desert island, at the very least replaced. At the moment this book goes on sale, the top three House Democrats will be 82, 83, and 82. President Biden is 79. Mr. Schumer, a sprightly 71, belongs in a Cub Scouts uniform by comparison. Hillary and Bill Clinton are 74 and 75. What few "young" figures are popular among party elites—Pete Buttigieg, Kamala Harris, Hakeem Jeffries—are deemed rising stars because they endorse and adhere to the same worldview as the ancient party power brokers.

It is lunacy to expect leaders to initiate a meaningful change of course when they are subject to no expectations, are in charge simply because they're in charge and haven't decided to retire, and have spent decades inside one system with space for a single worldview. As Nixon once said, "We are all Keynesians now," so too are "we" all neoliberals since Clinton. Reform doesn't come from octogenarians who regularly let slip that they yearn for the good ol' days when the congressional GOP wasn't like this. In these dire circumstances—make no mistake, they are now dire— the Democrats should be turning to younger, more aggressive leadership who, regardless of policy positions, are willing to fight and to recognize the GOP for what it is. You can imagine the names for yourselves, or consider the possibility that the right, confrontational leaders are out there waiting to be discovered. Don't fall for the Mayor Pete gambit, offering up a younger person who adheres to all the same flawed ideas as the dinosaurs who anointed him. A change of leadership won't solve things on its own, but without it, envisioning how the Democrats survive and eventually succeed is considerably more difficult.

So, that's it. Keeping things simple, my advice for the party is to be partisan and find leaders who will fight as hard and as pitilessly and as uncompromisingly as Mitch McConnell does. Bring back a Jim Wright, the disgraced Speaker of the House who was a crude, unprofessional, and lugubrious old-school fixer but who would have chewed glass to advance the Democratic agenda. If a given person can't be relied upon to burst into laughter and expletives upon hearing excuses involving the Senate parliamentarian, then that person is not leadership material, period.

A BOLD IDEA

But you want to hear some specific policy stuff anyway, don't you?

For generations the Democratic establishment has insisted that liberalism simply cannot win, and McGovern '72 is the definitive proof. Only moving to the right is a winning move; moving to the left is a death sentence. That's logically consistent only if we disregard the extent to which it becomes, and is, a self-fulfilling prophecy. Democrats have been left bashing and running away from liberalism of the New Deal vintage for decades now. How could the voting public possibly embrace ideas when both political parties join hands and agree that they are bad? Remember, both Bill Clinton and Barack Obama failed in a quest to cut Social Security. That was going to be their masterwork: a chance to be the Democratic president who enabled the Republicans' eight-decade quest to reform the most popular entitlement program in America. Think about that.

Imagine if instead of agreeing that government is bad and part of the problem, Democratic candidates *robustly and consistently* defended it? Not sporadically followed by retreat when right-wing media yelps but steadily. Public opinion can be led, not just followed. Following it is straightforward, albeit done inconsistently. Leading it, however, is much harder and pays off only over time. If the modern Democratic Party has proven one thing, it's that it doesn't want to do things that might not bear fruit immediately. The next election is always the only thing that matters. And that's a big stumbling block—it is undeniable that if the party were to reorient itself toward progressive, activist goals, it might cost them in the short term.

Read that again; it's important. Ideologically rebranding would *not* produce immediate success and would likely accomplish nothing unless accompanied by the kind of structural reforms and reoriented attitude described earlier. Republicans took decades of electoral drubbings on their path to the favorable position they've occupied since Reagan defeated Carter in 1980. If the prospect of doing worse in the short term is a deal breaker in your mind, consider that things aren't exactly going gangbusters for Democrats under the current strategy of prostrating themselves to an imaginary moderate. If your view of the last several decades of American politics—comprehensively, at all levels—is that the

Democrats are doing pretty good, we are inhabiting different realities. We are at an impasse, and I'm sorry you read this far.* If the argument against changing course is that it might give the Republicans the presidency in 2024, you'd best sit down before I tell you what the status quo is doing for Republican electoral odds in 2024 and beyond.

The long-term advantage is that every progressive policy that Democrats actively reject now had the potential to create loyal voters who would not need to be begged, threatened, shamed, and cajoled into coming out to vote. Forgiving student loan debt might offend moderates, but if enacted, it also has the potential to create a bloc of voters who will never, ever forget the president and the party who did that for them. Think of the people with decidedly nonliberal attitudes and beliefs who became loyal Democrats for life on the strength of what the New Deal did for them. What if forgiving student loan debt costs Democrats their congressional majority in the 2022 midterms, you ask? As with the ACA and 2010, the odds are outstanding that they're going to lose it anyway. "Let's do good stuff for people while we can" is worth a try given how poorly "don't do anything that might upset our idealized swing voter" has been working.

Think of what divesting the Democratic Party of antilabor, union-busting, big-tech worshippers could do to boost the confidence of tens of millions of working-class Americans—the working class of the present and not the past, people like Uber drivers, health-care workers, freelance anythings, day laborers, restaurant staff, package handlers—that the party is on their side rather than their bosses' side? It would be a relief to be rid of the awkward elite liberalism that tries to sympathize with working people who are exploited but insists that the people doing the exploiting aren't bad.

What if, instead of a world where people are oppressed but there are no oppressors, there was a party willing to state unambiguously that comically wealthy, powerful robber barons are the enemy of people who can't find an apartment for less than 80 percent of their income? It would hurt robber baron feelings, sure. But those working-class voters Democrats

---

* No refunds.

insist will only respond to Trumpian racism might find it more appealing than a party insisting that cool CEOs and complicated tax credits are going to fix our problems. It might take some time for this strategy to bear fruit, but both alternatives currently battling for supremacy in liberal circles—popularism and whatever this status quo is—are not exactly lighting up the scoreboard.

Another common criticism of this approach is that progressive policies appeal to younger voters who vote infrequently and who will become more moderate with age. This old saw certainly explains a generation like the boomers, who expressed liberal sympathies until they amassed a huge amount of wealth and pivoted to defending it. But will today's younger people experience the "amass wealth" part? Home ownership, savings, pensions, even simply having stable long-term employment—these are all things that theoretically make people more conservative with age but also things many under-forties can only experience in history books. If the economic and social structure that caused previous generations to drift rightward are gone, why should the effect be assumed to remain?

Any strategy comes with risk, and the approach presented here is not guaranteed to succeed. If the Republicans continue down their current path, there may soon not even be meaningful elections to compete in. When the futility of the current approach and its poor track record are properly considered, however, the risk of trying something different diminishes. It may work or it may not. We do know with a high degree of certainty that trying desperately to piece together just enough votes to beat some QAnon-brained Republican sociopath every couple of years (and spending the intervening years telling your voters why so little can be done with power) is a failure. It doesn't work nearly often enough to offset the damage Republicans do—often with Democratic assistance or at least acquiescence—and over time, things will only get worse. The lesser of two evils delivers evil more slowly but ultimately takes us to the same destination.

It is no doubt tempting, even addictive, for Democrats to continue to center a liberal base for whom politics is merely their favorite thing to watch on TV. Voters who have skin in the game, for whom politics is the difference between stability and grinding poverty, are more demanding and less forgiving. People struggling with debt, forced into demeaning and unremunerative jobs in lieu of stable and rewarding careers, unable to afford the basic cost of living, and vilified by a bipartisan elite consensus as lazy and spoiled cannot afford to settle for symbolic "wins" that don't solve problems. That the Republicans do not solve these core economic problems for voters either is not the point; the Democratic Party plainly needs to find a way to get better at winning these voters' loyalty. What they are doing now isn't working. The results speak with a clear voice.

THE MORAL

If you disagree with the vast majority of what you read in this book, if nothing at all seemed worth your while to read, I hope you can take just one thing away from it: what the Democrats are doing, and have been doing for a long time, is not working. A strategy that led us here has been, by definition, a failure. They have to try something different. And not in the marketing-branding sense of different, where old wine is repackaged in new bottles. Messaging is not the answer here, as if the right combination of buzzwords will make voters Democrats. The current approach that sets the bar at "not as bad as the GOP" has proven incapable of stopping Republicans from their mission to drag the country back to the Gilded Age. We are stuck in a cycle: Democrats win power when dissatisfaction with the GOP surges, talk themselves out of governing, and the GOP comes roaring back into power and goes on a rampage. Things slowly, gradually, consistently get worse. Slow disintegration isn't the big step up from rapid destruction that some liberals believe it is.

This strategy has persisted because it appeals to a specific kind of person who does not perceive anything wrong with this country that can't be solved by consistently voting for the blue team. People who are doing well financially, who are broadly successful, may reject my assertion that there are problems deeper than "more people need to vote for Democrats." To them, things are and always will be fine. These people spent the Trump years yearning to go back to the way things were under Obama without realizing that for Trump to happen, things must have been a lot less rosy under Obama for many Americans than they believe. The reality is that for decades the working class in the United States has been beaten down, falling further behind, working harder with less to show for it. It might be your first task to recognize that what seems fine to you might be—in fact, is—a system that has utterly failed millions of other people.

If we remain stuck in this cycle, the right *will* win. It will keep moving to the right while Democrats respond in kind to keep pace with the shifting center. What is happening in the United States and elsewhere with ethnonationalism becoming an open and explicit core of the appeal on the right is not a fad, and it doesn't lead anywhere good. Center-left parties like the Democrats will either figure out how to appeal to the working class and the poor that they once considered their core supporters, or we will all suffer the consequences. That, as I noted at the beginning, is why I wrote a book about the Democrats instead of another mind-numbing exploration of how the Republicans are very bad. By any meaningful definition, the Republicans and the conservative movement are winning. I hope we can agree at least on that and conclude from it that whatever the Democrats are doing to oppose them is not having the desired effect. Remember that the next time you hear that the answer to our problems is something you've been hearing for decades. If move to the center is supposed to work, why hasn't it worked? If nothing I suggested here strikes you as a good idea, maybe start by asking if it's time to try something, anything, that isn't the same tired nostrums self-declared political sages have been pitching for forty years.

ON MORALS AND VOTES

Now, the hard part.

Most of the Democrats' problems can be traced back to the fact that Republicans are bad. Very bad. Evil, even. Accordingly, Democrats can set their standards and expectations below sea level, and there is a built-in temptation to do as little as possible, to do nothing hard, and rely on the most convenient argument available to them: we are better than the Republicans. The GOP is sufficiently bad that this statement is almost bound to be true. For voters, the logic is simple: things will get worse right now if you do not vote for even the lamest Democrats. When Democrats are in office, anything they do is fine or at least excusable, because what the GOP would do is worse. Rationally, "vote blue no matter who" becomes a defensible argument.

Once voters accept the premise that they are *morally obligated* to support a political party no matter what it does, then the party has no incentive to respond to voters. None. An enthusiastic vote and a "lesser of two evils" vote count the same. There is no holding their feet to the fire once in office if they have a guarantee of perpetual electoral support. You can't pull them left; you can't pull them anywhere. They have no incentive to do anything but whatever best serves the interests of the wealthy and the powerful, declare it superior to whatever the GOP would have done, and remind you that you owe them continued support, *or else*. They're not just immune to being swayed in office; they don't even understand the concept of having to earn your vote. They believe it is owed to them, that by offering themselves as any alternative to the GOP, they have done you a favor.

So, try this. It's straight out of the playbook of how right-wing activists reshaped the GOP to their liking as the New Deal began to fall apart, and how the really goofy fringes of the right have taken over in the twenty-first century. Start by having some basic expectations and demands as a voter. If your attitude is "I'll vote for anyone as long as they're not a Republican," try a baby step like amending that to "almost anyone." If anyone claims that the argument this book presented is "do not vote," they are lying or intentionally misreading it. But I do believe that voting needs to become the least, not most, important thing you do if you sincerely want to see things change in this country. You should cast your vote with the understanding that it's not enough and that as long as you reward elected officials for doing little more than existing and calling themselves Democrats, those people will continue to do what is easiest, best, and most lucrative for themselves. Your alternative is to decline to vote for them. As one person, that's all you have control over.

I know, I know. I've heard every argument about how nonvoting or failing to vote blue makes things worse because it increases the likelihood of Republicans winning. But here's the thing: Republicans already are winning. When they're not winning elections outright, they're getting the political outcomes they want with alarming regularity. Look around you.

Look comprehensively at the political landscape, including state and local politics, unelected institutions like the courts, and the policy direction of the country over the past four decades. The right has won and is winning. So really, the argument that withholding a vote helps Republicans boils down to an argument over the pace of change. Things get worse either way, and we get to choose whether it happens faster or more slowly.

If "don't vote for people who don't support the most important things" sounds too simple, remember that it has worked on the right. In a *Washington Post* editorial, I once argued that the key to defeating the National Rifle Association was to think as they do, to be as fanatically uncompromising in favor of gun control as they are in opposition to it.[11] Republican elected officials didn't turn into gun extremists overnight.[12] It took years of NRA-guided voters telling their elected officials: "If you support gun control you lose our vote forever, period." Liberals fail to wield an equally powerful opposition in favor of gun control because—as with every issue—liberals willingly, reflexively accept excuses in lieu of outcomes. Compromise and giving the opposition some of what they want is centered in the process, and disappointment gives way to the "vote blue no matter who" imperative.

On the most basic level of understanding electoral politics, the flaws in this approach have to be apparent. If today's Republican Party looks like a bunch of militant activists with fringe beliefs controlling a cadre of elected officials who are terrified of displeasing them, it didn't used to be that way. The party's leaders happily played second fiddle to New Deal Democrats for decades, selling the idea of cutting deals to get a little of what they want to a well-off base that wasn't all that upset with the status quo. That is the role the Democratic Party has settled into since losing its dominant political position. Take what you can get. Cut a deal. Throw our own putative ideals under the bus to appeal to our opponents. Hey, where did our diehard supporters go? Why isn't anything getting better?

This is a deeply uncomfortable idea for liberals drilled on decades of Democratic strategy that tries a lot of messages but always, always boils down to "the Republicans are worse, aren't they?" Nothing will change if that argument is followed to its conclusion. The GOP will keep getting worse, and Democrats will continue to flail around wondering why "we are less bad" isn't a winning guidepost. Democrats try to make inroads with the working class in the same way Republicans say, after every election, that they need to be less racist and appeal more to people of color. They try it out, and when it doesn't work immediately or they feel themselves falling behind, they jettison it and rush back to what they know.* They revert to playing the greatest hits, which for Republicans is be racist and for Democrats is punching left to impress centrists.

How can that cycle be broken? Not easily and not without risk, certainly. You have to make demands, set conditions, and be firm. You have to have some expectations of the people you vote for. There will always be excuses and arguments, threats and extortionate blame shifts, pleas for one more chance. At some point you have to say *no*.† "Vote blue no matter who" is a mindset the Democratic establishment encourages among supporters because it benefits them. It takes all the pressure off. Deliver or don't deliver, whatever. Voters must support us; we're the only game in town! It's both deeply cynical and exploitative. The party encourages the mindset that all positive change left of the GOP must happen through Democratic electoral politics, which is why its answer to everything seems to be (and is!) to vote blue, but harder. The party will defer anything that is difficult and do only what suits its own interests because it has concluded that there is no alternative.

Except Americans do have an alternative, one that the voters Democrats struggle mightily to attract have been taking: they abstain. They give up. They walk away. Or they get so angry that they're easy prey for the right-wing outrage machine. There are always alternatives, and the last few decades are conclusive proof that Americans are all too willing to take them. Nobody has to vote for the Democratic Party.

---

* In a notable example, Republicans' postmortem on Mitt Romney's loss in 2012 concluded that the party needed to appeal more strongly to nonwhite voters. After a half-assed attempt to rebrand, the 2014 midterms almost immediately devolved into an extremely racist bout of fearmongering about a disease of African origin (Ebola) that a Black president was intent on spreading across the United States.

† Or not! If your personal calculus is that voting blue no matter who makes sense or is meeting your expectations and needs, by all means do it. I'm not here to dissuade anyone from voting.

In politics, as in life, it turns out that nobody owes anybody else a goddamn thing. To get something from voters—and this includes or should include you—requires making promises and following through on them. The cycle of promises made and fulfilled creates something called loyalty. It makes people want to vote for a party more than grudgingly. Right now, the Democrats are extremely effective at making a specific kind of voter excited about voting blue. Those are voters who make no tangible demands other than "not Republican," and Democrats have grown lazy catering to them.

This strategy has gone as far as it can go. To progress beyond the limitations of a politics in which Democrats, majority or minority, play second fiddle to Republicans hellbent on building some kind of Mayberry fantasy ethnostate, Democrats must convince more voters to vote for them more often. That really is it. What a simple statement. But it is, at its core, the whole problem. The options moving forward are simple: Scold voters about why they owe the Democratic Party even when it doesn't do the things they want, or start doing the things people beyond the well-off liberal base want. Keep things as they are now, or try something different. Be satisfied with slowing down the toboggan ride to hell, or insist that we find a different destination. Someplace a little better than hell. Peoria, say.

I don't have a ton of faith; they've resisted change this long, and they can resist it for the foreseeable future. Eventually, though, there will be a point when the political, economic, and social status quo in this country will be enough of a mess that, like Burgess Meredith's bespectacled bookworm in the classic *Twilight Zone* episode "Time Enough at Last," Democrats will emerge from the rubble of American democracy, survey the wreckage all around them, and finally, tentatively begin to consider the question, "Are *we* doing something wrong?" Then, and only then, can the long, difficult process of fixing this mess begin.

ACKNOWLEDGMENTS

I am deeply indebted (metaphorically) to Gary Morris of David Black Agency and to Ken Stern for introducing the two of us. Gary has been an agent-plus throughout this process, not only finding a home for the book but also serving as a sounding board, willing reader, and source of advice. Without him you'd be reading something else right now, and I'd be sitting at home thinking, "I'd like to write a book someday."

Everyone at Bold Type Books, Perseus, and Hachette Book Group has my sincere gratitude for taking a chance on me and on this book, for ushering a very clueless novice through the process and creating a final product of which I am extraordinarily proud. Editor Ashley Patrick did an incredible job taking a mess of raw material and patiently helping me turn it into something coherent. Ashley's guidance is the only reason this did not end up a four-volume set entitled *Everything That Has Ever Happened* with serially repeated jokes. She ensured I was never hamstrung. Our mutual favorite TV show is *The West Wing*.

Hillary Brenhouse, Remy Cawley, Claire Zuo, fact-checker Sara Krolewski, copy editor Kate Mueller, production editor Kelly Lenkevich, and countless others at Bold Type Books did their damnedest to make this book a success. No author could ask for more. Their professionalism and patience were invaluable.

I have relied heavily on advice, friendship, grounding, and support from friends and family so numerous that I'm bound to forget somebody. The list includes but is far from limited to: my dad, Edward A. Burmila Jr., the Moore family (John, Lucy, Isaac, Becky, and Kevin), Mike Konczal, Erik Martin, Dr. Matthew Gambino, Seth Wilson, Jim Coleman, Rick Erickson, Josh Ryan, Brenda Gregoline, Sally Harless, Tony

Madonna, Ryan Bakker, Helen Clarkson, and, of course, Marple and Olive.

The literally thousands of students who crossed paths with me during my time in academia, as well as countless colleagues and mentors in political science, all contributed to making me a better writer with a stronger understanding of politics. I couldn't begin to list them all. If you were one of them, thanks. I mean it.

Thanks also to the staffs at the various locations where research and writing took place: the UNC–Chapel Hill Davis Library, Northeastern Illinois University Libraries, and three Chicago haunts—Nighthawk, Crown Liquors (RIP), and Brew Brew.

Everyone who supported and read my writing online for over a decade kept me going toward this goal when it seemed like it would never happen. Podcast, blog, and social media followers helped me feel like there was somebody listening, and I was not simply some guy screaming out a window.

Finally, nothing I do would be possible without the love and support of my wife and seabird, Cathy Brigham. She neither flinched nor wept when I proposed writer and podcaster as a new career path at age forty. Let's do everything together, forever.

NOTES

INTRODUCTION

1. Obama press conference, January 29, 2009.

2. Paul Krugman has been the leading proponent of the size argument; "Too Little of a Good Thing" in the *New York Times*, November 1, 2009, is representative. Brad DeLong, in "Stimulus Too Small," *Wall Street Journal*, January 20, 2010; and Mike Konczal, John Aziz, Christina Romer, and countless others have made similar arguments.

3. See Dayen, D., *Chain of Title* (New York: New Press, 2017); or Dayen, "Obama Failed to Mitigate the Foreclosure Crisis," *Atlantic*, December 14, 2016.

4. Highlights of the jeering responses to the Beshear performance were compiled in Weiser, C., "KY's Steve Beshear's 'Diner' Response to Trump Gets Panned and Roasted," *Cincinnati Enquirer*, March 1, 2017.

5. For video and full transcript, see "Democratic Response to Trump's Address to Congress, Annotated," NPR, February 28, 2017, www.npr.org/2017/02/28/516829714 /democratic-response-to-trumps-address-to-congress-annotated; and "Democratic Response to Trump's Speech: Video and Transcript," *New York Times*, February 28, 2017, www.nytimes.com/2017/02/28/us/politics/democratic-response-video-transcript.html.

6. Barack Obama speech at Democratic National Convention, July 27, 2016.

7. Miroff, B., *The Liberals' Moment: The McGovern Insurgency and the Identity Crisis of the Democratic Party* (Lawrence: University Press of Kansas, 2009).

8. Lillis, M., "Pelosi Rejects Litmus Test on Abortion," *Hill*, April 24, 2018.

9. "Poll: Most Back Public Health Care Option," CBS News Online, June 19, 2009.

10. Woodward, B., *The Agenda: Inside the Clinton White House* (New York: Simon and Schuster, 2014), 227.

11. Quoted in Rhodes, B., *The World as It Is: A Memoir of the Obama White House* (New York: Random House, 2019).

12. See Sifry, M., "Obama's Lost Army," *New Republic*, February 9, 2017, https:// newrepublic.com/article/140245/obamas-lost-army-inside-fall-grassroots-machine.

13. See Hertel-Fernandez, A., *State Capture: How Conservative Activists, Big Businesses, and Wealthy Donors Reshaped the American States—and the Nation* (New York: Oxford University Press, 2019).

14. Skocpol, T., "A Guide to Rebuilding the Democratic Party from the Ground Up," *Vox*, January 5, 2017.

15. From Steve Jobs's biography, quoted in Lynley, M., "Why Steve Jobs Was Disappointed in Obama," *Business Insider*, October 24, 2011.

16. Clift, E., "Merrick Garland Would've Been a Great Justice. He's Not a Great A.G.," *Daily Beast*, June 21, 2021.

A NOTE ON LANGUAGE

1. Roberts, S. V., "Democrats: An Aye for Business," *New York Times*, March 1, 1981, 4.

CHAPTER 1: DEPRESSION INTERCESSION

1. This anecdote is documented in Egan, T., *The Worst Hard Time: The Untold Story of Those Who Survived the Great American Dust Bowl* (Boston: Mariner Books, 2006), 145–148.

2. Katznelson, I., *Fear Itself: The New Deal and the Origins of Our Time* (New York: Liveright, 2013).

3. Terkel, S., *Hard Times: An Oral History of the Great Depression*, 2nd ed. (New York: New Press, 1986), 434.

4. For a full history of the Democratic Party, see Witcover, J., *Party of the People: A History of the Democrats* (New York: Random House, 2003). For "party systems" and realignment, see Sundquist, J. L., *Dynamics of the Party System: Alignment and Realignment of Political Parties in the United States* (Washington, DC: Brookings Institution, 1973); and Key Jr., V. O., "Secular Realignment and the Party System," *Journal of Politics* 21, no. 2 (1959): 198–210. For the antebellum period, Reconstruction era, and Gilded Age, see White, R., *The Republic for Which It Stands: The United States During Reconstruction and the Gilded Age, 1865–1896* (New York: Oxford University Press, 2017). For 1896 to the New Deal, aka the Fourth Party System, see Hofstadter, R., *The Age of Reform: From Bryan to FDR* (New York: Knopf, 1956); Burnham, W. D., "Periodization Schemes and 'Party Systems': The 'System of 1896' as a Case in Point," *Social Science History* 10, no. 3 (1986): 263–314; and Gould, L. L., *America in the Progressive Era, 1890–1914* (London: Pearson, 2001).

5. Via the Living New Deal Project, which maintains a searchable map and database of New Deal projects by location.

6. Schivelbusch, W., *Three New Deals: Reflections on Roosevelt's America, Mussolini's Italy, and Hitler's Germany, 1933–1939* (New York: Macmillan, 2006).

7. See Selfa, L., *The Democrats: A Critical History* (Chicago: Haymarket Books, 2008), 51–53.

8. Ferguson, T., *Golden Rule: The Investment Theory of Party Competition and the Logic of Money-Driven Political Systems* (Chicago: University of Chicago Press, 1995).

9. In Grafton, J., ed., *Great Speeches: Franklin Delano Roosevelt* (New York: Dover Thrift Editions, 1999), 54.

10. Grafton, *Great Speeches*, chap. 2.

11. Rep. William Connery is quoted in Feldman, G., "Unions, Solidarity, and Class: The Limits of Labor Law," *Berkeley Journal of Employment and Labor Law* 15, no. 2 (1994): 187–272.

12. See Keynes, J. M., *The General Theory of Employment, Interest, and Money*. Reprint. (New York: Springer, 2018).

13. Plotke, D., *Building a Democratic Political Order: Reshaping American Liberalism in the 1930s and 1940s* (New York: Cambridge University Press, 2006).

14. See the description of "partisan regimes," of which the New Deal Democratic order is exemplary, in Polsky, A. J., "Partisan Regimes in American Politics," *Polity* 44, no. 1 (2012): 51–80.

15. Dwight D. Eisenhower, "Letter to Edgar Newton Eisenhower," November, 8, 1954, Teaching American History, https://teachingamericanhistory.org/library/document/letter-to-edgar-newton-eisenhower/.

16. Quote attributed to House Speaker Sam Rayburn (D-TX), in Krehbiel, K., "Unanimous Consent Agreements: Going Along in the Senate," *Journal of Politics* 48, no. 3 (1986): 541–564.

17. Quoted in King, A., *The New American Political System* (Washington, DC: American Enterprise Institute, 1990), 97.

18. Smith, J. S., *Building New Deal Liberalism: The Political Economy of Public Works, 1933–1956* (New York: Cambridge University Press, 2006).

19. See Morris, A. D., *The Origins of the Civil Rights Movement: Black Communities Organizing for Change* (New York: Free Press, 1984).

20. Maxwell, A., and T. Shields, *The Long Southern Strategy: How Chasing White Voters in the South Changed American Politics* (London, UK: Oxford University Press, 2019).

CHAPTER 2: THE TWIN TRAUMAS OF '68 AND '72

1. For a full transcript of address, see Barack Obama, "Transcript: Obama's Speech Against the Iraq War," January 20, 2009, NPR, www.npr.org/templates/story/story.php?storyId=99591469.

2. Keeanga-Yamahtta Taylor has written devastatingly about this, notably in "Joe Biden, Kamala Harris, and the Limits of Representation," *New Yorker*, August 24, 2020.

3. For Biden's remarks: Tau, B., "Biden Remembers McGovern," Politico, October 25, 2012. For criticism of Biden based on the remarks: Bauer, F., "Biden and McGovern," *National Review*, August 17, 2021.

4. See Risen, C., *A Nation on Fire: America in the Wake of the King Assassination* (Hoboken, NJ: Wiley, 2009).

5. See Cowie, J., *Stayin' Alive: The 1970s and the Last Days of the Working Class* (New York: New Press, 2010), chap. 2.

6. For an overview of those changes, see Marcetic, B., "The Secret History of Super Delegates," *In These Times* 40, no. 6 (June 2016); and Herndon, A., "Democrats Overhaul Controversial Superdelegate System," *New York Times*, August 26, 2018.

7. Sanchez, J., "Revisiting McGovern-Fraser: Party Nationalization and the Rhetoric of Reform," *Journal of Policy History* 32, no. 1 (2020): 1–24.

8. Dark, T. E., "Organized Labor and Party Reform: A Reassessment," *Polity* 28, no. 4 (1996): 497–520.

9. Compiled FEC data via OpenSecrets.org.

10. See Gould, L., *The Rise and Fall of the New Deal Order, 1930–1980* (Princeton, NJ: Princeton University Press, 1989), chap. 2.

11. An excellent summary of Wilson's key ideas appears in Hildreth, A., "The Importance of Purposes in 'Purposive' Groups: Incentives and Participation in the Sanctuary Movement," *American Journal of Political Science* 38, no. 2 (1994): 447–463.

12. Recommended reading on New Politics includes Hilton, A., "Searching for a New Politics: The New Politics Movement and the Struggle to Democratize the Democratic Party, 1968–1978," *New Political Science* 38, no. 2 (2016): 141–159; and Shafer, B. E., *Quiet Revolution: Struggle for the Democratic Party and the Shaping of Post-Reform Politics* (New York: Russell Sage Foundation, 1983).

13. This anecdote appears in Miller, J., *Democracy Is in the Streets: From Port Huron to the Siege of Chicago*, 2nd ed. (1994), 214. I thank Thomas Frank for bringing it to my attention in his *The People, No: A Brief History of Anti-Populism* (New York: Macmillan, 2020).

14. Details in this section are taken from David Paul Kuhn's exhaustive *The Hardhat Riot: Nixon, New York City, and the Dawn of the White Working-Class Revolution* (New York: Oxford University Press, 2020).

15. See Kuhn, *The Hardhat Riot*.

16. Quoted in White, T. H., *The Making of the President, 1972* (New York: Harper Perennial, 2010), 164–166.

17. For extensive detail, see Hilton, A., *True Blues: The Contentious Transformation of the Democratic Party* (Philadelphia: University of Pennsylvania Press, 2021).

18. This point about replication rather than recruitment is explored well in Geismer, L., *Don't Blame Us: Suburban Liberals and the Transformation of the Democratic Party* (Princeton, NJ: Princeton University Press, 2017).

19. Beyond the reductionist assumption that economic changes are inevitable, scholars have pointed out that even the framing of postindustrial is reductionist in assuming that such societies must, somehow, be fundamentally different; see Ferkiss, V., "Daniel Bell's Concept of Post-Industrial Society," *Political Science Reviewer* 9 (1979): 61–102.

20. Quoted in Alterman, E., *The Cause: The Fight for American Liberalism from Franklin Roosevelt to Barack Obama* (New York: Penguin Books, 2013), 261.

21. Quoted in Cowie, *Stayin' Alive*, 158.

22. Hilton, "Searching for a New Politics."

23. For a complete discussion see Hilton, "Searching for a New Politics."

24. Hilton, *True Blues*, chap. 4.

CHAPTER 3: THE WILDERNESS YEARS

1. See Ryan, A., *Dewey and the High Tide of American Liberalism* (New York: W. W. Norton, 1995); Laski, H., *The Rise of European Liberalism* (London: George Allen and Unwin, 1936); and Geuss, R., "Liberalism," in ed. R. Geuss, *History and Illusion in Politics* (New York: Cambridge University Press, 2001).

2. Roosevelt, F. D., *Public Papers of the Presidents of the United States: Franklin D. Roosevelt; 1938*, vol. 7 (New York: Macmillan, 1941), xxix.

3. For example, Sabin, P., "Environmental Law and the End of the New Deal Order," *Law and History Review* 33, no. 4 (2015).

4. Sabin, P., *Public Citizens: The Attack on Big Government and the Remaking of American Liberalism* (New York: W. W. Norton, 2021).

5. This section draws from Lawrence, J. A., *The Class of '74: Congress After Watergate and the Roots of Partisanship* (Baltimore, MD: Johns Hopkins University Press, 2018); Stoller, M., "How Democrats Killed Their Populist Soul," *Atlantic*, October 24, 2016; Owens, J., "Extreme Advocacy Leadership in the Pre-reform House: Wright Patman

and the House Banking and Currency Committee," *British Journal of Political Science* 15, no. 2 (1985); and Young, N., "Wright Patman: Congressman to the Nation, 1893–1953" (PhD diss., University of Texas, 1995).

6. Broder quoted in Jacobs, M., *Panic at the Pump: The Energy Crisis and the Transformation of American Politics in the 1970s* (New York: Macmillan, 2016), 136.

7. "A Bold and Balky Congress," *Time*, January 23, 1978, 8–16.

8. Jordan, H., *Crisis: The Last Year of the Carter Presidency* (New York: Putnam, 1982), 317.

9. Lydon, C., "Jimmy Carter Revealed: He's a Rockefeller Republican," *Atlantic Monthly*, July 1977.

10. Jordan, *Crisis*, 316.

11. All quotes from Schlesinger Jr., A., "The Challenge Facing Liberals," *Chicago Tribune*, July 5, 1979.

12. For an exhaustive narrative of 1970s energy politics, see Jacobs, *Panic at the Pump*. This section owes much to Jacobs's research.

13. Jacobs, *Panic at the Pump*.

14. "Fights Loom in Congress with Few New Initiatives Likely," *New York Times*, November 12, 1978.

15. Jacobs, *Panic at the Pump*, 194.

16. Jacobs, 198.

17. Stanley, T., *Kennedy vs. Carter: The 1980 Battle for the Democratic Party's Soul* (Lawrence: University of Kansas Press, 2010), 92.

18. Tolchin, M., "Carter Briefs House Democratic Chiefs," *New York Times*, January 23, 1979.

19. Jacobs, *Panic at the Pump*, 181.

20. Tolchin, "Carter Briefs House Democratic Chiefs."

21. See "Transcript of Press Conference at the American Bankers Association Annual Convention, New Orleans, Louisiana," October 9, 1979, Statements and Speeches of Paul A. Volcker, Fraser, fraser.stlouisfed.org.

22. For a useful summary, see Durand, C., "1979 in Reverse," *New Left Review*, June 1, 2021.

23. Quoted in Greider, W., *Secrets of the Temple: How the Federal Reserve Runs the Country* (New York: Simon and Schuster, 1989), 149.

24. Greider, *Secrets of the Temple*, 154.

25. Carter is examined in detail as a "disjunctive" president overseeing the final stage of a collapsing political regime in Stephen Skowronek's classic *The Politics Presidents Make* (Cambridge, MA: Harvard University Press, 1993).

26. Bibby, J. F., and B. F. Schaffner, *Politics, Parties, and Elections in America* (Chicago: Nelson-Hall, 1996).

27. McGirr, L., *Suburban Warriors* (Princeton, NJ: Princeton University Press, 2015).

28. Quoted in DiSalvo, D., *Engines of Change: Party Factions in American Politics, 1868–2010* (New York: Oxford University Press, 2010).

29. Historian Brent Cebul has written persuasively on the long history of economically moderate-to-conservative promarket views within the Democratic coalition. See Cebul, "Supply-Side Liberalism: Fiscal Crisis, Post-Industrial Policy, and the Rise of the New Democrats," *Modern American History* 2 (2019): 139–164.

30. Prominent examples of this view include Geismer, L., *Don't Blame Us: Suburban Liberals and the Transformation of the Democratic Party* (Princeton, NJ: Princeton University Press, 2015); Selfa, L., *The Democrats: A Critical History* (Chicago: Haymarket Books, 2012); Davis, M., *Prisoners of the American Dream: Politics and Economy in the History of the US Working Class*, 2nd ed. (London: Verso Books, 2000); Hedges, C., *Death of the Liberal Class* (New York: Bold Type Books, 2011); and basically everything Thomas Frank has ever written.

31. Schlesinger Jr., A., "For Democrats, Me Too Reaganism Will Spell Disaster," *New York Times*, July 6, 1986, 13.

32. Quoted in Baer, K. S., *Reinventing Democrats: The Politics of Liberalism from Reagan to Clinton* (Lawrence: University Press of Kansas, 2000), 73–74.

33. See Bertram, E., *The Workfare State: Public Assistance Politics from the New Deal to the New Democrats* (Philadelphia: University of Pennsylvania Press, 2015).

34. See Frank, T., *Listen, Liberal* (New York: Metropolitan Books, 2017), chapter 2.

35. Rothenberg, R., *The Neoliberals: Creating the New American Politics* (New York: Simon and Schuster, 1984).

36. Liechtenstein, N., "Labor, Liberalism, and the Democratic Party: A Fruitful but Vexed Alliance," in ed. J. Bell and T. Stanley, *Making Sense of American Liberalism* (Champaign: University of Illinois Press, 2012).

CHAPTER 4: INSURGENT MODERATES

1. This section draws from three thorough accounts of the early years of the Democratic Leadership Council, one of which is first-person and the others with access to the principals and archives directly: Baer, K. S., *Reinventing Democrats: The Politics of Liberalism from Reagan to Clinton* (Lawrence: University Press of Kansas, 2000); From, A., and A. McKeon, *The New Democrats and the Return to Power* (New York: Macmillan, 2013); and Hale, J. F., "The Making of the New Democrats," *Political Science Quarterly* 110, no. 2 (1995): 207–232. I am indebted to all of these authors for their research.

2. See Conroy, S., *Vote First or Die: The New Hampshire Primary; America's Discerning, Magnificent, and Absurd Road to the White House* (New York: PublicAffairs, 2017).

3. Baer, *Reinventing Democrats*, 34–38.

4. Granat, D., "Democratic Caucus Renewed as Forum for Policy Questions," *CQ Weekly Reports* 41 (1983): 2115–2119.

5. Baer, *Reinventing Democrats*, 41.

6. Committee on Party Effectiveness, *Rebuilding the Road to Opportunity: A Democratic Direction for the 1980s* (Washington, DC: Government Printing Office, 1982).

7. Hale, "The Making of the New Democrats," 211.

8. Cooper, D. N., *Rebuilding the Road to Opportunity, Not Just Filling in the Potholes: A Labor Perspective* (Storrs: Labor Education Center, University of Connecticut, 1983).

9. These are the terms used in the original language of 1982. Elving, R., "Debating Length, Language, Democrats Ponder Platform," *CQ Weekly Report*, June 11, 1988, quoted in Hale, "The Making of the New Democrats."

10. Hale, "The Making of the New Democrats."

11. See Borquez, J., "The Reagan Democrat Phenomenon: How Wise Was the Conventional Wisdom?," *Politics and Policy* 33, no. 4 (2005): 672–705.

12. Hale, "The Making of the New Democrats," 215–217.

13. Caddell, P., "A Party Afraid of the Truth," *Mainstream Democrat* 2, no. 4 (December 1990).

14. Galston, W., and E. C. Kamarck, *The Politics of Evasion: Democrats and the Presidency*, report, Progressive Policy Institute, September 1989.

15. Carmines, E. G., and J. A. Stimson, *Issue Evolution: Race and the Transformation of American Politics* (Princeton, NJ: Princeton University Press, 1989).

16. See Gilens, M., "'Race Coding' and White Opposition to Welfare," *American Political Science Review* 90, no. 3 (1996): 593–604; Peffley, M., J. Hurwitz, and P. M. Sniderman, "Racial Stereotypes and Whites' Political Views of Blacks in the Context of Welfare and Crime," *American Journal of Political Science* (1997): 30–60; and Wetts, R., and R. Willer, "Privilege on the Precipice: Perceived Racial Status Threats Lead White Americans to Oppose Welfare Programs," *Social Forces* 97, no. 2 (2018): 793–822.

17. Hale, "The Making of the New Democrats," 221. See also Grim, R., *We've Got People: From Jesse Jackson to Alexandria Ocasio-Cortez, the End of Big Money and the Rise of a Movement* (New York: Strong Arm Press, 2019).

CHAPTER 5: IT'S BILL CLINTON'S DEMOCRATIC PARTY NOW

1. Berke, R. L., "Brown Renews His Battle Against the Moonbeam," *New York Times*, April 12, 1992.

2. Broder, D., "The Evolution of Bill Clinton as a Different Kind of Democrat," *Chicago Tribune*, December 10, 1992. Even a month after the election, journalists were still exploring the question of what exactly this different democrat was.

3. For example, Locin, M., "Clinton Says He Is a 'New Democrat,'" *Chicago Tribune*, October 22, 1992.

4. Baer, K., *Reinventing Democrats: The Politics of Liberalism from Reagan to Clinton* (Lawrence: University Press of Kansas, 2000), 198, 204.

5. Berke, R. L., "Clinton: Getting People off Welfare," *New York Times*, September 10, 1992.

6. Gilens, M., "Racial Attitudes and Opposition to Welfare," *Journal of Politics* 57, no. 4 (1995): 994–1014.

7. Peffley, M., J. Hurwitz, and P. M. Sniderman, "Racial Stereotypes and Whites' Political Views of Blacks in the Context of Welfare and Crime," *American Journal of Political Science* (1997): 30–60.

8. Hale, J. F., "The Making of the New Democrats," *Political Science Quarterly* 110, no. 2 (1995): 228.

9. Lewis-Beck, M. S., and T. W. Rice, *Forecasting Elections* (Washington, DC: CQ Press, 1992).

10. Lacy, D., and B. C. Burden, "The Vote-Stealing and Turnout Effects of Ross Perot in the 1992 US Presidential Election," *American Journal of Political Science* (1999): 233–255.

11. Alvarez, R. M., and J. Nagler, "Economics, Issues and the Perot Candidacy: Voter Choice in the 1992 Presidential Election," *American Journal of Political Science* (1995): 714–744.

12. Belkin, A., and G. Bateman, eds., *Don't Ask, Don't Tell: Debating the Gay Ban in the Military* (Boulder, CO: Lynne Rienner, 2003).

13. A remarkable history of deficit politicking in the US: Kelton, S., *The Deficit Myth: Modern Monetary Theory and the Birth of the People's Economy* (New York: Hachette, 2020).

14. Contemporary views on the benefits of deficit reduction are captured in Mann T., and C. Schultze, "Getting Rid of the Budget Deficit: Why We Should and How We Can," *Brookings Review* 7, no. 1 (1988).

15. Woodward, B., *The Agenda: Inside the Clinton White House* (New York: Simon and Schuster, 1994), 70–71.

16. Woodward, *The Agenda*, 90.

17. Woodward, 115.

18. Woodward, 249.

19. Woodward, 129.

20. Woodward, 126.

21. Woodward, 37.

22. Woodward, 112, 262.

23. Woodward, 206.

24. Woodward, 297.

25. Woodward, 155.

26. Woodward, 162, 170.

27. Woodward, 233.

28. Hero, J., et al., "Understanding What Makes Americans Dissatisfied with Their Health Care System: An International Comparison," *Health Affairs* 35, no. 3 (2016): 502–509.

29. Blendon, R. J., and K. Donelan, "Public Opinion and Efforts to Reform the US Health Care System: Confronting Issues of Cost-Containment and Access to Care," *Stanford Law and Policy Review* 3 (1991): 147.

30. Nather, D., "How Clinton WH Bungled Health Care," Politico, February 28, 2014.

31. In Bob Woodward's book *The Agenda* (New York: Simon and Schuster, 1994) is an example of Clinton lauding the supposed willingness of moderate Republicans to "get something done" while lambasting the unreliable and demanding Democratic caucus (pages 179–181).

32. Quoted in Rushefsky, M. E., and K. Patel, *Politics, Power and Policy Making: The Case of Health Care Reform in the 1990s* (Armonk, NY: M. E. Sharpe, 1998).

33. Blendon and Donelan, "Public Opinion and Efforts to Reform," 148.

34. Two examples are Greenberg, S. B., "Third Force: Why Independents Turned Against Democrats—and How to Win Them Back," Democratic Leadership Council, 1994; and Starr, P., "What Happened to Health Care Reform?," *American Prospect*, Winter 1995, 20–31.

35. Selfa, L., *The Democrats: A Critical History* (Chicago: Haymarket Books, 2008), 51–53.

36. Quoted in Cornwell, S., "From 'Hillarycare' Debacle in 1990s, Clinton Emerged More Cautious," Reuters, June 6, 2016.

37. Donnelly, K. P., and D. A. Rochefort, "The Lessons of 'Lesson Drawing': How the Obama Administration Attempted to Learn from the Failure of the Clinton Health Plan," *Journal of Policy History* 24, no. 2 (2012): 184–223.

38. These data are presented clearly in Lopez, G., "The Simple Truth About Why Mass Incarceration Happened," Vox, August 30, 2015.

39. For example, Alexander, M., *The New Jim Crow: Mass Incarceration in the Age of Colorblindness* (New York: New Press, 2012).

40. A la Marcetic, B., "Joe Biden, Mass Incarceration Zealot," *Jacobin*, August 9, 2018.

41. See Mancillas, L. K., *Presidents and Mass Incarceration: Choices at the Top, Repercussions at the Bottom* (Santa Barbara, CA: ABC-CLIO, 2018).

42. See Sacco, L. N., *The Violence Against Women Act: Overview, Legislation, and Federal Funding*, Congressional Research Service, Washington, DC, May 26, 2015.

CHAPTER 6: RED TIDE

1. Coppins, M., "The Man Who Broke Politics," *Atlantic*, October 17, 2018.

2. Quoted in Strahan R., and D. J. Palazzolo, "The Gingrich Effect," *Political Science Quarterly* 119, no. 1 (2004): 99.

3. Quoted in Zelizer, J. E., *Burning Down the House: Newt Gingrich, the Fall of a Speaker, and the Rise of the New Republican Party* (New York: Penguin Press, 2020), 305.

4. For an extensive look at the relationship between the two see Gillon, S. M., *The Pact: Bill Clinton, Newt Gingrich, and the Rivalry That Defined a Generation* (New York: Oxford University Press, 2008).

5. Shafer, B. E., "The Partisan Legacy: Are There Any New Democrats? And by the Way, Was There a Republican Revolution?," in ed. C. Campbell and B. A. Rockman, *The Clinton Legacy* (London: Chatham House, 2000).

6. Gillon, *The Pact*, 38–50.

7. Fineman, H., "The Warrior," *Newsweek*, 1995, 28–33.

8. Zelizer, *Burning Down the House*, is encyclopedic on the details of this battle, and the summary version I offer here is based on that work.

9. Rosenson, B., "Ethics Evolving: Unethical Political Behavior Viewed Through the Lens of US House Ethics Investigations, 1798–2011," *Public Integrity* 16, no. 3 (2014): 227–242.

10. Quirk, P. J., "Coping with the Politics of Scandal," *Presidential Studies Quarterly* 28, no. 4 (1998): 898–902.

11. Flippen, J. B., *Speaker Jim Wright: Power, Scandal, and the Birth of Modern Politics* (Austin: University of Texas Press, 2018).

12. Campbell, J. E., "Introduction: Forecasting the 2018 US Midterm Elections," *PS: Political Science and Politics* 51, no. S1 (2018): 1–3.

13. Aldrich, J. H., and D. W. Rohde, "The Republican Revolution and the House Appropriations Committee," *Journal of Politics* 62, no. 1 (2000): 1–33.

14. Sinclair, B., "Transformational Leader or Faithful Agent? Principal-Agent Theory and House Majority Party Leadership," *Legislative Studies Quarterly* (1999): 421–449.

15. See Owens, J. E., "The Return of Party Government in the US House of Representatives: Central Leadership-Committee Relations in the 104th Congress," *British Journal of Political Science* (1997): 249–250; and Strahan and Palazzolo, "The Gingrich Effect," 89–114.

16. Owens, "The Return of Party Government," 254.

17. Aldrich, J. H., and D. W. Rohde, "The Transition to Republican Rule in the House: Implications for Theories of Congressional Politics," *Political Science Quarterly* 112, no. 4 (1997): 541–567.

18. Quoted in Owens, "The Return of Party Government," 262.

19. 1978 speech by Gingrich, *Frontline*, PBS, www.pbs.org/wgbh/pages/frontline /newt/newt78speech.html.

20. The rise of conservative media has been covered voluminously elsewhere, for example, Barker, D., *Rushed to Judgment: Talk Radio, Persuasion, and American Political Behavior* (New York: Columbia University Press, 2002); and Jamieson, K. H., and J. N. Cappella, *Echo Chamber: Rush Limbaugh and the Conservative Media Establishment* (New York: Oxford University Press, 2008).

21. Lehmann, C., "The Eyes of Spiro Are upon You: The Myth of the Liberal Media," *Baffler*, Spring 2001, 23–38.

22. Stahl, J., *Right Moves: The Conservative Think Tank in American Political Culture Since 1945* (Chapel Hill: University of North Carolina Press, 2016).

23. Andrew, R., "War of Ideas," *Stanford Social Innovation Review* 3, no. 1 (2005): 18–25.

24. McDonald, L., "Think Tanks and the Media: How the Conservative Movement Gained Entry into the Education Policy Arena," *Educational Policy* 28, no. 6 (2014): 845–880.

25. Gillon, *The Pact*, 122.

26. A prime example is the role quasi-academic think tanks played in elevating climate skepticism from conspiracy theory to a policy position with the outward trappings of legitimacy; see Jacques, P., R. Dunlap, and M. Freeman, "The Organisation of Denial: Conservative Think Tanks and Environmental Scepticism," *Environmental Politics* 17, no. 3 (2008).

27. Quoted in "The Politics of Slash and Burn," *New York Times*, September 20, 1990.

28. Coppins, "The Man Who Broke Politics."

29. Quoted in Gillion, *The Pact*, 141.

CHAPTER 7: THE SENSELESS HABITS OF HIGHLY DEFECTIVE PEOPLE

1. Brady, D. W., et al., "The Perils of Presidential Support: How the Republicans Took the House in the 1994 Midterm Elections," *Political Behavior* 18, no. 4 (1996): 345–367.

2. Quoted in Curry, G., and T. Hardy, "Despite Rise in Party Stature, Blacks Fret," *Chicago Tribune*, July 16, 1992.

3. Quoted in Grover, W., and J. Peschek, *The Unsustainable Presidency: Clinton, Bush, Obama, and Beyond* (New York: Springer, 2014), 63.

4. Quoted in Berke, R. L., "Moderate Democrats' Poll Sends the President a Warning," *New York Times*, November 18, 1994.

5. Quoted in Richter, P., "Clinton Hints at Pursuing Less Liberal Agenda," *Los Angeles Times*, November 11, 1994.

6. Baer, K. S., *Reinventing Democrats: The Politics of Liberalism from Reagan to Clinton* (Lawrence: University Press of Kansas, 2000), 232–235. Clinton would write a thank-you note to From, reading, "It was helpful—at least it was what I really wanted to say."

7. Osborne, D., "Can This President Be Saved? A Six-Point Plan to Beat the One Term Odds," *Washington Post*, January 8, 1995.

8. In Berke, "Moderate Democrats' Poll Sends the President a Warning."

9. By Al From, Will Marshall, Bruce Galston, and Doug Ross.

10. See Congressional Research Service Report for Congress, *The National Performance Review and Other Government Reform Initiatives: An Overview, 1993–2001,* June 4, 2001.

11. Schneider, W., "The Deficit: Budget Balancing; Clinton Infuriates Almost Everyone," *Los Angeles Times,* June 18, 1995.

12. Frum, D., "When the Economy Turns," *Weekly Standard,* February 1, 1999.

13. Quirk, P., and W. Cunion, "Clinton's Domestic Policy: The Lessons of a 'New Democrat,'" in ed. C. Campbell and B. Rockman, *The Clinton Legacy* (London: Chatham House, 2000).

14. Quoted in Brownstein, R., "Clinton's Odyssey Toward Center May Offer Lesson for Republicans," *Los Angeles Times,* December 2, 1996.

15. McGovern, G., "A Word from the Original McGovernik," *Washington Post,* December 25, 1994.

16. Yang, J. E., "Looking Back to Theodore Roosevelt, Gephardt Calls for 'New Progressivism,'" *Washington Post,* December 3, 1997.

17. Yang, J. E., and P. Baker, "Gephardt Speech on Party Angers Some Democrats," *Washington Post,* December 6, 1997.

18. Schlesinger and Gephardt quoted in Burns, J. M., and G. Sorenson, *Dead Center: Clinton-Gore Leadership and the Perils of Moderation* (New York: Scribner, 1999), 160.

19. Waddan, A., *Clinton's Legacy: A New Democrat in Governance* (New York: Springer, 2001), 20.

20. Steven M. Gillon's *The Pact* (New York: Oxford University Press, 2008) makes this point in voluminous detail.

21. Woodward, *The Choice* (New York: Simon & Schuster, 1996), 17.

22. Quoted in Harris, J., *The Survivor: Bill Clinton in the White House* (New York: Random House, 2005).

23. Tedlow, R., *New and Improved: The Story of Mass Marketing in America* (Cambridge, MA: Harvard University Press, 1996), 372.

24. Paraphrasing a memorable analogy from Mattson, K., "Micro Man," *Guardian,* April 11, 2008.

25. Devroy, A., "Clinton's Holiday from Polls," *Washington Post,* July 5, 1997.

26. Just one example: Kornhauser, M. E., "People Don't Like Paying Taxes. That's Because They Don't Understand Them," *Washington Post,* April 14, 2017.

27. This summarization appears on Wikipedia and is derived from Department of Treasury, IRS, Publication 596, "Earned Income Credit (EIC)," for use in preparing 2018 tax returns.

28. Smith, M. D., "The Seductive Danger of Symbolic Politics," *Nation,* January 21, 2016.

29. For a fuller review of Clinton's relationship to labor, see Moberly, R. B., "Labor-Management Relations During the Clinton Administration," *Hofstra Labor and Employment Law Journal* 24 (2006): 31.

30. Sapiro, V., and D. Canon, "Race, Gender, and the Clinton Presidency," in ed. C. Campbell and B. A. Rockman, *The Clinton Legacy* (London: Chatham House, 2000), 194.

31. Walton Jr., H., *African-American Power and Politics: The Political Context Variable* (New York: Columbia University Press, 1997), 28.

32. Quoted in Sapiro and Canon, "Race, Gender, and the Clinton Presidency," 176.

33. Marnin, J., "Just 60M Americans Participated in 401K Plans Last Year, but Most Funds Saw Boost," *Newsweek.com*, August 19, 2021.

CHAPTER 8: THE MYSTERIOUS WORLD OUTSIDE WASHINGTON, DC

1. Winter, M., *All Politics Is Local: Why Progressives Must Fight for the States* (New York: Bold Type Books, 2019).

2. New documents and evidence draw out and underscore this position in Plokhy, S., *Nuclear Folly: A History of the Cuban Missile Crisis* (New York: W. W. Norton, 2021).

3. Shafer, B. E., and W. J. M. Claggett, *The Two Majorities: The Issue Context of Modern American Politics* (Baltimore, MD: Johns Hopkins University Press, 1995).

4. Hertel-Fernandez, A., *State Capture: How Conservative Activists, Big Businesses, and Wealthy Donors Reshaped the American States—and the Nation* (New York: Oxford University Press, 2019), 235.

5. Green, E., "The Ideological Reasons Why Democrats Have Neglected Local Politics," *Atlantic*, January 4, 2017.

6. Transcript available at https://politics.uchicago.edu/news/entry/watch-genforward -are-campaigns-hearing-millennials.

7. For a view on ALEC's mammoth influence, see Nichols, J., "ALEC Exposed," *Nation*, August 1/8, 2012; or Collingwood, L., S. El-Khatib, and B. Gonzalez O'Brien, "Sustained Organizational Influence: American Legislative Exchange Council and the Diffusion of Anti-sanctuary Policy," *Policy Studies Journal* 47, no. 3 (2019): 735–773.

8. Mutnick, A., S. Kapos, and O. Beavers, "Illinois Dems Carve Up Liberal Giant-Slayer's District in New Congressional Map," Politico, October 29, 2021.

9. For example, Prince, M., "Dan Lipinski Stands Against Nike After It Pulls Patriotic Sneakers," *Daily Caller*, July 3, 2019.

10. Eubank, N., and J. Rodden, "Who Is My Neighbor? The Spatial Efficiency of Partisanship," *Statistics and Public Policy* 7, no. 1 (2020): 87–100.

11. Winburn, J., *The Realities of Redistricting* (Lanham, MD: Lexington Books, 2008), 1.

12. Sam Rosenfeld and Daniel Schlozman, in their forthcoming book *The Hollow Parties*, cover this exhaustively.

13. Title of a 2019 working paper by Rosenfeld and Schlozman.

14. Schlozman, D., and S. Rosenfeld, "The Hollow Parties," chap. 6 in ed. F. E. Lee and N. McCarty, *Can America Govern Itself?* (New York: Cambridge University Press, 2019), 120–152.

15. For example, Dickinson, T., "No We Can't," *Rolling Stone*, February 2, 2010.

16. Dickinson, "No We Can't."

17. See, for example, Otterbein, H., and A. Thompson, "Down-Ballot Dems Split from Biden on Door-Knocking," Politico, September 14, 2020.

18. Berman, R., "The Democrats Whose 2020 Goal Is Grander Than the Presidency," *Atlantic*, April 17, 2019.

CHAPTER 9: THE BUSH YEARS

1. The dynamics of the third party / independent effects on the outcome are explored in many studies, for example, Hillygus, D. S., "The Dynamics of Voter Decision Making Among Minor-Party Supporters: The 2000 Presidential Election in the United States," *British Journal of Political Science* (2007): 225–244; and in nonacademic analysis, Leonhardt, D., "Was Buchanan the Real Nader?," *New York Times*, December 10, 2000.

2. See Mebane Jr., W. R., "The Wrong Man Is President! Overvotes in the 2000 Presidential Election in Florida," *Perspectives on Politics* (2004): 525–535.

3. Erikson, R. S., "The 2000 Presidential Election in Historical Perspective," *Political Science Quarterly* 116, no. 1 (2001): 29–52.

4. All taken from Pomper, G. M., "The 2000 Presidential Election: Why Gore Lost," *Political Science Quarterly* 116, no. 2 (2001): 201–223.

5. Jacoby, W., in ed. H. F. Weisberg and C. Wilcox, *Models of Voting in Presidential Elections* (Redwood, CA: Stanford University Press, 2004).

6. "The Kerry bandwagon had been set in motion by the desire to get behind someone who could defeat Bush, not by a positive attraction of support to the candidate," in Campbell, J. E., "Why Bush Won the Presidential Election of 2004: Incumbency, Ideology, Terrorism, and Turnout," *Political Science Quarterly* 120, no. 2 (2005): 228.

7. Sixties leftover Todd Gitlin may have coined, or at least popularized, the phrase in a 2003 interview: McClure, L., "Anyone but Bush," *Salon*, July 20, 2003.

8. Thomas, E., and the Special Project Team, "The Inside Story: How Bush Did It," *Newsweek*, 2004.

9. Campbell, "Why Bush Won the Presidential Election of 2004," 227.

10. Selfa, L., *The Democrats: A Critical History* (Chicago: Haymarket Books, 2012), 85.

11. Fahey, A. C., "French and Feminine: Hegemonic Masculinity and the Emasculation of John Kerry in the 2004 Presidential Race," *Critical Studies in Media Communication* 24, no. 2 (2007): 132–150.

12. For ABC News polling, see Trei, L., "Why Bush Won in 2004," Stanford News Service, November 17, 2004.

13. Jacobson, G. C., "Polarized Politics and the 2004 Congressional and Presidential Elections," *Political Science Quarterly* 120, no. 2 (2005): 199.

14. Recommended readings include Rosenfeld, S., *The Polarizers: Postwar Architects of Our Partisan Era* (Chicago: University of Chicago Press, 2018); and Layman, G. C., T. M. Carsey, and J. M. Horowitz, "Party Polarization in American Politics: Characteristics, Causes, and Consequences," *Annual Review of Political Science* 9 (2006): 83–110.

15. Jacobson, "Polarized Politics," 218.

16. See the monograph Poole, K., "Picture of a Polarized Congress," https://legacy.voteview.com/pdf/ViewpointPolarization.pdf. Ask Keith about trains too.

17. A good review of his politics and career is in Nichols, J., "Do Not Hire This Man," *Nation*, December 3, 2020.

18. Bendavid, N., "The House Rahm Built," *Chicago Tribune*, November 12, 2006.

19. See Hart, P. T., K. Tindall, and C. Brown, "Crisis Leadership of the Bush Presidency: Advisory Capacity and Presidential Performance in the Acute Stages of the 9/11 and Katrina Crises," *Presidential Studies Quarterly* 39, no. 3 (2009): 473–493.

20. "Emanuel Key to Dems' Success," Associated Press, December 10, 2006.

21. Pilkington, E., "Pro-gun, Anti-abortion, Fiscally Conservative: Meet the Neo-Dems," *Guardian*, November 9, 2006.

22. Gerstein, J., "Emanuel in Line for Big Promotion After Leading Fight for House," *New York Sun*, November 9, 2006.

CHAPTER 10: OBAMA COMETH

1. Klein, E., "Could This Time Have Been Different?," *Washington Post*, October 8, 2011.

2. Newton-Small, J., "Why the Democrats—and Obama—Forgave Lieberman," *Time*, November 18, 2008.

3. For structural economic problems facing the Obama presidency: Epstein, R., "The Economic Consequences of the Obama Reelection: How Stagnation Has Vanquished Growth," *Southern Economic Journal* 80, no. 2 (2013): 282–298.

4. Quoted in Gopnik, A., "Liberal in Chief," *Atlantic*, May 15, 2016.

5. Berman, A., "Obama: Triangulation 2.0?," *Nation*, February 7, 2011.

6. "Triangulation 2.0? Clinton Visits White House," RealClearPolitics video, December 10, 2010.

7. Foer, F., and N. Scheiber, "Nudge-ocracy," *New Republic*, May 6, 2009.

8. All Foer and Scheiber quotes from "Nudge-ocracy."

9. Meacham, J., "We Are All Socialists Now," *Newsweek*, February 6, 2009.

10. Schaller, T. F., "The Democratic Party in the Age of Obama: Yes We Can or No We Can't?," *New Labor Forum* 19, no. 3 (2010).

11. Lind, M., *The New Class War* (New York: Penguin, 2020).

12. Kurtz, H., "Obama Reps Woo Liberal Elite at Aspen Ideas Festival but Face Angry, Disappointed Supporters," *Daily Beast*, June 29, 2011.

13. See "Remarks by the President at the GLACIER Conference—Anchorage, AK," August 31, 2015, White House, President Barack Obama, obamawhitehouse.archives.gov.

14. Goodell, J., *The Water Will Come: Rising Seas, Sinking Cities, and the Remaking of the Civilized World* (New York: Little, Brown, 2017), 76.

15. Goodell, *The Water Will Come*, 81.

16. Goodell, 84.

17. Hayes, C., "Barack Obama: Pragmatist," *Nation*, December 10, 2008.

18. Sargent, D., "Postmodern America Didn't Deserve Jimmy Carter," *Foreign Policy*, July 24, 2021.

19. Weinraub, B., "Mondale Staff Worries: Will Voters Pick Him?," *New York Times*, December 26, 1983.

20. Broder, D., "Dukakis' Lessons of Defeat, Victory, and Growth," *Washington Post*, June 29, 1987.

21. Germond, J., "Black Leaders Adopt New Pragmatism to Avoid Backlash on Clinton," *Baltimore Sun*, September 30, 1992.

22. Goodman, P., "From Welfare Shift in '96, a Reminder for Clinton," *New York Times*, April 11, 2008.

23. "Which Al Gore?," *Economist*, August 12, 2000.

24. Sunstein, C., "The Empiricist Strikes Back," *New Republic*, September 10, 2008.

25. Seitz-Wald, A., "On Historic Night, Hillary Clinton Favors Pragmatism over Flair," NBC News, July 29, 2016.

26. Pritchard, S., "Pragmatic Progressivism: How Democrats Can Win the Presidency," *Carolina Political Review*, November 20, 2018.

27. Obeidallah, D., "Democrats' 2018 Midterm Hopes Strengthened by Decline of Liberal 'Purity Tests,'" NBC News online, March 19, 2018.

28. Viser, M., and A. Linskey, "'The Art of the Possible': Biden Lays Out Pragmatic Vision for His Presidency," *Washington Post*, March 25, 2021.

29. Walsh, E., "Pragmatic Centrist in Debt to JFK," *Washington Post*, June 15, 2003.

30. Comment from Democratic Sen. Jay Rockefeller, a key architect of the bill, "ObamaCare Is 'Just Beyond Comprehension,'" March 12, 2013, YouTube video, 0:57, www.youtube.com/watch?v=DTfpkRLrPo8.

31. For example, Kimberly, L., "Opposing Medicaid Expansion," *U.S. News and World Report*, December 4, 2015.

32. Garfield, R., A. Damico, and K. Orgera, "The Coverage Gap: Uninsured Poor Adults in States That Do Not Expand Medicaid," Medicaid, Kaiser Family Foundation, January 21, 2021.

33. Quoted in Beam, C., "Brown and Blue," *Slate*, January 20, 2010.

34. James E. Campbell is the most prominent proponent of this "exposure" and "surge and decline" conception of congressional elections; see, for example, Campbell, "The Presidential Surge and Its Midterm Decline in Congressional Elections, 1868–1988," *Journal of Politics* 53, no. 2 (1991): 477–487.

35. See the Kaiser Family Foundation tracking poll at www.kff.org/interactive /kff-health-tracking-poll-the-publics-views-on-the-aca.

36. Smiley, T., "A Letter to Obama: In Gratitude and Love," *Time*, January 10, 2017.

37. D'Antonio, M., "Unfinished Business (and Failures)," in *A Consequential President: The Legacy of Barack Obama* (New York: Thomas Dunne Books, 2017), 231–233. The author quickly excuses Obama's "no-win situation" with race, although the connection is not apparent on economic policy and regulatory issues.

38. Tillery Jr., A. B., "Obama's Legacy for Race Relations," in ed. B. A. Rockman and A. Rudalevige, *The Obama Legacy* (Lawrence: University Press of Kansas, 2019), 73–74.

39. Via Twitter.com, https://twitter.com/BreeNewsome/status/1415302063366496258 ?s=20, July 14, 2021.

40. Tillery, "Obama's Legacy for Race Relations," 75.

41. Selfa, L., *The Democrats: A Critical History* (Chicago: Haymarket Books, 2008), 81.

42. Selfa, *The Democrats*, 71.

43. See "Raising the Floor: Sharing What Works in Workplace Diversity, Equity, and Inclusion" (blog), November 28, 2016, White House, President Barack Obama, obamawhitehouse.archives.gov.

CHAPTER 11: DR. NO

1. Kalman, L., "The Constitution, the Supreme Court, and the New Deal," *American Historical Review* 110, no. 4 (2005): 1052–1080.

2. See Pareene, A., "Nihilist in Chief," *New Republic*, March 21, 2019.

3. See Blum, R. M., *How the Tea Party Captured the GOP* (Chicago: University of Chicago Press, 2020) on this point. Tea Party activists routinely voiced complaints about the establishment GOP in addition, obviously, to liberals and Democrats.

4. See Berman, R., "Mitch McConnell's Slipping Grip on the Republican Party," *Atlantic*, January 4, 2021, which discusses McConnell's limitations but, as much writing of that period did, pronounces the GOP dead prematurely.

5. See an extended discussion in Jentelson, A., *Kill Switch: The Rise of the Modern Senate and the Crippling of American Democracy* (New York: Liveright, 2021).

6. Uscinski, J. E., *Conspiracy Theories: A Primer* (Lanham, MD: Rowman and Littlefield, 2020).

7. Karabell, Z., "Here's What Happens to a Conspiracy-Driven Party," Politico, January 30, 2021.

8. See, for example, Fisher, M., "Probing the Tea Party's Conspiracy Theory Fringe," *Atlantic*, February 11, 2010.

9. Skocpol, T., and V. Williamson, *The Tea Party and the Remaking of Republican Conservatism* (New York: Oxford University Press, 2016), 104–110.

10. Newport, F., and A. Dugan, "5 Ways America Changed During the Obama Years," Gallup, January 27, 2017, news.gallup.com.

11. On this point, see extended treatment in Peck, R., *Fox Populism: Branding Conservatism as Working Class* (Cambridge, UK: Cambridge University Press, 2019).

12. Information in this section relies on Atlas, John, *Seeds of Change: The Story of ACORN, America's Most Controversial Antipoverty Community Organizing Group* (Vanderbilt University Press, 2010), and "The Fall of ACORN: A Timeline," *Week*, January 8, 2015.

13. Connolly, along with Rep. Hank Johnson in the following paragraph, are both quoted in Carter, Zachary D., and Arthur Delaney, "How the ACORN Scandal Seeded Today's Nightmare Politics," HuffPost, April 5, 2018.

14. Dreier, Peter, and Christopher R. Martin, "How ACORN Was Framed: Political Controversy and Media Agenda Setting." Perspectives on Politics 8.3 (2010): 761–792.

15. See Cooper, R., "The Tyranny of the Congressional Budget Office," *Week*, May 18, 2020

16. For a discussion of latent biases in the CBO's methods, see DiVito, E., and M. Konczal, "Five Reasons Why the CBO Underestimates Federal Investment." Roosevelt Institute, June 7, 2021.

17. Pareene, A., "The Real-Life Victims of Democrats' Irrational Deficit Paranoia," *New Republic*, May 5, 2021.

18. Levitz, E., "Dems Nix Anti-Recession Policy After Learning It Would Help Too Many People," *New York Magazine*, May 14, 2020.

19. Drew, E., *On the Edge: The Clinton Presidency* (New York: Touchstone Books, 1995), 87.

CHAPTER 12: IF YOU'RE WAITING FOR A SIGN, THIS IS IT

1. A comprehensive discussion of gender and the 2016 election is provided in Heldman, C., M. Conroy, and A. Ackerman, *Sex and Gender in the 2016 Presidential Election* (Santa Barbara, CA: ABC-CLIO, 2018).

2. Frank, T., *The People, No* (New York: Metropolitan Books, 2020).

3. For example, Alexander, M., "Why Hillary Clinton Doesn't Deserve the Black Vote," *Nation*, February 10, 2016.

4. Lauter, D., "Why Did Trump Win? Democrats Stayed Home," *Los Angeles Times*, November 11, 2016.

5. "Hillary Clinton's Cynical Race Appeals: The Revenge of Neoliberal Identity Politics," *Salon*, February 19, 2016.

6. See, just for starters, Ditonto, T., "Direct and Indirect Effects of Prejudice: Sexism, Information, and Voting Behavior in Political Campaigns," *Politics, Groups, and Identities* 7, no. 3 (2019); and the collected work of Prof. Carol Heldman on unconscious sexism.

7. Reich, R., "The Democratic Party Needs to Clean House," *Newsweek*, November 10, 2016.

8. Devine, C., "What if Hillary Clinton Had Gone to Wisconsin? Presidential Campaign Visits and Vote Choice in the 2016 Election," *Forum* 16, no. 2 (2018).

9. Parenti, C., "Garbage In, Garbage Out," *Jacobin*, November 17, 2016.

10. Morrill, J., and F. Clasen-Kelly, "Hillary Clinton Fighting 'Enthusiasm Gap' Among Some Black Voters," *Charlotte Observer*, September 7, 2016.

11. Murphy, P., "Democrats Worry About Hillary Clinton's Ground Game," *Daily Beast*, October 17, 2016.

12. On the question of race and turnout in 2016 see Fraga, B. L., et al., "Why Did Trump Win? More Whites—and Fewer Blacks—Actually Voted," *Washington Post*, May 8, 2017; and Green, J., and S. McElwee, "The Differential Effects of Economic Conditions and Racial Attitudes in the Election of Donald Trump," *Perspectives on Politics* 17, no. 2 (2019): 358–379.

13. Farley, J., "Five Decisive States: Examining How and Why Donald Trump Won the 2016 Election," *Sociological Quarterly* 60, no. 3 (2019): 337–353.

14. Monnat, S., and D. Brown, "More Than a Rural Revolt: Landscapes of Despair and the 2016 Presidential Election," *Journal of Rural Studies* 55 (2017).

15. Mutz, D., "Status Threat, Not Economic Hardship, Explains the 2016 Presidential Vote," *Proceedings of the National Academy of Sciences* 115, no. 19 (2018): E4330–E4339.

16. Grimmer, J., and W. Marble, "Who Put Trump in the White House? Explaining the Contribution of Voting Blocs to Trump's Victory," working paper under review (2019): 3, https://williammarble.co/docs/vb.pdf.

17. Research shows definitively that voters changing their vote preference from one election to the next is less influential to electoral outcomes than changes in turnout from one election to the next. In other words, who does or does not show up to vote explains two different election outcomes better than the theory that certain voters changed their minds from one to the next. See Hill, S., "Changing Votes or Changing Voters? How Candidates and Election Context Swing Voters and Mobilize the Base," *Electoral Studies* 48 (2017); and Fraga, B., *The Turnout Gap: Race, Ethnicity, and Political Inequality in a Diversifying America* (New York: Cambridge University Press, 2018). This does not imply that changing minds is irrelevant, though; see Hill, S., D. Hopkins, and G. Huber, "Not by Turnout Alone: Measuring the Sources of Electoral Change, 2012 to 2016," *Science Advances* 7, no. 17 (2021).

18. Hopkins, D., and S. Washington, "The Rise of Trump, the Fall of Prejudice? Tracking White Americans' Racial Attitudes via a Panel Survey, 2008–2018," *Public Opinion Quarterly* 84, no. 1 (2020): 119–140.

19. Representative of the many published papers on this topic are, for sexism: Cassese, E., and M. Holman, "Playing the Woman Card: Ambivalent Sexism in the 2016 US

Presidential Race," *Political Psychology* 40, no. 1 (2019): 55–74; and for racism: Pettigrew, T., "Social Psychological Perspectives on Trump Supporters," *Journal of Social and Political Psychology* 5, no. 1 (2017): 107–116. For an overview of both: Schaffner, B., M. MacWilliams, and T. Nteta, "Understanding White Polarization in the 2016 Vote for President: The Sobering Role of Racism and Sexism," *Political Science Quarterly* 133, no. 1 (2018): 9–34.

20. Morgan, S., "Status Threat, Material Interests, and the 2016 Presidential Vote," *Socius* 4 (2018).

21. See for example Sides, J., M. Tesler, and L. Vavreck, *Identity Crisis: The 2016 Presidential Campaign and the Battle for the Meaning of America* (Princeton, NJ: Princeton University Press, 2019).

22. Sharp, L., "Branding Hillary," *Baffler*, May 2021.

23. Sullivan, J., "The New Old Democrats," *Democracy*, June 20, 2018.

24. Carnes, N., and N. Lupu, "It's Time to Bust the Myth: Most Trump Voters Were Not Working Class," *Washington Post*, June 5, 2017.

CHAPTER 13: LESSONS LEARNED

1. Masket, S., *Learning from Loss: The Democrats 2016–2020* (New York: Cambridge University Press, 2020), 61.

2. To cite but a few examples: "Health Care Powered Democratic Wins in 2018," *New York Times*, September 2, 2020; "Democrats Ran and Won on Health Care; Now What?," CNN, November 17, 2018; and "The One Issue That's Really Driving the Midterm Elections," *Atlantic*, November 2, 2018.

3. Hall, C., and J. Tolbert, "Health Care and the Candidates in the 2018 Midterm Elections: Key Issues in Races," Kaiser Family Foundation, October 22, 2018.

4. Scott, D., "What the New Democratic House Majority Might Actually Pass on Health Care," Vox, November 12, 2018.

5. Cauterucci, C., J. Craven, and R. Hampton, "There's Something Icky About the Internet's Ecstatic Stacey Abrams Worship," *Slate*, January 7, 2021.

6. See Third Way, Collective PAC, and Latino Victory, "2020 Post-Election Analysis," ThirdWay.org.

7. Ghitis, F., "What Democrats Need to Learn from Trump's Better-Than-Expected Showing," CNN, November 4, 2020.

8. Burns, A., "Democratic Report Raises 2022 Alarms on Messaging and Voter Outreach," *New York Times*, June 6, 2021.

9. Lewis, C. M., "Third Way to Nowhere," *Baffler*, June 30, 2021.

10. Giridharadas, A., "Welcome to the New Progressive Era," *Atlantic*, April 14, 2021.

11. Krugman, P., "How Democrats Learned to Seize the Day," *New York Times*, February 8, 2021.

12. Levitz, E., "Biden's COVID-Relief Bill Is a Big F**king Deal," *New York Magazine*, March 9, 2021.

13. Benen, S., "The Democrats' Preoccupation in 2021: Learning Lessons from 2009," MSNBC, February 1, 2021.

14. Pareene, A., "Have Democrats Learned Their Lesson?," *New Republic*, March 11, 2021.

15. Milbank, D., "'Moderate' Joe Biden Has Become the Most Progressive Nominee in History," *Washington Post*, October 27, 2020.

16. Zhou, L., "Progressives' Biggest Fear About the Build Back Better Act Has Come to Pass," Vox, December 19, 2021.

17. Karson, K., and M. Khan, "Pelosi Backs Kennedy over Markey in Contentious Massachusetts Senate Race," ABC News online, August 20, 2020.

CHAPTER 14: THE LAST CHAPTER PROBLEM

1. Greenberg, D., "Why Last Chapters Disappoint," *New York Times*, March 18, 2011.

2. See, for example, Moncrief, G., and J. A. Thompson, "On the Outside Looking In: Lobbyists' Perspectives on the Effects of State Legislative Term Limits," *State Politics and Policy Quarterly* 1, no. 4 (2001): 394–411.

3. Olson, M. P., and J. C. Rogowski, "Legislative Term Limits and Polarization," *Journal of Politics* 82, no. 2 (2020): 572–586.

4. For just one exploration of this issue, see Wootson Jr., C., "New Generation of Activists, Deeply Skeptical of Democratic Party, Resists Calls to Channel Energy into the 2020 Campaign," *Washington Post*, June 13, 2020.

5. Illing, S., "Wokeness Is a Problem and We All Know It," Vox, April 27, 2021.

6. For example, Boch, A., "Increasing American Political Tolerance: A Framework Excluding Hate Speech," *Socius* 6 (2020); or Rosenfeld, M., "Moving a Mountain: The Extraordinary Trajectory of Same-Sex Marriage Approval in the United States," *Socius* 3 (2017).

7. Geismer, L., and M. Lassiter, "Stop Worrying About Upper-Class Suburbanites," *Jacobin*, January 1, 2021.

8. Klingelhöfer, J., "The Swing Voters' Blessing," *Journal of Economic Behavior and Organization* 174 (2020).

9. Quirk, P., and W. Cunion, "Clinton's Domestic Policy: The Lessons of a 'New Democrat'," in ed. C. Campbell and B. Rockman, *The Clinton Legacy* (London: Chatham House, 2000), 225.

10. Cook, C., "Just Who Are These Undecided Voters, Anyway?," Cook Political Report, September 10, 2019.

11. Burmila, E., "To Beat the NRA, Think Like the NRA," *Washington Post*, February 18, 2018.

12. See the excellent background in Newirth, M., "Death Travels West, Watch Him Go," *Baffler*, April 2001.

INDEX

© Jim Colman

Ed Burmila has taught and written on American politics for two decades. He holds a PhD in political science, spent ten years as a professor, is a veteran blogger and podcaster, has published original research in several academic journals, and has contributed to popular outlets such as *The Nation* and the *Washington Post*. His heart lives in Chicago; the rest of him lives in North Carolina with his wife, Cathy, and two dogs.